Paul Powell
of Illinois

T0288315

Paul Powell of Illinois

A Lifelong Democrat

Robert E. Hartley

Southern Illinois University Press

Carbondale and Edwardsville

Library of Congress Cataloging-in-Publication Data
Hartley, Robert E.
    Paul Powell of Illinois : a lifelong Democrat / Robert E. Hartley.
    p.   cm.
Includes bibliographical references (p.   ) and index.
    1. Powell, Paul, 1902–1970. 2. Legislators—Illinois—Biography. 3. Illinois—Politics
and government—1951– 4. Illinois—Politics and government—1865–1951. 5. Illinois.
General Assembly—Biography. I. Title.
F546.4.P6 1999   98-51443
977.3'04'092—dc21   CIP
[b]
ISBN 0-8093-2271-4 (alk. paper)
ISBN 0-8093-2272-2 (pbk : alk. paper)

The paper used in this publication meets the minimum requirements of American
National Standard for Information Sciences—Permanence of Paper for Printed Library
Materials, ANSI Z39.48-1984. ⊗

To those who instilled an appreciation of Illinois history:
Dave Felts, Bob Howard, Ed Lindsay, Bob Sink.

To those who urge fresh inquiry:
Dave Kenney, Jim Nowlan, Bob Reid, Paul Simon.

Contents

Illustrations

Preface

THE NEWS CYCLE OF A PROFESSIONAL POLITICIAN IS PREDICTABLE. THE news follows the person, and as he or she progresses through the chairs of public service, appropriate attention is paid. The attention reflects the height of achievement.

Then comes a time when the news stops. Perhaps a career is cut short by losing an election or failing to receive a much-sought appointment. The individual returns to private life. Others remain in the political arena for decades and finally decide to retire to a quieter life and news oblivion. Of course, there are those whose public activities are ended by death.

In virtually all those circumstances, the news cycle is completed. The news and the news people go elsewhere, and the person is remembered mostly in history books and by relatives and friends.

That is the familiar cycle. Once in a great while, however, the cycle is interrupted by events after retirement or death that overshadow everything that came before. For that to happen and to catch the fancy of a fickle public requires a nearly cataclysmic event, one that carries an easily remembered tag line.

In life, Paul Powell was a public figure of authority and notoriety, and the news followed him for about thirty-five years. Then, on October 10, 1970, he died. In death, Paul Powell became a mystery and a curiosity, and his story was all about big money.

Instead of the news and news people leaving him for other news makers, they found Powell more interesting in death than in life. The reason for this exception is what happened after October 10, 1970. Only a full telling of the story, including the incredible events in the hours after he died and the finding of $800,000 in cash, some in a shoe box, can help to explain why Powell is remembered so vividly thirty years later.

Simply stated, Powell became a living tag line: "$800,000 in shoe boxes." Mention his name, the money, or the shoe box across Illinois today, or even outside the state, and reaction is predictable. People first fumble over the words and his name, then they put them together from memory. This is truly a phenomenon.

Intriguing as the story of his cash may be, however, there is much more to understand about Paul Powell in life and death. The story always has been there; it just was covered by the weight of unanswered money questions: Where did the money come from? How did it get in the hotel closet? Who in their right mind would accumulate all that money in cash and not put it in a bank?

Those questions are worth probing, and that is one objective of this narrative. Another objective is to bring a measure of perspective to a political life that covered a generation in Illinois history. The Powell story before death is almost as intriguing as after October 10, 1970.

Looking for insight about Powell is a harrowing experience. It traverses the highs and lows of Illinois politics and public issues. To get beyond the tired clichés about Powell and down to the hard-core questions of public policy is a challenge. We can start the quest by using two comparisons of Powell with historical figures and by taking a look at public policy questions of the 1990s.

John Alexander Logan, a child of early southern Illinois, was born near Murphysboro and was reared before the Civil War along the Big Muddy River. As a local, state, and national politician and as an officer and leader of men in the Civil War, he blazed a trail of pragmatism and heroism unrivaled in the state's history. His story, his geography, his zeal for patronage, and gut appeal to local constituents created a mold for political behavior in the 1930s, 1940s, and 1950s. Paul Powell was the John A. Logan of his time.

In his two-volume biography of Logan, historian James Pickett Jones tells how an upbringing in southern Illinois shaped Logan's early ideas and thoughts about partisanship and slavery and his strong appeal to those who migrated from the Deep South and border states. Logan learned early that he had to represent the feelings of his constituents in order to build loyalty. He knew instinctively the importance of political jobs to an area starved for employment and decent wages.

Jones explains the change in Logan from fierce Democrat and Abraham Lincoln doubter to Union general, associate of Ulysses Grant, and finally—in the most dramatic change of all—Unionist Republican. Logan cared little for party designation; he looked high and low for coalitions that cut across regional, party, and personal lines. The political people of both parties distrusted him and tried to deny Logan higher office. The word *pragmatist* fails to do justice to Logan's willingness to seek comfort in any political shelter.

Logan's most determined fight came over the issue of civil service at the state and federal levels. Simply, he opposed it with every nerve and bone in his body. Spoils—the fruits of political victory—and patronage were the nutrients of Logan's career. Without patronage, Logan faced the mercy of unfriendly political contemporaries. Without patronage, Logan would not have survived.

A second, more familiar, contemporary parallel is the political and personal life of Lyndon Baines Johnson, native of the Texas hill country, political pragmatist, coalition builder, and master legislator. The application to Paul Powell, about whom we can use all of the above descriptions with the substitution of southern Illinois hill country, is stunning.

Think about what we know of Lyndon Johnson. Born of humble parents who scratched out a living from marginal soil, Johnson saw politics as a way out. Johnson's biographers tell us how his early life in Texas marked him with drive and ambition and with a desire to make sure he did not have to live that life for long. He never really left the hill country, though, and when he retired from the presidency in 1969, he returned to his ranch there and to the people with whom he felt most comfortable.

Johnson rose from the Depression as did Powell. Once elected, he brought home as much patronage and political pork as he could, building a level of trust and loyalty among his people to be utilized in political wars as well as in ongoing social contact. Once in the U.S. Senate, and eventually the leader of his party in that body, Johnson became the master compromiser, driven to pass legislation almost without regard for party loyalty. His deals with Sen. Everett Dirksen of Illinois are legendary, as are the corners he cut. There is his controversial victory for the U.S. Senate in 1948, and there always were questions about the connection of his personal fortune and legislation he championed.

We see now from his biographers how LBJ made sure legislation passed that lined his pockets and provided opportunity for personal wealth. Differences of scale aside, Powell and Johnson were political twins.

Finally, we need to address Powell and his times in comparison with political activism in the 1990s. How should Powell's actions and attitudes be evaluated in the context of our modern political environment?

Alan Dixon, former state legislator, state official, and U.S. senator has seen a lot and speaks carefully about most of it. In a discussion of Powell, Dixon cautioned the author to remember that when he ran for statewide office for the first time in 1970, the same year Powell died, there were no laws or regulations regarding accountability for campaign contributions. Everyone was on the honor system. Most elected officials played it straight, but a few did not. The law clearly stated that if you converted campaign money to personal use, federal taxes had to be paid. But who was to say whether the $100 bill someone put in your hand on the campaign trail should be declared?

The standards of honesty in government of thirty or forty years ago were different because of the times, not because of the issues. The term *conflict of interest* occasionally arose in newspaper editorial pages and even in campaign speeches. Media and political critics frequently pursued Powell for his open conflicts and his defense of them. There were members of the legislature who confronted Powell's flexible standards toward lobbyists and their favors.

Powell proved a master at collecting campaign contributions, and he bragged openly about pocketing the leftovers. His coziness with the statehouse media gave him latitude that might not be extended today. But we know from experience that those who cut matters close legally and ethically do so more comfortably if the press is otherwise occupied or just amused.

We learn that Powell operated as he did in large part because he was encouraged by those who hung around him and wanted the spoils. Manipulating public policy at the state level appeared to be acceptable as long as the public got more universities, hard roads, and public aid—how and under what conditions barely received attention. Perhaps those who watched Powell at work and approved are as responsible as he was for the results.

One reason we should be concerned today no matter what state or what part of the nation we live in is that as the federal government system pushes more and more policy decision making down to the state level, there is more opportunity for manipulation and more temptation to cut corners. This fact alone argues that we should look toward today's media and the watchdogs of government with much higher expectations than ever before.

These parallels and observations argue that Powell's story—over and above "$800,000 in shoe boxes"—is timeless. The issues raised by his life and politics are as fresh as cable news.

Acknowledgments

AFTER THREE BOOKS AND COUNTLESS NEWSPAPER AND HISTORY ARTICLES about Illinois, I can honestly say that the depth of my gratitude to Illinoisans is bottomless. They are courteous and patient, informative and informed, and they know a good story when they hear it. Any writer who expects to pursue the life and times of a complex political personality such as Paul Powell needs the generosity and understanding of such people.

My gratitude extends statewide. The quest brought me in contact with the unvarnished observations of Mel Lockard in Mattoon, the humor and memory for detail of Royce Hundley in Vienna, the bluntness and friendliness of Leo Brown and David Rendleman in Carbondale, and the richness of experiences from Abner Mikva in Chicago. On the trail of a good Illinois political yarn, there will always be disappointments and a few unproductive ventures. The turndowns came from a few who have kept their silence for decades. There is, after almost thirty years, still a stigma attached to being too close to Powell.

With only an exception or two, everyone asked was cooperative and made time available. For those who chose to speak but asked for anonymity, I am grateful for their contributions. I discovered a deep desire by almost everyone to talk about Powell, explain his actions, and acknowledge his shortcomings.

Fortunately, there were those who counseled as often as I sought their help and guided me to information that enriched the story. They are proof of the importance of keeping in touch with Illinois issues since leaving the state in 1979. High on that list are Paul Simon, who saw the book potential early; Jim Nowlan, who never refused the call for a name, a lead, or a piece of information; Dave Kenney, a counselor with uncommon good sense; and Gene Callahan, who simply has more useful information about people than any Illinoisan I know.

Gerald Fitzgerald Sr., a former member of the Illinois Racing Board, read portions of the manuscript and shared his knowledge of horse racing. In Vienna, Gary Hacker, a man with a passion for oral history and getting accurate infor-

Acknowledgments

mation about Powell, made his files available and guided me to helpful people. Rose Mary Orr, a walking storehouse of information about Powell's hometown, came to my rescue when called. My longtime colleague and friend Bob Reid, University of Illinois professor of journalism, gave up valuable time to read and comment with his usual extraordinary thoughtfulness.

Through the years of research into Powell, I leaned heavily on professional researchers, archivists, and keepers of files. I believe they all became fascinated with the subject, and this interest increased their value to the project. In no particular order, they are researchers Claire Martin, who scoured the papers of Powell for me, and Peggy Turk Sinko, my right arm in Chicago; Cheryl Schnirring and Mary Michals of the Illinois State Historical Library; Tom Wood, oral history archivist at the University of Illinois at Springfield; Judy Travelstead, librarian at the *Southern Illinoisan* in Carbondale; Stephen Kerber, archivist of Southern Illinois University at Edwardsville; and the staffs of the *St. Louis Post-Dispatch* library and the St. Louis Mercantile Library.

Mary Hartley—who said she spent as much time with Paul Powell as with her husband during the project—liked the idea from the start and made countless contributions.

Paul Powell
of Illinois

1

A Son of Southern Illinois

P AUL POWELL'S PROMINENCE IN ILLINOIS POLITICAL HISTORY IS
assured. Not because of his thirty-five years in state government, thirty
of which were spent in the state legislature. Not because he served three
terms as Speaker of the House. Not because of the thousands of laws he
authored or caused to be enacted.

He takes a place in Illinois infamy because $800,000 in cash was found in
a Springfield hotel room after his death on October 10, 1970.

As a result Powell is remembered far and wide in Illinois and beyond. His
legislative career, the contributions he made, and the controversies he
spawned are virtual footnotes. In full view, however, Powell was a more powerful state leader than some of the governors who served during his time.

Nevertheless, after nearly three decades, public curiosity lingers about the
finding of the money and its origin. Sparked by occasional news articles, the
search is alive for more facts about the money and those who handled it. This
reflects an enduring fascination with the marriage of money and politics in
Illinois.

The singular curiosity overlooks the fact that Powell amassed a huge fortune during his years in state government, thanks in large part to the way he
conducted himself and the laws he nurtured to passage. At his death, his
estate exceeded $3,200,000, including the $800,000. In 1970 dollars, that was
astounding. In today's dollars, that still looks pretty big.

There is much more to learn about Paul Powell.

If history has treated southern Illinois as "the Other Illinois" for more than
150 years, as historians record, then no wonder its people have shared a deep
inferiority complex. Shunned, as it were, by the more prosperous and
haughty northern two-thirds of the state and the Chicago urban center in
particular, southern Illinois has been left to its own devices. Residents have
scrambled for everything from food to respect.

This is the picture drawn by scores of historians who probed the beginnings and subsequent life of the lower third of Illinois.[1] The harsh reality

of soil, weather, and rivers provides a perfect backdrop for the life of Paul Powell, product of pioneer parents, son of deep southern Illinois, champion of regional interests.

Tens of thousands of years ago the die was cast for southern Illinois. Glaciers dropped down from the north with sheets of ice that carved modern Illinois's physical features. When the glaciers had receded—the Illinoisan and Wisconsinite glacial drifts were the most recent and notable—the deep soil so conducive to quality farming across the prairie stopped short of southern Illinois. The glaciers left gently rolling countryside to the north, known as "God's Country," and jagged hills and a stubborn clay soil to the south.[2]

By some measurements, a century ago the yield of crops in the north was a third more and the price of land almost twice as high as in southern Illinois. All was not despair. In deepest southern Illinois, a spur of the Ozark Highland was left, which provided spectacular scenery and land adaptable to fruit growing.

The counties of southern Illinois are surrounded on three sides by huge river systems: the Ohio on the south, the Mississippi on the west, the Wabash on the east, and smaller but formidable rivers on the north. As one historian noted, "From Southern Illinois country to the north, south, east, west there are 15,000 miles of navigable rivers."[3] By all rights, this should have been the land of plenty, with access to major markets. Instead the rivers flooded, making life periodically miserable in the valleys, and the water washed away the topsoil. As settlers found, the rivers brought floods and devastation rather than prosperity.

In the settlement history of Illinois country from 1810 to 1830, the people came to southern Illinois first, up and over from the mid-South and Deep South, from Kentucky, Tennessee, the Carolinas, and Virginia. Many were seasoned pioneers, held back from moving for years by Indian warfare. Some were small farmers driven from their southern homes by rapid expansion of the plantation system, especially in the western Carolinas, Georgia, and eastern Tennessee. Families came from the hill regions of the South, and they retained the ways of mountain people.[4] They found game in the woods, fish in the rivers, and game birds in the flyways. Southern Illinois felt like home.

The settlers discovered familiar surroundings across southern Illinois and into southern Indiana. Historian Ray Allen Billington said they were influenced more by the region's natural vegetation than by the soil differences such as "the densely wooded section of southern Illinois and Indiana where a thick forest of hardwoods covered the land. Particularly prized were the silt-filled river bottoms, even the hilly portions were eagerly sought after, for the plentiful timber promised profitable farming to westerners who judged the richness of land by the density of its forests."[5] The wooded stretches of southern Illinois offered adequate soil and familiar vegetation. Yes, it felt like home, but the rugged land exacted a toll and made tedious times more so.

These southerners were not easily discouraged, however, and that had a lot to do with their strengths and convictions. Historian Paul Angle described them as "generous, hospitable, hardy, independent, brave and intelligent, but undisciplined by education. Their superstitions were many and strong, their prejudices deep and unyielding." Quick to anger, independent, used to scrambling for their livelihood, they started feuds and ended them, too. Angle found that to be the heart of his tale of vengeance, violence, and murder in *Bloody Williamson*.[6] Angle called them "jealous of family honor and quick to resent an insult. Given what they considered sufficient provocation, they could kill with little compunction." The consensus among historians is that southern Illinoisans were a contentious and troublesome lot.

They also brought along strong Protestant religious feelings. They were fundamental Methodists and Missionary Baptists and Campbellites (Disciples of Christ), with a deep distrust of education and outsiders. They lived by simplistic codes, with the family providing the essential focus of social life and social control. As we learn from their chronicles, southern Illinoisans did not look to the city or state to provide for needs. They took pride in what they produced and how they helped each other.

In the early years of Illinois, this cultural closeness reflected their southern roots, but as time passed the reality of their isolation from the north of Illinois shaped attitudes and behavior. After statehood in 1818, they kept in touch with large concentrations of settlers in the southern and central parts. Vandalia, on the northern edge of southern Illinois, was the home of the state legislature until 1837, reflecting those early migration patterns. But as the state grew and more people settled in the north, and particularly the Chicago area, political centers of power shifted that direction, and a deeper isolation of the south set in. While southern Illinoisans had themselves for comfort and counsel in the early years, eventually the isolationist feeling combined with a fierce independence of government and an impatience with the realities of the river country to lead the people toward deepened insecurities, animosities, and violence.

They lived in the region called "Egypt" or "Little Egypt." There are a dozen stories of how Egypt got its name, but historian Robert Howard offered an explanation that rings true with other Illinois historians. In his one-volume history of Illinois, he first disposed of various unfounded theories, one being that the area resembled the delta of the Nile—which it does not. Howard wrote that the naming occurred after an incident during the deep snows and low temperatures of northern regions in 1830. Suffering was widespread and food was scarce in the north parts, but the people were relieved by supplies of meal and feed transported from the older and milder southern counties. "The people remembered the account in Genesis of a Mediterranean famine in which the people of the north received help from Pharaoh's court in Egypt." Howard said the name *Egypt* first began to appear in print about 1843.[7]

Pride notwithstanding, life in southern Illinois toward the end of the nineteenth century reflected deep disillusionment and bitterness. For all the promise of the land and the rivers and the discovery of mineral deposits, which led to enormous mining operations, the blossoming for the people had not occurred. Too often, residents watched their hopes swept away by floods and swallowed by absentee mine owners.

When people talk today about "deep southern Illinois," they are talking about country that includes Vienna, Illinois, and Johnson County (named for Richard M. Johnson of Kentucky, who served as vice president with President Martin Van Buren).[8] Lying almost dead center in the county, Vienna is about fifteen miles due north of the Ohio River as it winds toward a joining with the Mississippi. The town sits near the furthest southern point of the state and relates in latitude to the mid-South, the Southwest, and central California.

The settlement of Vienna occurred much as with other small towns in southern Illinois in the first decades of the 1800s. Settlers drifted from the southern states of Tennessee, Kentucky, North and South Carolina, and Arkansas to farm and found the hilly, timbered countryside friendly and similar to the places they had left. That familiarity can be understood from this historical description: "It is a picturesque region. The hills and valleys, the bluffs and gaps, beautiful farms, quiet homes nestling among the hills, cattle on a thousand hillsides, all give the visitor a surprise and interest from every angle of observation."[9] That picture survives today, for surprisingly little has changed in terms of geography and farming patterns.

There are other distinct features of the region, which add to the beauty but have also made this portion of southern Illinois less productive than other parts of the state. Mel Lockard, a native of nearby Union County, wrote in his autobiography of growing up in southern Illinois about the reality of the landscape: "I always wished my granddad had settled a little farther north, up here near Mattoon, where some of the most fertile land in the world is. . . . It turned out to be worth about $3,000 an acre and my granddad's land is still worth little in comparison."[10] The agriculture story of Johnson County is the story of small farms with small crops, dependence on livestock, and fruit trees.

Johnson County is rugged, featuring giant rock formations and low elevation swamps. A conspicuous ridge runs from east to west across the northern part of the county, dividing the waters of the Cache River and Bay Creek, running south, and the waters of the Big Muddy and Saline Rivers, running north. The northern part of the county has little tillable land. The southern part is lowland, with boggy river bottoms. Unlike many counties of southern Illinois, this region has no deposits of coal. Some of the finest cypress swamps in the Midwest occur in the county. One legend is that cypress timbers from Johnson County were sent to Chicago to help rebuild the city after the disastrous fire of October 1871.[11]

As with many small communities of the early 1800s, Vienna developed along trails that were popular with military movements and early settlers. Vienna was at or near the crossing of the road from Golconda to Jonesboro and the road from Fort Massac to Kaskaskia, the territorial capital of Illinois. In his conquests of the late 1700s, General George Rogers Clark traveled through the county from Fort Massac to Kaskaskia. On February 27, 1837, Vienna was incorporated as a village, and in a few years the population had grown to about 150 people, with three stores and a courthouse.[12]

Johnson County—and most of the regions of southern Illinois—sent fathers and sons to fight in the Civil War in large numbers compared with total population. Along with much of the southern third of the state, Johnson County residents had strong southern sympathies and were torn over which side to support in the war. Finally, with strong leadership from politicians who supported the Union, the citizens of Johnson County fought with General U. S. Grant and the southern Illinois Union general, John A. Logan, in spite of Democrat leanings.[13]

Robert B. Powell and his wife, Paul's grandparents, started a family in Benton, Arkansas, before the Civil War. She gave birth to Thomas B. Powell on April 11, 1858, but the vagaries of health and care in those times claimed both parents soon thereafter.[14] Thomas, orphaned by age seven, and a sister came to Johnson County and Vienna in the care of Maj. Andrew Jackson Kuykendall, who reared Thomas to adulthood. Kuykendall, a lawyer, earned a reputation as the county's most noted citizen, and military hero. As described in one county history, he "was an ardent Democrat but a loyal one.

His influence for the Union was felt far and near."[15] He served four years in the Illinois House, fourteen years in the state Senate, and one term as a congressman after the Civil War.

The family roots put down there by Thomas early in the second half of the nineteenth century deepened and remained until the death of his youngest son, Paul Taylor Powell, in October 1970. Then the Powells were gone from Vienna and southern Illinois. The memories linger on in a two-story frame house that Thomas built in 1884 and that is now a memorial to his youngest child. It sits a block north of the county courthouse in Vienna and just across the street from the town square.

For nearly a century, the Powell family was a fixture in Vienna, involved in its growth, sharing disappointments, surviving disasters, and celebrating joys. The Powells participated in all of those experiences, but no more so than many other pioneer families of southern Illinois. The difference between the Powells and all the others was Paul, who left the most indelible imprint of any individual on the history of Vienna.

Thomas became a stalwart citizen of Vienna from early times. He married Rosa Johnson and reared at least four children, named John, Thomas, Ira, and Gertrude. At the same time he studied and learned to be a pharmacist, starting as a clerk in the local drugstore owned by a "Dr. Damron."[16] After two years as clerk, Thomas purchased the establishment and began a business career in Vienna that lasted until his death in 1924 at age sixty-six. Notable among his achievements was the construction and ownership of a "brick block" (which included a drugstore) on the town square. The building stands today as a survivor of several fires that destroyed much of the community at various times over the years.

After the death of his first wife, before 1900, Thomas married Vinna Hartwell, fourteen years younger, of nearby Marion, and they began a family of their own. To Thomas and Vinna were born two sons, Hartwell, the elder by two years, and Paul, who was born January 21, 1902, in the house that his father built. Hartwell, described by Vienna residents as an easygoing and good-natured boy, one day went outside of town with a friend to knock apples out of a tree. He used the butt of a gun he carried to hit the apples. The gun accidentally discharged and killed Hartwell, who was fourteen.[17] From that point on, Paul assumed the position of caretaker for his remaining family, the house, the family history, and the memories of his parents and Hartwell. His mother Vinna, a musician, lived in the family home until her death in 1941. By the time Paul died in 1970, he had buried his brother, both parents, and two wives.

Thomas set a standard for community service and public involvement that must have impressed and influenced Paul. First, he was a lifelong Democrat, a source of pride with his son. As many business people did in a small town, Thomas took his turn as a public official and leading citizen. He served the county four years as deputy sheriff and tax collector, was mayor of Vienna in 1891, and put in more than four years as postmaster. He belonged to the Independent Order of Odd Fellows (IOOF) lodge, and the Powells were loyal members of the Christian Church. Vinna gave piano lessons to many of the children of the community for a number of years, on a piano still in the Powell home.

When Thomas died, on May 28, 1924, he left the house, the brick block, and the drugstore to his children from both marriages and Vinna.[18] Over the years Paul was asked frequently about the tough financial times he experienced growing up, while at the same time being the child of the local druggist and pharmacist, and a landowner. Powell said his father had been generous to a fault all his life and died owing much more than he had in assets. He replied: "It is true my father operated a small drugstore. I can remember when I was in there as a small boy, men would come in and say, 'Uncle Tom I need some pills for the bellyache but I haven't any money.' There wasn't anybody who walked out of there without pills for the bellyache. The reason my father was a man of humble means was because he signed his name on too many notes that he had to pay off."[19]

By the turn of the century, the population of Vienna had reached 1,217. To the present day, the number has rarely exceeded that and often has fallen below 1,000. An opera house was built in 1896, and a Carnegie Library in 1910. Vienna Township High School moved into its own building in 1918. Despite bad fires in 1884 and early 1900, the business district grew to serve a wide region. The roads were still dirt, and the streets of town were crushed rock. "Hard roads" and concrete sidewalks were in the future.

The earliest recollections of Paul Powell come from his record in high school and as a budding businessman in his teenage years. Referred to as a "serious boy" by one of his childhood friends, Paul actually was known to most of the town as Tadie. Unable to pronounce his middle name, Taylor, as a youngster, it came out as Tadie, and to this day many who remember him from personal involvements call him by that name.[20]

Among the recollections of his school days, there are no indications of future greatness, certainly no more than other students of note. He once served as the students' representative to the teachers, and he recalled later, "I sat in with the teachers, and I stood up for the students." Church was important to the Powell family routine, and Paul recalled that he and his brother Hartwell each put fifty cents in the collection plate every week, "but they never let me pass the collection plate."[21]

As with any high school, and especially small schools, boys who played football or basketball are often remembered for their feats. Powell, a good-sized boy, played football and in his senior year served as team captain. Royce Hundley, a few years younger than Powell and a schoolmate, remembers that the football coach introduced the then little-known tactic of on-side kicks to the game played locally. In those surprise situations, Powell did the kicking.[22] In Powell's senior year, the team had a particularly good record and is remembered fondly as "the team of 1919–20" in Vienna.

But for young Powell there was more to life than church, school, and athletics. By about age fifteen, he had become an entrepreneur of note. Almost directly across the street, south from his home, Powell opened a dry-cleaning establishment in the back of a barbershop. Many Vienna residents tell the story of the cleaning work, but details were added by Levi Locke, a life-long friend of Powell: "When he was 16 years old he opened up a cleaning store. In those days you cleaned clothes by beating them with a stick, brushing them, and using some white gasoline. Then, to press a suit, you'd use 16-pound irons you'd heat on the stove. Well, Powell had no patience for that. So he bought the first Hoffman steam presser that anybody around here had ever seen. He'd be there on Saturday doing 25 suits at $1.50 each. Folks had to have a pressed suit for Sunday church."[23]

When Powell graduated from high school, he sold the cleaning establishment and went on to other ventures. His later notoriety led to many stories of his devotion to making money. Longtime friend Joe Throgmorton said, "He hustled papers, shined shoes, washed collars, anything to make a dollar when he was in school."[24] Hundley called Powell "the most grown up young man—he was a hustler, all business." At least one friend remembers he organized an amateur football league. While stories have him involved in everything from selling radios to used cars to running a grocery store that specialized in fresh vegetables, he is best remembered as going into debt to start the town's first full-blown restaurant.

The business started as a confectionery, then became a small cafe, and finally blossomed into a restaurant called Powell's Cafe, where all the clubs and organizations in town held their meetings. The printed statement for customers said proudly, "A good place to eat."[25] He ran the businesses from three different locations on the town square over the years. The cafe business continued until after he became a member of the Illinois state legislature in 1935. In fact, this business contact laid the groundwork of contacts, friends, and name-recognition that later served him well in launching a political career.

"That's really what afforded Paul to meet the town's folk on a regular basis," recalled old friend Paul O'Neal, who first met Powell in 1925. "Paul was always accommodating and eager to help people. Every group in this area would have its dinners at that restaurant, and Paul would give them a break on the cost. People remembered him."[26]

Shortly after graduation from high school, Powell married his childhood sweetheart, Violet Price, known by the young people of Vienna as Piggy. Her ancestors had first come to Johnson County about 1840, and she lived on a farm near Vienna with her parents. Violet was born a year before Paul. Hardly anyone has a harsh word for the memory of Violet. Retired dentist Hundley says: "She was one of the sweetest girls that ever grew up in Vienna. . . . And she had a soprano voice that was beautiful."[27]

Mrs. Levi Locke remembered the two of them as a young couple: "He was such a nice-looking young man, who didn't like to part his hair. He was very mannerly and very much in love with Violet, who was a beautiful, quiet-spoken brunette."[28] Paul and Violet seemed to be the perfect couple, hard working, church-going, and happily a part of Vienna. At the cafe, "she would play the piano and people would dance," Hundley added.

Then two events jolted Powell's young life. First, his father died in 1924, leaving his mother and him as family survivors without much in the bank and a list of notes signed by Thomas. "I learned a lot from my father," Powell often said. The second setback for Powell occurred in 1925, when Violet, who had gone to Murphysboro to visit her parents, was killed by a tornado that swept across southern Illinois that day. "I think Paul's life would have been a lot different if she had lived, because she was so sweet," Hundley surmises.

Powell dedicated himself to the cafe and to getting involved in public matters in the community. This led him to his first elections for public office and a first taste of public service. He loved every minute of it. In 1928 citizens elected him to the school board, and he served six years. In 1930, at age twenty-eight, he was elected mayor of Vienna, a job that paid him $10 a week. Recalling that feeling of being mayor, Powell once said, "I think my head got bigger when I got to be mayor than any other office I ran for."[29] He served as mayor until he entered the legislature, and during that time he also served as a Democratic precinct committeeman.

As he launched his elective career, Powell married Daisy Butler on June 13, 1929. He met Daisy at the county courthouse, where she worked as a court reporter. Daisy was born August 11, 1897, in Villa Ridge, in Pulaski County, just north of Cairo at the confluence of the Ohio and Mississippi Rivers. Her father taught school, and they were pioneers of the most southern region of the state.[30] She had two brothers, Edward, who died in a car accident near Mattoon in 1938, and Glenn, who lived much of his life in New York State and who preceded Daisy in death.

A small woman, Daisy stood her ground against all comers and earned a lifelong reputation as sharp tongued and sassy. "She was nice, but she had a temper and was just the opposite of his first wife," according to Mrs. Levi Locke. "She'd stand right there and tell you just what she thought. Her hair was a kind of goldie color."[31] Daisy always considered Powell bright and smart politically, and she urged him to take up more and more of a political life. She worked with him in the restaurant business before he became a legislator and was one of the first employees of the old Illinois Public Aid Commission created in 1935 . She helped set up the public aid program in Illinois and was district supervisor of twelve counties in southern Illinois until resigning because of ill health.

For all the pleasant moments of their marriage, there were many more unpleasant ones, according to friends, relatives, and associates of both Paul and Daisy. For most of the last twenty years of her life, she suffered a variety of ailments that immobilized her at different times. She suffered from cancer, and then lived in pain with an abdominal ailment, and eventually died April 26, 1967, due to physical handicaps caused by old X-ray therapy.[32] She also suffered a broken hip in later years. She rarely set foot in Springfield during Powell's years as a legislator and secretary of state and lived most of her time either in Vienna or in Chicago, where she stayed in a hotel suite so that she could be near her doctors.

Daisy's isolation from her husband and his career as a politician and major state officeholder resulted in bitterness toward him, accusations of neglect, and threats to disclose his love affairs with various women with whom he worked in Springfield. Powell's friendship—assumed to be much closer than just a friendship—with Lucille Koval and Marge Hensey, a divorcee who Powell called Little Bit, was hardly a secret to anyone with curiosity. As secretaries and friends, they went public places with him, campaigned with him, and were known to frequent his living quarters at the St. Nicholas Hotel in Springfield. Hensey was staying in a two-bedroom hotel suite with Powell in Rochester, Minnesota, when he died. Koval had talked with him by telephone the day before his death.

As the years passed and the estrangement hardened, Daisy did not keep her criticism of her husband's social life to their private conversations.

Depending on what had occurred most recently, she chose almost any public location to announce Powell's latest sins. Royce Hundley remembers seeing Daisy one day at the drugstore in Vienna: "She cussed every breath, saying, 'you know he brought that bitch down to the DuQuoin state fair. Why didn't he leave her in Springfield.'"[33]

Powell left behind a stack of letters Daisy wrote to him over a five-year period from 1959 to 1964. They tell a story of domestic unhappiness, jealously, and anguish in the lives of this married couple. Daisy's rambling letters, filled with expletives, referred to the other women in Powell's life as "bitches and whores." She accused him of ignoring her and of being mean and nasty for flaunting his women in public and sneaking them in and out of the St. Nicholas Hotel.

She appeared highly indignant that Powell would take them to their Vienna home. In one letter she said, "I guess you and your girl friends are having a time, but couldn't you get to a motel rather than taking them in my home that I worked so hard on."[34] She frequently accused her husband of giving her jewelry and her keepsakes at the house to his women friends.

Mingled with the complaints about Koval and Hensey, who she rarely mentioned by name but about whom she repeated unflattering gossip, Daisy dished up political advice and admonished him for not attending to political details. She feared he would squander his political capital by being known in political circles as a cad and womanizer. She warned him of fading political clout and cautioned Powell not to trust Chicago Mayor Richard Daley. In a letter mailed March 25, 1963, she wrote: "Do you think for one minute Daley intends for you to be secretary of state or anything else if he ignored you on that luncheon yesterday? . . . Why can't you see that? But the SB can use you in the legislature to get his program through for Chicago and all the state officials are afraid of their appropriations so they have to smile to your face and then hate you for the first time in your political history. . . . Your political career comes first with me."[35]

Daisy kept him informed of her health problems and sufferings and blamed Powell for causing her mental and physical grief. She often threatened to expose him publicly or show up where he was likely to be accompanied by one of his woman friends. Those threats were in the early letters. As the years passed and her health worsened she dropped the threats and said she would never do anything to ruin his political career. She complimented him on his political skills and for being smart and successful, then cursed him for failing to call or for arguing with her on the telephone.

Daisy reminded Powell of her loyalty to him and her interest in his political career. In a letter that she signed "Whether you like it or not," Daisy reminded him of an early political decision and how she counseled him at the time: "I have always wanted you to be somebody and if you remember I absolutely refused to let you be a motorcycle cop and wear a cap when you knew you had more brains than that. I also remember first time you ran when you called me and said you didn't know whether to file your petition for representative as Eddie Barrett and John Stelle said you couldn't win and you said it was snowing. I told you to file that d—— petition as you had promised your people to do so and whether you got beat or not you had to file and to h—— with Eddie Barrett and John Stelle. I didn't know at that time I would be bypassed but if I had I would still have given you the same answer."[36] Barrett and Stelle were longtime political associates of Powell.

The early letters carried the traditional greeting of "Dear Paul," but in time she dropped any semblance of affection. The last letters simply began without a greeting. The letters from the first years ended with closings such as "With love, Daisy," but in a 1961 letter she closed simply with "Good-bye." Once in 1963 she closed, "Just little old me," and a few months later, "Nothing left of me." With declining civility and health, she wrote longer, rambling treatises that deteriorated with each page, often concluding with details of her physical misery.

The briefest letter from Daisy among those in Powell's files was mailed on November 16, 1960: "I found the most unusual Xmas present for you & bought it & am going to put on it, from 'old shit ass to old shit ass.'"[37]

Among Powell's personal files, there were just two letters he wrote to Daisy, written in 1963 after his heart attack. At that same time, Daisy wrote the most sympathetic letters, expressing concern about his health and begging him to slow down or pay the ultimate price. She wrote to counsel caution, and remind him that if he became ill, his girlfriends would abandon him. Powell's letters are milder than Daisy's, and yet there are references to contentious moments between them and her unwillingness to answer his telephone calls.

In the letter of March 6, 1963, Powell said: "I don't intend to bawl you out any more even if you accuse me of being a horse thief—and when I come up to see you hope we have an enjoyable visit. The only reason I am coming to Chicago is to see you and you only because I do care whether you believe it or not, so there."[38] In the second letter, filled mostly with idle chatter about business affairs, Powell concluded, "I hope soon you will start to answer the phone and if you won't fuss at me I promise that I won't fuss and will visit with you on the phone—try it once and see." He signed it, "With love, Paul."[39]

The outpouring of affection for Daisy at her funeral in Vienna is remembered to this day by those who attended. More than five hundred floral pieces filled the Powell residence, the front porch and yard, and the porch and yard of an adjoining residence. Hundreds of people filled the Vienna High School gymnasium for the service, and there were more flower arrangements there. Powell turned out the state's highest ranking officials for his wife's funeral, including Gov. Otto Kerner, Lt. Gov. Samuel Shapiro, State Auditor Michael Howlett, and many other Democratic party officials.[40] Those who attended Powell's funeral services in Vienna about three and a half years later remarked that he did not receive nearly as much floral attention as Daisy. She was buried in the Vienna cemetery with Violet.

After all those years of running the restaurant and meeting people and then taking his chances as a candidate for the school board and mayor, there had to be a next step for one who struck others as a natural campaigner. His instincts with people, his willingness to listen and be sympathetic, worked in his favor. He learned well.

Once he told a political associate: "Don't ever turn down a drink or something to eat when you're campaigning. I don't care if they hand you a glass of muddy river water, you take a big gulp and tell 'em how good it is."[41] Through all the years, he remained loyal to his Vienna friends and those who put him in the highest ranks of the state's officials. About those loyalists he said, "The horses that do the pullin' in the field are the first ones to get the hay throwed to 'em."

There are as many stories about Powell's days in Vienna as there are people to tell them. His political beginnings remain unclear, except for one friend who claimed credit for turning Powell toward Springfield. The story came from Paul O'Neal, one of Powell's Vienna regulars. Through frequent publication, his story has become the tale of record. "He really didn't have much interest in politics but did it because it was the right thing to do and his mother would be proud of him. . . . Paul and I were in this cabin, actually a still, when I asked him to run for the House. He told me that he didn't have any money, but I answered that we could make up a batch of liquor and he could have the first hundred or two hundred bottles. I gave him some money, too."[42]

In his autobiography about growing up in southern Illinois, Mel Lockard devoted a chapter to his friendship with Powell, including one story about Powell's political beginnings: "The state senator from Jonesboro, Illinois, R. Wallace Karraker, who was a Democrat, gave Paul less than fifty bucks to go to Springfield to get a job. He got a job up there and he kinda liked the way things looked and he came back and he started runnin' for the state legislature and he was never defeated for a state office."[43]

With those first whisky flavored campaign funds, Powell bought a box of matches with his name printed on them and went to the mining areas of his district to distribute them. "He promised that if they voted for him, he'd always take care of them," O'Neal said. "And so long as I knew Paul Powell, he took care of them or anyone else who needed it."

Whether he produced jobs when requested or not, Powell developed a reputation for holding court with anyone who wanted to talk. O'Neal remembers managing the line of people who came to see Powell about work. He said there would be sometimes twelve to fifteen people waiting to see him. The meetings generally were held in his home, in a wood-paneled family room filled with pictures, books, fancy liquor bottles, mementos, an ever-present telephone, and later in his career, several television sets.

O'Neal is one of several friends, associates, supporters, and benefactors who since Powell's death in 1970 have spoken frequently about the man. Mostly they have praised him; usually they have pointed out his good qualities and the reasons they remain loyal even after his death. They tell a story of truthfulness, honesty, compassion, feeling, and commitment to good works. Mostly they are men who have their roots deep in southern Illinois soil and who want the world to know that whatever happened a couple of hundred miles off in Springfield or further in Chicago did not necessarily have any connection to what happened in Vienna and Johnson County. These stalwart friends have not varied their stories or shirked in their loyalty.

They have included O'Neal, a political helpmate; Throgmorton, friend, local druggist, and fellow investor in income-producing real estate; C. L. McCormick, a Republican legislator from Powell's district, who remained a close friend and political soul mate; Hundley, retired dentist whose remembrance of Powell is sprinkled with candor; Lockard, a southern Illinois boy who grew up in nearby Cobden, managed banks, and eventually went off to make his fortune in Mattoon (and write a book about his life); Clyde Choate, legislative sidekick and compatriot, who lives in Anna and presents an unambiguous picture of the man he knew better than anyone; and the late Clyde Lee, who disclosed little of his longtime association with Powell.

Powell befriended any number of people, found them jobs, gave them money, or guided them to lives that turned out well. Among those he touched deeply is James "Stud" Walker, a retired Vienna businessman and former sales manager of more than passing note. Born twenty-one years after Powell, he could have been the son never born. He likes to talk about a nearly wasted youth, during which he acquired his nickname. As Walker sees things, Powell might have been the reason for his successes, and his stories of Powell the friend, adviser, counselor, and teacher are convincing.[44]

Walker almost took over the insurance business that Powell began so that he could supplement his legislative salary and provide a means for deducting the costs of his political travel throughout southern Illinois. Powell took Walker to Springfield to register for a license, but when Walker got back home, he decided that wasn't for him. Powell continued to sell insurance until the last year of his life. Among other ventures, Walker ran for election as county clerk, and he won, thanks in large part to Powell's long memory.

The job was open due to the death of the Democratic incumbent, and the incumbent's wife was slated by the Democrats to run for her husband's position. Walker received the Republican nomination and launched his campaign knowing he was climbing uphill. "She had the sympathy of the community," Walker says. "She needed the job. I was already employed." Late in the campaign, Walker saw Powell, who asked how things were going. Walker said he was going to be wiped out by the sympathy vote. Powell simply told him not to give up.

According to Walker, on the weekend before the election, he heard that Powell had instructed his Democratic friends in Vienna to vote for Republican Walker: "I saw Daisy after the election and she said 'I voted for you, you Republican son of a bitch and I've been sick ever since.' That was Daisy for you." Walker later learned that the woman candidate and her family had supported an opponent of Powell in an earlier election, and Powell had not forgotten. The tide turned with Powell's endorsement of Walker. "Powell was awfully good to me," he acknowledged.

In a lengthy discussion of Powell, Walker echoes the sentiments of others who praised the man: "He had to excel in whatever he did. He liked to be complimented. He was a man of his word. There was something about his personality—you couldn't help but like Paul Powell. I trusted him." Moreover, Walker said, Powell "was my hero because he was a self-made man. He was not the most polished man in the world, but he talked the language of the common people." He also left Walker with some valuable lessons in local politics.

At one point early in his work life, Walker was an employee of the Illinois Veterans Commission, a political appointment he received from a Republican. Although Illinois law stipulated that no employees of the commission could engage in partisan politics, the man who appointed him told Walker he had to campaign for Republican candidates to return the favor for his employment. Powell heard about Walker's work for the Republicans and called his young friend: "Stud, I want to see you in Springfield." Walker was "scared to death." He was called before the commission in Springfield, without any guidance or advice from Powell before Walker arrived in Springfield. Finally before the hearing, Powell counseled, "Relax, you're not going to get fired, you're just going to get your ass out of politics."

At the hearing, the charges against Walker were read, and he admitted guilt. "I'm guilty and I apologize," he said. Then Powell testified: "I've known this boy all his life—he's doing a helluva good job. I don't want him to lose his job. Everybody likes him and I like him. Furthermore, he's here at state expense and he can take me out to dinner tonight." The commissioners laughed, of course, and Powell got his way. In the end Walker promised to stay out of politics while working for the commission, and he kept his job. "That was the end of the politics for the Republicans," Walker stated. He also noted that Powell often "cussed me like a son."

For all the favors and advice—Powell encouraged him in several career business ventures—Walker seized one big opportunity to repay Powell. In 1961, while Powell served his third term as Speaker of the Illinois House of Representatives, the local community organized a testimonial event patterned after a popular television show of the time called *This Is Your Life.*

Walker produced the night for Powell with relish—one thousand people packed the high school gymnasium—and brought a virtual truckload of the legislator's associates to Vienna. They included Lt. Gov. Sam Shapiro and Delyte W. Morris, president of Southern Illinois University, along with former childhood friends and classmates. The newspaper report said Walker "was never in better form" as master of ceremonies.

Before the event, however, Walker remembers one tense moment. Walker learned that Powell's wife Daisy had threatened to attend the event and expose her husband's extramarital activities. Walker contacted Powell and told him of the rumor. Powell promised that Daisy would be in Chicago on the night of the party, which she was. Powell "apologized" to the audience for her absence, noting her poor health.[45]

In an emotional but controlled response to the night of reminiscences, Powell said: "Tonight my heart is full. Tonight is the greatest honor I have ever received." He spoke with reverence of his father and mother, his brother, and his first wife Violet. He remembered being a member of the first high school class that graduated from the new building. He ran through the list of community activities and honors and added, to the crowd's amusement, "I have done a lot of things I am glad these men didn't talk about."[46]

This was the moment a local boy, Walker, and his mentor, Powell, both dreamed of. The event captured the depth of feeling for Powell by so many of his friends and neighbors.

2

A Full Life of Politics

THROUGH THIRTY YEARS OF SERVICE IN THE ILLINOIS HOUSE OF
Representatives, no one matched Paul Powell for staying power. In this
century, no other Democrat dominated the party and the actions of the legislature for so long.

His colleagues through those times—Republicans, Democrats, downstaters, Chicagoans—credit his talent and ability. Those characteristics alone,
however, were not enough to rank him at the top for so long. The key to his
run of power in the legislature was an artful determination to make full-time
work out of a part-time job and a devotion to political purpose that, when
combined with skills, made him peerless.

When Powell first went to Springfield for a legislative session in the 1930s,
the trip by car from Vienna took hours over two-lane roads that were prim-
itive by today's standards—"hard roads" people called them then—and
unimaginable to anyone now under sixty years of age. There were no interstate highways. Dim lighting alongside roads and through towns made night
driving hazardous, and the day of the twenty-four-hour fast-food restaurant, where a weary traveler could stop for a cup of coffee and a sandwich or
hamburger, did not exist.

Traveling simply took longer, living was harder than today, and conven-
iences in the Depression era were fewer and more modest than any time
since. The 1930s were not that far from a time when people got from one
point to another in southern Illinois by walking or riding horses.[1]

At that time people in southern Illinois knew their elected officials by personal contact and occasional mentions in the local weekly newspaper. The
weekly often published interpretations directly from the elected officials and
let readers know when officials were in town. Still, the most effective and
convenient means of contact for citizens was at an office where citizens
received a handshake and a kind word and had an opportunity to ask a favor.

Rep. Clyde Lee of Mt. Vernon started an insurance business so that he
would have an office on Main Street, where he welcomed citizens and voters.[2] Powell worked out of his home, just a few steps from the town square,
where he greeted citizens. Most officials in southern Illinois never missed a

county fair or community festival. Rarely did these contacts lead to lengthy discussions of public policy or the high-blown strategies of the legislature. In most rural parts of Illinois, citizens viewed local officials and members of the state legislature as opportunities for government jobs; patronage was the elixir of local politics.

The legislature in Springfield that Paul Powell entered in 1935 was a part-time activity. The legislature met in regular session every two years, on the odd number year. Rarely did a governor call a special session. The legislature and governor transacted the state's business from about February through June, with vacations, recesses, and short workweeks providing ample time for the part-time jobs they needed to supplement government work.

When Powell entered the legislature, his salary for the two-year session was $5,000. At the end of his first decade, legislative salaries had advanced to $6,000 for a biennium; in 1955 legislators received $10,000 for two years; and in 1963, Powell's last session, the salary had grown only to $12,000 for two year's work.

In contrast to today, Illinois legislators of 1935 were barely known outside their own districts; they earned relatively low salaries, had no staff, telephones, or offices, and had almost no allowances for incidentals such as travel, postage, and office supplies.[3] Powell's other businesses and part-time jobs allowed him to deduct his political travels from taxable income.

Lobbyists and their expense accounts, easily available in trade for votes, supplemented government pay. Lobbyists for large businesses and organizations paid for meals, drinks, incidental expenses, entertainment, and trips. Campaign contribution limits, public disclosure of income, and declaration of lobbyist expenses were unheard of.

While the compensation and dreary conditions may have frightened some from seeking legislative office, there never seemed to be any shortage of aspirants. In order to overcome the puny pay, the legislature took care of members' interests by passing laws that assisted landowners and businesses. There are no quotes from Powell's long state government career in which he complained about the pay, but he did comment on the opportunity to make money: "I didn't know what money was until I went to Springfield. I watched those Chicago boys taking it in and said to myself, 'You country boy. Who needs to run a restaurant when you can get into this?'"[4]

With a smattering of part-time business activities, such as selling insurance policies, consulting work for John Stelle's ceramic company in Indiana, income from farmland, and a few small business ventures, Powell added enough income that he could devote most of his time to politics. In 1945, for example, Powell's federal income tax return showed $2,500 from the state for legislative services (one year of a two-year term) and $900 from Arketex Ceramic Corporation in Brazil, Indiana, a company owned by John Stelle. He had dividend and interest income of $356.93. His insurance business lost $91.52 on income of $360.48. After deductions for expenses in the legislature, and for taxes, Powell showed a net income of $3,203.12 for tax purposes.[5] While not excessive for its time, this income level and pattern permitted Powell to devote full time to politics. These sources of income carried Powell until the early 1950s, when he began to receive large amounts of dividend income from racetrack investments.

Rep. Anthony Scariano of Chicago, who entered the legislature in 1957 and battled constantly with Powell over many issues, reflected about Powell's full-time devotion to politics: "He darned well had to [work full-time] as busy as he was out taking care of his constituents downstate. He had people help him with automobile licenses and hunting licenses and all the favors, the constituent favors, that a member of the legislature is expected to do for his constituents, especially in the downstate areas".[6] Scariano added that the demand for patronage jobs kept Powell busy. "It was a full-time job for him."

For a snapshot of the legislature dating back to Powell's beginning, two experienced observers of Illinois politics, Sam Gove and Jim Nowlan, caught the flavor in a few words:

> [The legislature] is a fiercely partisan body where horse trading and sophisticated political stratagems are often more important to the lawmakers than the particular issues to be decided. It is tied closely to business and special interests by high-pressure lobbying and generous contributions to election campaigns. . . . Control has always been shared with the governor, whose veto can destroy years of work, and has always been well guarded by the majority and minority leaders of the House and Senate, known most recently as the Four Tops. Along with the governor they control legislation in Illinois, and to have an influence on them, a legislator must be savvy, well-connected, willing to bend and tough in the trenches.[7]

Powell could not have chosen a better time than 1934 to seek election to the legislature. The legislature of 1935–36 had large majorities of Democrats in both the Senate and House, thanks to the Franklin D. Roosevelt landslide of 1932. In Powell's first term, Democrats led in the Senate by 35 to 16, and in the House by 84 to 69.[8] This comfortable working majority for the Democrats continued only one more two-year term before Republicans began to make inroads, coinciding with Roosevelt's election to a third term as President and the election of a Republican governor in Illinois in 1940.

Personally, Powell did not need Roosevelt's coattails. By virtue of a provision in the 1870 constitution called cumulative voting, each of the fifty-one districts had two members from one party and one from the other, thus virtually guaranteeing a "minority" party representation. District 51 voters, Powell's home ground, historically elected two Republicans and one Democrat. For the next thirty years, when Powell was in the legislature, District 51 always sent two Republicans and Powell.

The cumulative voting concept, long a part of the Illinois political picture, had its roots in the years following the Civil War, when political regionalism in Illinois alarmed many of the state's officials. The patterns of partisanship followed established geographic lines, and nothing resembling a two-party system existed in all sections. Republicans had majorities in the central and northern parts of the state, and Democrats had strength in the western and lower portions of the state. In order to discourage these patterns and more evenly distribute party representation, those attending the 1870 convention devised a cumulative voting provision.[9]

In order to provide a "minority" party member from each district, voters could cast one vote for each of three candidates, one and a half for each of two, or three votes for any one candidate. The final option, all three votes for one, was called "plunking." Thus, Powell, who never had majority support in his district, could cultivate a solid minority vote to cast all three votes for him, and it was enough to win third place. This resulted in a "safe" seat for him.

Cumulative voting may have given minority representation throughout the state for a number of years, but the practice had its downside. It weakened political party discipline and allowed the minority representative to build long-term power centers independent of party affiliation or party workers. Furthermore, academics have discounted the impact of cumulative voting on political sectionalism by noting that most of the time minority party members voted with their majority colleagues from the same district.

Powell made the case for doubters. While he pledged public allegiance to Democratic party politics, he thumbed his nose at the discipline when coalitions were necessary to achieve his goals. He, as other southern Illinois political leaders before and after him, knew when to jettison party labels to achieve results. This pragmatic approach without loyalty to party label served Powell and his predecessors well and reflected the southern Illinois region's cultural disdain for loyalty to political parties and party authority.

For all of Powell's popularity at home, the partisan numbers would never have broken favorably for him in the district. An analysis done for Powell of voting patterns in District 51 from 1948 to 1954 demonstrates the size of

Republican strength in the district and in Johnson County, Powell's home.[10] In the 1948 election, when Democrats won across the state on the strength of Harry Truman's victory, Republicans outvoted Democrats in the district by 4,123 votes, and Johnson County went Republican 7,336 to 4,320. In the off-year election of 1950, the Republican majority increased to 12,822 in the district but narrowed in Johnson County with 7,297 for Republicans and 4,588 for Democrats.

In the Eisenhower landslide victory year of 1952, the Republican vote majority expanded to 22,266, and Republican voters nearly doubled the count on Democrats in Johnson County, 9,540 to 4,739. In the off-year election of 1954, Democrats gained ground in the district and trailed by 3,984 votes. In Johnson County, Democrats came closer than any of the three previous elections by polling 5,072 votes to 7,657 for Republicans. Judging from these numbers, without cumulative voting District 51 might never have elected a Democrat to the legislature.

The political tide in the legislature began to turn back toward Republican domination with the 1939–40 session, when Democrats lost the House 80 to 73 but kept the Senate, 31 to 20. Beginning with the session of 1941–42, at the outset of World War II and the third term for President Roosevelt, Republicans grabbed a majority in both houses.[11]

Until the election of 1948, Republicans held the governorship and both houses of the legislature. During that time, the turnover in ranks of Democrats caused by service in World War II and attrition of ranks due to Republican successes worked in Powell's favor. Comfortably in place thanks to cumulative voting, he became a fixture in the House and moved up to the leadership position of minority whip in the 1945–46 session.

From 1945 through the end of his days in the Illinois legislature in 1964, Powell served in leadership positions in all but four years. His positions of authority included three terms as speaker and four sessions as minority leader.[12] By the very nature of those leadership positions, Powell kept the counsel of the highest elected officials of the state. Because governors had a major role in the legislative process, Powell had a very direct and personal relationship with most of the men who served in that office from 1935 to 1965. Often as not, Powell and governors cooperated, regardless of party affiliation, to move serious legislation and keep the wheels of government turning. As secretary of state, from 1965 to 1970, Powell had a different but no less close relationship with the chief executives.

Governors during Powell's legislative time were Henry Horner, Democrat, 1933 to 1940; John H. Stelle, Democrat, 1940 to 1941; Dwight Green,

Republican, 1941 to 1949; Adlai Stevenson, Democrat, 1949 to 1953; William Stratton, Republican, 1953 to 1961; and Otto Kerner, Democrat, 1961 to 1965. Kerner served until being appointed a federal judge in 1968, and Samuel Shapiro, a Democrat, took over and filled out Kerner's term through 1968. Richard B. Ogilvie, a Republican, took office in 1969 and was governor when Powell died.

The relationship between Powell and any governor was complex. As Speaker and even as minority leader, Powell had considerable influence on the legislative agenda. The degree of success a governor had in pushing his bills and budget depended on Powell and the personal chemistry between them. Powell's desire to hold statewide office was one of the worst kept secrets in Springfield and made the governors naturally leery of becoming too dependent. Maybe as a result Powell developed a personal relationship with only one, John H. Stelle, who served in the position only because of the death of Governor Horner. Other governors came and went from Powell's life, but they never forgot him.

Henry Horner

As a junior member of the legislature during much of Horner's terms in office, Powell followed the lead of existing party leadership. He ably repre-sented the interests of southern Illinois in dealings with Horner, but the two did not have occasions to build a close working partnership. Generally speaking, Powell supported Horner to the extent that party leadership sup-ported him. Occasionally when Chicago support abandoned the governor, Powell extended a friendly hand. They kept some distance because Horner was in another league from Powell. The governor was a wealthy Chicagoan, a bachelor, an intellectual, and a world class collector of Lincolniana, and his friends were the elite of Chicago. Furthermore, John H. Stelle, Powell's southern Illinois associate, was Horner's most hated rival. There was tension in the governor's relationships with all southern Illinois legislators.[13]

Balancing relationships in his first years provided Powell with one of his biggest challenges. On the one hand, he believed in supporting his Democ-ratic governor. On the other, he could see that he should avoid choosing up sides between the two adversaries. Both Horner and Stelle believed in aggres-sive approaches to governing, and they had strong and determined con-stituencies. That Powell, still wet behind his legislative ears, could maneuver between them was an indication of his political instincts.

John H. Stelle

No word better describes Stelle than *provocateur*. He played more bad guy leading roles than a cinema villain of the time, Edward G. Robinson. His name evoked fear, anger, hatred, and disrespect, from the tip of southern Illinois to the Chicago Loop.

Among enemies, his name stood for betrayal and gamesmanship.[14] At the same time, he enjoyed acclaim for driving a hard southern Illinois bargain with Chicago Democrats, and like many other controversial politicians, he commanded the deepest loyalty from those he helped. Powell became a close friend and business partner.

Stelle's statewide political star rose rapidly and fell as fast. In all, he had an active political life on the state scene of less than a decade. He reached the pinnacle of state office—the governor's chair, by "accident"—after climbing relentlessly through lesser state posts, only to become a footnote in state history.[15] He understood statewide politics better than most outside the population centers and, consequently, became an ally of the Chicago Democratic machine.

Together they were formidable for the Republicans to beat. Without the Chicago link, Stelle would have been a strictly local politician long ago forgotten. Instead, because he dared to play on the statewide level and do the bidding of the Chicago machine, he left a bitter memory with many he encountered. Ultimately he earned the disrespect of mainstream Democrats, too, by supporting high-profile Republicans such as Dwight Eisenhower.

The Stelle family was a fixture in southern Illinois, specifically in Hamilton County, where the county seat is McLeansboro. A fourth generation resident of the county and son of a county judge, Stelle became a successful and creative businessman, farmer, and lawyer. He raised thoroughbred horses on his farm and raced them at county fairs throughout the state. He served gallantly in battle as a private, lieutenant, and then captain during World War I, in which he was wounded and gassed. Like many other ambitious and patriotic men, after the war he joined the American Legion and developed those contacts as a political constituency.

Riding that wave as a Democrat, Stelle looked for opportunities to break into the statewide political picture. Democrats, suffering greatly at the hands of Republicans during the 1920s, welcomed a new face and new energy, and especially if he brought along votes. His first political activity came as a result of his American Legion connections. In 1928 he helped form a downstate

Democratic organization, and in 1930 he worked on the campaign of James Lewis, candidate for U.S. Senate. In 1932 he became director of organization for the Democratic state central committee.[16]

The sponsor of Stelle's political elevation from southern Illinois was Edward J. Barrett, a Chicago Democrat who years later became a close associate of Mayor Richard J. Daley. Barrett had served in World War I, became active in the American Legion, and subsequently aligned himself with the political machine of Patrick Nash and Edward J. Kelly, which dominated the city and state political picture for most of the 1930s. Barrett cultivated the Stelle connection and friendship in order to establish a link to southern Illinois Democrats and to start his own statewide quest.

Barrett cemented the relationship by appointing Stelle assistant state treasurer in 1931. This brought Stelle into the orbit of Kelly and Nash. In 1933 Barrett was elected state auditor, and he appointed Stelle as assistant. In the same year, Kelly was appointed mayor to succeed Anton Cermak. Two years later Kelly was elected mayor of Chicago. Thanks to Barrett and Kelly, Stelle was elected state treasurer in 1934.[17]

In 1932 Mayor Cermak wanted an independent Democrat to run against incumbent Republican Gov. Len Small, and he settled on Judge Henry Horner, a German Jew reared in the Hyde Park area of Chicago. After Cermak's assassination, Kelly became mayor and soon declared Governor Horner too independent. Leading to the 1936 gubernatorial campaign with the Horner relationship in complete disarray, Kelly sought a friendly Democrat who could beat Horner and be more compatible with the Chicago machine.

Determined to overthrow Horner, in January 1936, the Kelly machine announced its support of Dr. Herman Bundesen, Chicago health commissioner, for governor. The choice shocked downstate Democrats because they had believed Kelly would anoint Bruce Campbell of Belleville to run against Horner. To assuage downstate Democrats, Kelly agreed to slate Stelle as lieutenant governor.[18]

In those days the governor and lieutenant governor candidates of a party ran separately and not as a team. This occasionally resulted in the election of a governor and lieutenant governor who did not see eye to eye. That is exactly what happened in 1936. Horner easily beat back the challenge of Bundesen, but Stelle won the lieutenant governor race, although the only county he carried outside Cook was his own. Immediately he became Governor Horner's worst nightmare.

Consider the position this put Powell in as a new state legislator from southern Illinois. Powell had been in the state legislature just two years at the time of Horner's reelection. At that point his loyalties were to the mainstream Democratic party, not the Chicago branch. Powell supported Horner's reelection and remained a friend until the governor's death in 1940. All indications are that Powell and Horner had a frank, if not cozy, relationship during that time.

Horner's biographer recalled a conversation between the two over a Horner-proposed increase in the sales tax that epitomized their candor. Powell showed a stack of telegrams opposing the tax increase to Horner. The governor thumbed through the telegrams and turned to Powell: "That one cost a buck! That one costs 75 cents! I'm interested in the people who don't have a buck, who don't have a nickel."[19]

Stelle, on the other hand, carried on constant war with Horner, as Kelly's principal agent in Springfield. Upon the death of Horner on October 6, 1940, Stelle became governor of Illinois, to the disgust of Horner's loyalists and to the cheers of those who had followed Stelle in his quest to unseat Horner, one way or another. The new governor cleaned house of Horner's friends and backers during his ninety-nine days as governor, firing more than 250 state jobholders.[20]

Although they had worked together on some issues, Powell and Stelle remained separated to a great extent over the issue of Governor Horner. After the swearing in of Stelle, Powell walked to the lieutenant governor's office and offered to make peace, knowing what Stelle had in store for Horner's followers. Powell feared Stelle would purge his patronage jobs. Years later, Powell told a reporter, "But it [the change of governors] only cost me four jobs."

Stelle ran for governor in 1940 and lost badly; he then returned to southern Illinois, where he devoted much of his time to national American Legion affairs and to horse racing. Horner's biographer characterized Stelle's postgovernor career this way: "Out of office and back at McLeansboro, he frequently raised his voice as a southern Illinois Democrat who had Republican friends in high places."[21] Not the least interested in Adlai Stevenson either as governor or president, he made speeches for Eisenhower in 1952. Stelle supported winning GOP candidates for governor in Illinois (Stratton) and Indiana, where he had business interests. In 1956, when Stevenson again carried the party's national banner, Stelle, Powell, and their associates refused to back Stevenson and instead supported Missouri Sen. Stuart Symington.[22]

After losing the 1940 gubernatorial race, Stelle maintained close political contact with Chicago Democrats, especially Barrett. In 1952, Stelle wanted Barrett to run for governor, but the Chicago machine did not choose him.

With his friend rejected, Stelle supported Republican William Stratton. Powell assumed the role of booster for Barrett by attempting to put Barrett's name in play for governor in the 1960 race, but Mayor Daley did not consider it.

Barrett had a successful political career at the state level until 1956; he then became a close associate and confidant of Daley, being elected to and serving in the sensitive position of county clerk and providing an important link for Powell to the Daley organization. Barrett was charged and convicted in federal court in 1973 on charges of bribery and mail fraud. Barrett's prosecutor was James R. Thompson, who later served four terms as governor.[23]

This practical political streak—some called it lack of loyalty to anything but personal interests—became common ground for a lasting friendship between Stelle and Powell. An older Stelle explained the way he cultivated Chicago Democrats and teamed up with Republicans to get things accomplished: "There I was, three hundred miles south of Chicago. I had to have a foothold in Chicago. Without it I would have been dead as a mackerel."[24] Powell might have written that statement about himself.

Stelle and Powell worked to pass the Illinois Harness Racing Act in 1945, which established pari-mutuel betting for harness racing. Together they promoted the breeding of horses in Illinois, racing at county fairs, and the pulling together of politics and racing. Along the way they helped each other earn thousands of dollars. One writer said of Stelle, "In horse racing circles he was the most influential downstater."[25] Until Powell came along.

Stelle's business interests ranged widely as he operated in the political background. He held extensive oil interests in Illinois and at one time had involvement in more than twenty syndicates that developed Illinois oil fields. The family business in Indiana—Arketex Ceramic Corporation—enjoyed huge success nationally and kept his family fed for years. Still, horse breeding and racing were Stelle's first loves.

In 1953 Stelle and a handful of southern Illinois politicians formed Cahokia Downs racetrack near East St. Louis, and he brought Powell into that orbit immediately. Stelle had more than 15 percent of the stock in Cahokia Downs, plus $50,000 in debentures. Powell and Stelle, among others, later organized and successfully operated the Egyptian Trotting Association. Stelle's stake in Egyptian Trotting amounted to 12,500 shares of common stock, the largest single holding. Those holdings, as it turned out, were inflated because they included shares owned by Powell.[26]

As a leading promoter of Cahokia Downs and as its longtime president, Stelle covered for Powell and protected his friend's holdings from public disclosure. The common stock holdings of Powell in Cahokia Downs would have been subject to public knowledge except that Stelle held them in his name while Powell paid taxes on the income. This way of concealing ownership was extended by Powell to many politicians who subsequently invested heavily in his racetrack ventures. He frequently arranged for little-known people to have their names used for racetrack stock held by well-known politicians such as Chicago's Dan Rostenkowski.

At his death, on July 5, 1962, Stelle's estate, valued at $1,500,000, went to his widow, Wilma, who lived at McLeansboro, and two sons, John A. of Brazil, Indiana, and Russell T. Stelle of Terre Haute, Indiana. John A., or John Albert as he became known to Illinois politicians, stepped into his father's racetrack shoes immediately. He succeeded his father as a trustee of Cahokia Downs Voting Trust. John A. also picked up where his father left off in helping Powell. The stock in Cahokia Downs and Egyptian Downs belonging to Powell was transferred in name to the younger Stelle.[27]

Dwight Green

There certainly was no reason for Powell to have a feeling of closeness to Governor Green, a Republican attorney who built his reputation on the prosecution of Al Capone and whose home territory was Chicago. That high-profile court drama earned Green a reputation that he rode to election in 1940 and reelection in 1944, but he had little exposure to downstate Democrats or even to the issues and concerns of southern Illinois, except when he needed their votes in the legislature. He got the votes by offering patronage jobs to the economically deprived lower third of the state.[28]

While Green prevailed, Powell earned his first leadership position as minority whip in 1945. In party affairs, Powell served as downstate director of the Democratic State Central Committee, expanded his exposure to party leaders in Chicago, and put himself in a position to help Democratic candidates for governor.

In the wake of World War II, the GOP continued to dominate state politics, and Powell found himself a leader of diminishing forces in Springfield. As matters shaped up for the 1948 campaign, Green and the Republicans looked formidable. State Democrats fretted over a damaged Harry S. Truman at the top of the ticket, an incumbent Republican governor, and no Democrat of stature to contend for governor. Chicago machine Democrats decided the chances of unseating Green would be better with a reform governor candidate, and they finally chose political neophyte Adlai E. Stevenson to carry the banner. Powell, who had stepped into party leadership downstate, became campaign manager outside Chicago for the Democratic ticket headed by Truman and Stevenson.

Adlai E. Stevenson

Truman swept Illinois like a prairie breeze; Stevenson won by more than a half million votes over Green, and Democrats took over the state House of Representatives. The outcome threw Powell and Stevenson together, as unlikely a pair as could be encountered in politically diverse Illinois.

Before Stevenson took office, Powell was embroiled in the contest of his life, and it proved to be an early test of the relationship. Powell wanted to be Speaker of the House, and he wanted Stevenson's blessing. But the governor-elect waffled, fearing an alliance with Powell would anger Chicago Democrats and make him too beholden to the southern Illinois wing of the party.

Stevenson's biographer stated it this way: "He [Stevenson] was haunted by the Horner story. He thought that because Horner had gotten himself at odds with the Chicago organization, therefore to win he had to turn to the downstaters who were worse than anyone in Chicago—John Stelle and the rest of them—and therefore Horner's whole ability to work in the public interest was compromised. Nobody in the Chicago organization ever seemed as evil as John Stelle or Paul Powell. Stevenson felt it was vital not to be driven into the arms of the southern Democrats."[29]

The Stelle connection with Powell and the fear Stevenson felt toward southern Illinois drove the governor-elect to neutrality in the race for Speaker. This was a sharp blow to Powell, who thought Stevenson could do no less than repay him for the campaign help.[30]

Powell never forgot the rejection, and it colored the relationship with Stevenson for years. Longtime Springfield reporter, historian, and author Robert P. Howard recalled the edge on the relationship between Powell and Stevenson: "I'm sure that Adlai had a certain fondness for him when Paul was speaker. Paul never could understand Stevenson because Stevenson was a moral man who didn't think that there should be any shenanigans going on."

Howard remembered Powell telling him of a conversation with Stevenson during which Powell said, "You ought to leave some poontang in for the boys." Howard said Stevenson had no idea what Powell was talking about. When among friends and Stevenson's name came up, Powell quipped that he was going to write a book about the governor and that the title was "Hypocrites I Have Known."[31]

During those four years, Stevenson and Powell wore happy faces in public to demonstrate cooperation and achievements, hoping that would help the party retain advantages in 1952. Although Stevenson's total legislative achievements were modest, the two did their best to smile in public. There was no better example than toward the end of Stevenson's term in 1951, when Powell helped the governor pass a gas tax and raise truck license fees after a terrible fight in the legislature. Stevenson personally thanked Powell for his help, and Powell, always prepared to characterize a tough decision in terms of money, replied, "I'm mighty glad to have your thanks, Governor, because it cost me $50,000."[32]

Stevenson helped Powell, too, namely on a bill that permitted harness racing and pari-mutuel betting at racetracks in summer months. This also showed a practical side of Stevenson often missing in accounts of his administration. Powell told associates that he put it on the line politically with Stevenson when the Speaker asked for a signature on the bill. Stevenson allegedly opposed the bill, but then he heard Powell say: "You're thinking about running for governor again. Have you any other ideas of running for office? Every county fair in the state of Illinois, they'll all be against you because this is going to help them."[33]

While there may not have been any love lost between Stevenson and Powell, when the governor decided to run for president against Dwight Eisenhower, the political roof fell in on Powell and the party, in effect killing Democratic chances to retain the governorship and a majority in the House. Eisenhower swamped Stevenson, took Illinois in a gallop, and brought into the state's executive office a Republican, William G. Stratton. Powell might have taken Stevenson for another term if it had meant continuing as speaker, but Stratton turned out to be a digestible alternative.

William G. Stratton

By comparison, the Stratton years for Powell were congenial, although from 1952 to 1958 Democrats in the legislature did not fare well. Republicans dominated the House, and Powell slipped out of top party leadership.

Chicago legislative Democrats became more aggressive in the quest for leadership positions after the election of Daley as mayor in 1955, leaving Powell on the sidelines for the first time since 1945. Powell served as minority leader in the sessions of 1951 and 1953, but in the sessions of 1955 and 1957,

Joseph De La Cour, a Chicago Democrat, took charge with Daley's blessing. Powell did not bow out of the action, however. He worked diligently for his agenda and looked for opportunities to help Stratton. The strategy paid off before the end of Stratton's second term.

Many downstate Democrats considered Stratton agreeable and easy to work with, including associates of Powell and persons close to the business of horse racing. Clyde Lee, who during Stratton's terms invested in racing operations at Cahokia Downs, Chicago Downs, and Egyptian Trotting, considered Stratton friendly to racing interests: "I'd say Governor Stratton was more interested in the State Fair than any governor that I served under. He was always at the fair during fair week and attended our meetings. . . . If we had any problems, we could go in and talk to him about them."[34] A governor sympathetic to the state fair and county fairs quickly moved to the top of the favored list with downstate legislators. Lee said: "Stratton was, in my book, an outstanding governor. I believe he had about as close a knowledge of everything that was going on in the state of any governor I ever served under."

While there is no such accolade from Powell on record, his actions and the observations of others might be taken as confirmation of Lee's declaration. Powell's work on Stratton issues drew this assertion from former legislator Anthony Scariano: "Powell certainly helped Stratton win the 1956 gubernatorial election. They exchanged favors for each other."[35]

For this and other favors, Stratton's opportunity to return the favor occurred early in 1959. With Democrats in control of the House (91 to 86) for the first time since 1949, Powell seemed poised to return as Speaker. However, Chicago Democrats had other thoughts and pushed De La Cour forward for the job. Powell needed the votes of Republicans to break the Democratic deadlock and be elected Speaker. At a key moment, Stratton addressed Republicans at a reception, saying, "I'd like for you to vote for Powell on the second ballot."[36] Republicans and downstate Democrats elected Powell as Speaker, and the victory worked for Stratton, too. Later in 1959, Powell provided enough Democratic votes to pass a half cent sales tax increase that Stratton had promoted.

Powell spoke publicly about Stratton late in 1959, in what must be viewed as a pat on the back and encouragement for the governor to seek a third term in 1960: "In my opinion Stratton is stronger now than he was three years ago. If anybody thinks [he] is easy, he is whistling in the dark."[37] Stratton did seek a third term, was nominated, and lost to Otto Kerner.

Powell surfaced briefly in Stratton's life a few years after the gubernatorial term ended, on an issue that in retrospect had serious meaning. It began four years after Stratton left office, when he was indicted for violating income tax laws regarding political contributions. Many elected officials rushed to Stratton's defense, including Sen. Everett Dirksen, who said that a governor has ceremonial duties that are official in part, for which use of unrestricted contributions is justified. Powell, among many others, contributed money to Stratton's defense, causing a reporter to ask why he aided a Republican. "If they get Bill Stratton on this charge, they'll get us all," Powell said. After a costly trial, ending in Stratton's acquittal, Powell wrote the former governor: "I am herewith enclosing my personal check in the amount of $500 to assist you in a small way in paying part of your legal expenses incurred in what I consider a great victory, not only for yourself but every other person who is in political life."[38]

Otto Kerner

After the election of 1960, with John F. Kennedy in the White House and Otto Kerner in Springfield, Republicans maintained a slight majority in the state House (89 to 88). In what must count as a political miracle, Powell was chosen as Speaker with renegade Republicans providing the margin of victory. Upon his election, Powell addressed the Democratic caucus and offered this comparison of Gov. Otto Kerner with former Gov. Adlai Stevenson: "Now boys this here Governor Kerner is a real governor—not like Stevenson. If you got problems you can come in and talk to him. He won't give you that highfalutin' talk."[39]

Described by one observer of Springfield affairs as "proud, handsome, urbane, courteous and naive," Kerner might have passed for another version of Stevenson, except that he did not surround himself with quality people, and his allegiance to Mayor Daley prevented him from demonstrating much independence.

Although there is nothing on the record to show that Powell and Kerner enjoyed a close association or shared common interests in horse racing, it was the sport that eventually brought riches to Powell, and Kerner to his knees. In 1973 Kerner was convicted of conspiracy, mail fraud, income tax evasion, and making false statements in income tax returns, involving the purchase of racetrack stock from Mrs. Marjorie Lindheimer Everett, a dominant figure in Illinois racing.

After receiving stock from Everett, Kerner appointed her friends to racing boards, gave her tracks the racing dates she requested, signed legislation she desired, and fired a harness racing board chairman who insisted that a competing track deserved consideration.[40] All of this occurred while Powell was active in racetrack affairs, but it came to light after Powell's death.

Samuel Shapiro and Richard B. Ogilvie

For the last six years of his life, Powell held one of the state's most influential political jobs, secretary of state. With roles changed and Powell less dependent on or able to help a governor, his relationships with Gov. Samuel Shapiro and Gov. Richard B. Ogilvie had few legislative highs or lows. Powell did not hold Shapiro in particularly high esteem because of political differences they shared when each served in the legislature. Powell believed Shapiro, a downstater, had played his cards too closely with Richard Daley.[41]

Ogilvie served as governor less than two years before Powell's death. In that period, nothing occurred to draw them close. Prior to his governorship, however, Ogilvie served in key Cook County positions of sheriff and chair of the Cook County Board, both traditionally held by Democrats. During Powell's terms as secretary of state, issues arose over the involvement of his office with Chicago crime figures and a secretary of state investigator whose actions created headlines. While Ogilvie and Powell did not have direct conflicts during those episodes, people who worked for Ogilvie and people who worked for Powell did. Not surprisingly, the two principals did not find comfort in each other's company.

In nearly a lifetime of state and local politics, Powell discovered over and over that his own knowledge and experience counted for little without the help of others. He honed an ability almost unmatched to mobilize coalitions inside the legislature and found that the favors he spread among colleagues paid off for years. Powell also demonstrated a willingness to help people and organizations in need from one end of the state to the other. Those people became his most ferocious defenders.

On the flip side, those who found Powell and his manner offensive attacked relentlessly from within and battled him through the media and in public forums. Now, nearly thirty years after his death, the feelings about Powell are as intense as they were in his prime. But quarrel as they might over Powell's motives and legacy, his friends and enemies agree on one truth about Paul Powell: He was unforgettable.

When it came to an opinion of Paul Powell, it did not make much difference on which side of the fence elected officials, public figures, and just plain people found themselves. In a chorus, they sang his praises as legislator, master of the bully pulpit, friend in need, believer in his causes, and manipulator of the system. He may have been, as his longtime friend state Rep. Clyde Choate said at the funeral service, "the most unforgettable man ever to walk these halls."[42] Or, maybe his banker friend Mel Lockard caught the essence of Powell: "Paul was always a good friend of mine because we came from the same part of the state and because we trusted one another."[43] Powell's antagonist Adlai E. Stevenson explained him another way: "He knew the shortest distance between two points as a curve."[44]

Paul O'Neal, once chairman of the Johnson County Democratic organization and the person credited with getting Powell his first political job, provided the local perspective of Powell's work: "I was with him when he'd go into places and people would be putting hundred dollar bills in his pocket. But he was a good man and a savior to southern Illinois. He was our Mayor Daley. Look at all the jobs and people he helped. He never turned anybody down. If he couldn't help you, he'd tell you straight out. But he'd never just rush you right out the door."[45]

You might expect his longtime associates to speak well of him, and they did without prompting. John S. Rendleman, who learned the ways of state politics at Powell's knee and eventually became the executor of his estate, identified his mentor as "one of the smartest men ever sent to the legislature of the State of Illinois."[46] That was in 1964, just four years before Rendleman became chancellor of the Edwardsville campus of SIU.

Powell's generosity for those who needed help, often with money, added considerably to his reputation as a friend in need. W. J. Murphy, a Republican representative from Antioch, Illinois, in the 1950s and 1960s, and a loyal Powell supporter and solid vote for racetrack legislation, came upon hard financial times during 1969. He had invested several hundred thousand dollars in a resort in Wisconsin Dells, Wisconsin, and found himself deeply in debt.

In a July 1969 letter to Powell, Murphy said that the financial situation resulted from his lengthy absence while serving in the legislature and from heavy summer rains that had delayed construction. He asked Powell to buy a share of the resort. Rather than become a partner, Powell loaned his legislative friend $15,000 on terms of Murphy's choice.[47] Powell's letter with check enclosed to Murphy on August 11, 1969, said: "You can make the due date any time you wish and, naturally, if at that time you are unable to pay the principle you can always renew it. The time and rate of interest will be left entirely up to you because the interest does not mean anything to me as long as I can assist you in this small way."[48] The loan was still on the books when Powell died a year later.

Powell also knew how and when to reward someone for loyalty. In 1951, when newspapers revealed the dealing that resulted in the establishment of the Chicago Downs harness racetrack, they disclosed that legislators had been placed on the organization's payroll. Furthermore, the newspapers divulged they were hired on the recommendation of Powell, and all of them had been visible in efforts to pass legislation in 1949 that created Chicago Downs.

One of the employed legislators was W. B. Westbrook, a Republican from Harrisburg in Powell's home district and a longtime cohort in county fair activities. When asked about placing his friends on the payroll, Powell, never offering an excuse, said: "There's nothing secret about working there. Some of them have worked around tracks for years and are a lot of protection to the bettors. It is better to hire them than to pick touts off the street."[49]

The strongest sentiments about Powell during his life and after were inspired by his years in the legislature. The inevitability of working hundreds of issues, asking for or demanding favors and support, rejecting countless requests for special legislation, and overseeing political fights by the score all shaped the public image of Powell. Few saw Powell as closely through the years as longtime Springfield reporter Robert Howard, who first met Powell in the 1930s: "He had charisma. He had brains, but he also was the type of personality that you would remember. . . . You couldn't help but like the man. . . . He had a down-to-earth way of speaking. He was totally friendly; he had this southern twang in his voice. But he had the personality. You would have to know definitely that he was a crook before you would turn completely against him, even if he didn't vote for your bills; it was hard to dislike him."[50]

Hard, perhaps, but not impossible. He had plenty of enemies and opponents, and among the most articulate and persistent through the years were two Chicago area Democrats with strong moderate to liberal credentials. Abner Mikva and Anthony Scariano were among a small band of legislators who warred with Powell on budgetary issues, racetrack legislation, and other subjects dear to Powell. They worked with others who shared their points of view, including downstaters Paul Simon and Belleville's Alan Dixon, both of whom later went on to serve in the U.S. Senate. Mikva and Scariano both entered the House of Representatives in the mid-1950s, at the peak of Powell's power and influence. They never made Powell's hit parade.

In the early 1960s no one on the Democratic side of the House battled Powell more than Mikva, Democratic representative from the University of Chicago area, later a member of Congress from Illinois, a federal appeals court judge, and eventually legal counsel to President Bill Clinton. Although he fought Powell on a variety of issues, in 1961 and 1963 Mikva went after one of Powell's favorite subjects: racetracks. Mikva mounted efforts to increase the state's take from racetracks, but Powell defeated him soundly. Mikva acknowledged that he never beat Powell on a racetrack issue. In a letter to the author, Mikva succinctly summed up his lasting impression of Powell: "I did not like him or trust him, but his influence was great, and he had great talent."[51]

Mikva's legislative sidekick, Scariano, shared a disdain for the Powell agenda and worked as hard against it as he did the agenda of Mayor Daley, another official with whom he disagreed openly. Speaking after he left the legislature and became a judge, Scariano painted Powell as a self-centered, grasping individual without the slightest ethical standard. Scariano believes Powell did anything necessary for money and power: "Paul Powell was for Paul Powell. I don't think he was the competent legislator that some people say he is. Everything he got in the legislature was through either ill-gotten power or ill-gotten gains."[52]

Scariano's criticism tied Powell closely to lobbyists, special interests, and campaign contributions:

> Paul Powell's power was built on the jobs that he could get people. Paul Powell's power came from lobbies and he could get a lot of favors from lobbies. Paul Powell's power came from his being given a certain amount of money in the form of campaign contributions. Paul would go to different people and put two hundred dollars on this guy, a few hundred on this guy . . . and he'd buy himself votes in that legislature. He'd help these people out during the election campaigns. . . . Paul always got enough money to help these people and then have something left over for himself. That's power. That's how power was built, by Powell at least, on jobs that he could get from state institutions, from private industry in lobbies he could command a lot of favors.

During the first sixty years of the twentieth century, Powell held the office of Speaker of the House more than any Democrat. But that achievement did not impress Scariano: "Powell could have accomplished what he did without being speaker. He may have had a certain amount of power with respect to calling bills or not calling bills, assignments to committees and that sort of thing. But Paul Powell never exercised that in my opinion in a fair, even-handed or honest way. He had people to pay off and he paid them off. He had lobbies to take care of and he took care of them. When you're just a traffic cop regulating the flow of bills, what competence does it take except a guy who knows how to wield the gavel. If you call that competence, he was a competent speaker."

Finally, Scariano played back a lasting criticism of Powell's coziness with horse racing: "You couldn't touch racetracks while Paul was there. We didn't increase racetrack taxes during all the time that Paul Powell was in the legislature. Every tax on the books was being increased, all sorts of new taxes came in, but you could never touch the racetracks."

Liberals and anti-machine legislators found Powell an easy target, but one of the most prominent friends of Adlai Stevenson wrote glowingly of Powell's reputation in Springfield. John Bartlow Martin, writer for and adviser to Stevenson and student of the Illinois legislature, wrote a two-volume biography of the governor.

During his description of Stevenson's four years in Springfield, Martin analyzed Powell's skills: "Now Paul Powell was a formidable figure. He was almost surely the most powerful downstate Democratic politician [in 1948]. A rangy man with a southern Illinois drawl, given to using slang, possessor of a loud florid oratorical style, a man of undistinguished appearance, when he arose on the floor of the House of Representatives he suddenly became a commanding presence that dominated the House."[53]

At another point in his book, Martin wrote: "Powell was a man of great native ability and intelligence. He knew every highway and byway in Springfield, especially the byways. He was a fearsome alley fighter, a slashing, devastating debater. He knew every pressure point in the Illinois legislature, knew what made each vote turn. He sought power and it flowed to him."[54]

That power also came from his voice. Friends and enemies credited Powell with an oratorical style that literally could change votes and move audiences. In a time now when oratory changes hardly anything in legislative arenas, it is difficult to imagine someone so persuasive. One example of his pulpit power occurred in 1961. The result, as the Associated Press reported, was a dramatic switch of votes on a bill to authorize Chicago to grant a lease for construction of a big hotel at O'Hare International Airport on city property. To help sell the bill, Powell stepped to the floor from the Speaker's rostrum and delivered one of the homespun talks for which he became famous. The bill got 94 votes, 5 more than needed for approval. The week before, the bill had received only 84 votes.[55]

Maurice Scott, who earned a reputation as one of the state's most credible tax experts and who worked with Powell on many financial issues, recalls a time when Powell turned on his verbal charm to defeat a bill: "There was a bill a number of years ago to increase the salaries of the legislators. Well, there was some criticism in the press and so forth—not like today, that bill was in the early days when they were making $2,500 a year. Well, I remember Paul getting up on the legislation to oppose it. I remember one of his remarks. He said, 'You know, if we get this salary up too large, why, the people will be electing some smart people and we'll be out of a job.' It brought down the house, but killed the bill."[56]

As controlled as he appeared to be in public, Powell had a long memory and seldom forgot unpleasant encounters. His experience with Governor Stevenson is a good example. More than a decade after his direct dealings with Stevenson, he perpetuated the image of the governor as a wealthy, pampered, overindulged dandy. Proving that he could carry a grudge to another generation, Powell did everything possible to thwart the statewide political career of the governor's son, Adlai E. Stevenson III.

In 1968, Adlai III, who started his own political march in 1964 as a state representative and then won as state treasurer in 1966, wanted to make another leap. He hoped to be slated by the Democratic organization either to run for governor or U.S. senator. All contenders for slating had to appear before the party's hierarchy, headed by Mayor Daley. Powell, too, sat on the slating committee.

Stevenson argued that he deserved an upgrade to top of the ticket. Reflecting the civic unrest and Vietnam War subjects as intense political issues, he was quizzed at length on his loyalty to the Democratic ticket and to President Lyndon Johnson's war policies. Powell went after the younger Stevenson on these subjects. Does this mean that you would not support all Democrats? Would you take the ticket from the top to the bottom? Riled by Powell, Stevenson fired back, "You have your loyalties and I have mine," and then he walked from the room. Daley, sensing disapproval among the mainstream Democrats in the room but also recognizing the power of Stevenson's name on the ticket, reminded slatemakers "that Adlai is a Stevenson. Generations of Stevensons have supported the Democratic ticket."[57] Stevenson was not slated for governor or the senate that year.

With an opportunity to square accounts on the public record at Powell's death, Stevenson, then the party's candidate for U.S. Senate, spoke carefully of his family nemesis: "His death leaves an emptiness in Illinois politics that will never be filled. I will miss him and so will countless others." Later, after discovery of the $800,000 in cash, Stevenson got in this final word, with a suggestion for Powell's epitaph: "It will be difficult to fill his shoebox."[58]

Taking the measure of Powell requires more than a shoe box full of one-liners, although that is often the way Powell treated serious subjects. The media contributed to this joke-book aspect of Powell's career that made for chuckles and anecdotes on the speaker's trail but added little to an understanding of the man. In some respects those most capable of providing a meaningful assessment have refused to comment or have offered a cleansed version.

Nonetheless, Powell spent countless hours developing his personality with the media. With an innate understanding of the power of newspapers in his time, he cultivated the Springfield press corps, stayed away from journalists who lived and worked in the big cities, and snubbed editorial pages. His favorite comment about the press—with variations to suit the audience or circumstance—was "I don't care what you say about me, just don't forget me."[59]

Reporters in Springfield were torn over their relationship with Powell. They investigated his actions and revealed his weaknesses, but they were fascinated by the man, his words, and his power. Twice they named him the most effective legislator in the state. They kept files of his quips and one-liners and never missed an opportunity to tell a Powell story. Until he became a statewide public official, investigative reporters outside Springfield paid little attention to Powell.

Reporter Howard acknowledged many encounters with Powell over the years, and he put the man in perspective: "He was an important politician and also a public official you needed to keep in touch with. Also, he was very entertaining. He would talk forever, and use his southern Illinois twang. Sometimes I thought he was filibustering and just talking while he was thinking—thinking when he was talking and deciding later on just what he would say of consequence."[60]

In their roles as observers, many journalists saw how Powell's style, his methods, and his effectiveness worked together. O. T. (Jack) Banton, legislative correspondent for Lindsay-Schaub newspapers during the Powell heydays, expressed the blend this way: "His southern drawl, and what is often described as his Will Rogers flavor of dry humor enables him to apply soothing syrup effectively when House battles grow tense, and to be respected and obeyed when he whacks the gavel."[61]

Shelby Vasconcelles spent a lifetime working as a staff member with the press at the Illinois state capital in Springfield. As much a fixture there as the House and Senate chamber pillars, Vasconcelles watched legislators come and go and observed the press in its good moments and its bad. He remembered Powell as frequenting the pressroom and having a "good relationship with the press."

Vasconcelles said: "Paul Powell came from down in the southern part of the state and he used to come in there and he'd tell the fellows from Chicago—what we called metropolitan newspapers—that everybody in his home town was real happy because they put his name in the Chicago papers. He didn't care how they put it in, or what they said about him, but he said 'As long as you put it in there, it makes me happy.' He said 'You can say anything you want.' And that's the way he was. If he really had something to say he'd say it."[62]

His position and rank in the legislature made him of special importance to Chicago political columnists who not only wrote about happenings in Springfield but also were part of the lobbying action. Among columnists such as George Tagge of the *Chicago Tribune*, this was especially true. Tagge worked as hard for the *Tribune*'s favorite Chicago civic projects and politicians as he did gathering material for his well-read column. One of the items Powell carried on his person at death was a tattered copy of a Tagge column dating back to 1949.

Tagge exerted significant influence throughout the state by virtue of the *Tribune*'s circulation. Longtime Springfield *Sun-Times* correspondent Thomas B. Littlefield wrote: "Political Editor George Tagge wore several hats in Springfield, as reporter, ex officio lobbyist for his newspaper, and as a kind of father confessor of the Republican party. . . . Tagge could interview a Republican legislator for a news story, lobby in behalf of a bill to increase legal advertising rates and offer counsel on campaigning tactics, all at the same time."[63]

Representative Scariano explained how Powell worked: "You had numerous instances where he was very friendly with some newspaper people. And whenever the particular reporter thought that a bill was harmful to his particular paper, well he'd go talk to Paul. And we'd see the results of it. Sometimes he was rather outspoken about it, too. Sometimes they'd climb on him mercilessly, but they didn't refrain from looking him up when they needed him. They had respect for that kind of power and they closed in on it whenever it served their own particular purposes."[64]

When the editorial pages of the metropolitan daily papers in St. Louis and Chicago took a swing at Powell, they often bounced him hard. This represented the institutional view of Powell, an elitist approach to a man who thought of himself as a populist. Of all the newspaper editorial pages that found Powell a favorite target, none hit harder at his style, his choice of subject matter, and his flexible ethical standards than the *St. Louis Post-Dispatch*. On the other hand, Chicago newspapers often treated Powell's behavior and comments as more of the same from a man who would not change no matter what they said. Editorialists knew Powell was most inclined to ignore editorials.

The *Post-Dispatch* demonstrated how it would watch Powell carefully as he ascended to a position of power in Illinois state government. The paper nipped at Powell on the eve of the 1949 vote for Speaker of House, at a time when Powell clearly was the leading contender. The paper had a major stake in Stevenson's success, and it feared Powell's motives. In a December 1948 editorial titled "The Danger in Paul Powell," the paper said in conclusion: "The Democrats in the House should look over their membership and see whether they may not do better than take a leader who seems only to 'smell the meat a-cookin'.' . . . The possibility of a Speaker of the John Stelle school of pie counter politics should be a warning to everyone in Illinois who wishes to see the November victory made good in legislative practice."[65]

Given another chance to swing at Powell as a result of revelations about Chicago Downs stock ownership in 1951, the *Post-Dispatch*, after pointing out the relationship of Powell to 1949 legislation and the holdings of his wife, Daisy, in Chicago Downs, said, "Just how different is it to participate in the passage of a bill for a money bribe as against bonanza stock or a lavishly paid job?"[66] Then and later there is no indication that the paper ever held much sway with Powell.

Three months and countless revelations after Powell's death, the *Post-Dispatch* seemed rather mellow, if still snippy, about Powell. In an editorial titled "Paul Powell, American," the paper commented on plans of a harness racing group in Illinois to award a $2,000 college scholarship for the best essay on "Paul Powell and Americanism": "A scholarship aspirant might accurately point out that Mr. Powell proved that public service can be a rewarding career. Equipped with little more than a lot of initiative and a sizable closet, the engaging rustic from Little Egypt rose to important heights in state government."

Often less inclined to take politics with as straight a face, the Chicago newspapers grew accustomed to Powell in the same manner they accepted the raw power and marginal ethics of Chicago's elected officials. In 1951, after newspaper accounts of Powell's stock ownership in Chicago Downs and assistance in putting his legislative pals on the racetrack payroll, the *Chicago Daily News*, one of the more liberal institutions in the city, spoke editorially under the heading "Gifts for Favors." At no time did the editorial mention Powell by name, although it was clear he was the target. "A public man of sensitive scruples will not embrace these opportunities. . . . It is a matter of common observation that scruples in high places do not seem as sensitive as they ought to be, and as we believe they were in earlier days."[67] A glancing blow compared with the *Post-Dispatch*.

Some eighteen years later, the *Daily News* editorialized in the wake of information that Powell had been on the Chicago Downs payroll as a consultant for many years, in addition to being a substantial holder of stock in the track operation. Rather than nail Powell to some public post, the editorial, titled "'Moonlighter' Powell," concluded: "But we're forced to concede at the same time that Powell has never made any secret of his moonlighting, declaring 'This income has kept me free from bribes or acting in any way in conflict of office.' That is Vienna sausage however you slice it, but the voters have gone on buying it."

After a series of articles in 1966 alleging Powell associations with mob-related people, the *Daily News* again offered its editorial thoughts with sarcasm scarcely hidden: "Time has amply established that friendly Paul Powell is the people's own choice, and that whatever he has cost the taxpayers is a modest price for the services of such a man."[68]

Once in a great while an editorial page would pause to reflect on actions of the legislature, and Powell would get the kind of mention that made his scrapbook. One such editorial appeared in June 1955, in the *Chicago Tribune*, under the headline "Men Who Make Our Laws." Written at a time when he had slipped out of House leadership, thanks to Mayor Daley, the *Tribune* went out of its way to be reflective:

> Powell is just as much a leader without title as he was when speaker of the house at the 1949 session. Certainly he is as much a leader as when he was elected spokesman for Democratic minorities in four general sessions. This year he has no title, by order of Cook county party brass hats. And still some go so far as to say he is "leader of both sides of the house." . . . Powell can shout, but this has little to do with the fact that he is the best orator in the legislature. Whether he is loud or quiet, the members listen closely. . . . High school was his top mark in education until he used the world—and particularly the legislature these 22 years—for a textbook. No lawyer, he goes to the heart of laws.

Through everything, for more than thirty-five years in Springfield, Powell's friends were willing to forget and forgive. There was, and still is, an amazing tolerance for his behavior, even to the graft that seemed to be part of his method of operating.

Powell's style in Springfield was to promote a coziness with hangers-on, some members of the press, and generally with those who liked to stay in his good graces. This gave him a platform for his folksy humor and anecdotes and added to his legend. The location for much of this schmoozing was the St. Nicholas Hotel, which ultimately played a center stage role in discoveries of cash after his death. But while living, Powell was bigger than life at the

St. Nick. It was his home, and he maintained it as much more than just a place to put his head at night. He managed during his secretary of state years to have the state pay for lodging at the St. Nick.

Gene Tyhurst, who managed the St. Nick during many of Powell's years in Springfield, talked after the death about the politician's routine and revealed more of the relationships Powell had with legislators and hangers-on: "The man brought in over 80 per cent of our business and we were grateful, so we paid his room bill. And if someone didn't pick up the meal tab, we would upon occasion. But Powell used to call every month and nervously ask how much he owed. The hotel wasn't the same after he died. He was the spirit of the St. Nick."[69]

Tyhurst described the suite where Powell lived and where he met with people of all stations in life: "He kept his storage room, which was located next to his suite, stuffed with goodies and gifts. When you visited his room, he let you in and then locked the door behind you. It gave you an eerie feeling. He did a lot of wonderful things for people, even though he was such as character, and the hotel staff loved him. The man who had the key to his room and cleaned up for him was said to have sold the key for $400 after he died."

Howard, a true habitué of Springfield, while working there or in retirement, adds flavor to event time at the St. Nick with Powell performing and also describes a kind of lasting impression of Powell:

> When he was secretary of state, he would announce new programs for his office—change on the driver's license system or something like that—with a luncheon at the St. Nick—invite the pressroom and the proper members of his staff and any old friends who were around. There he would just hand out the press release. The luncheon would be delayed while the bar was open and Paul would tell stories about the early days of campaigning in the Depression, and his relationship with John Stelle. In the Depression, people from southern Illinois especially were short on money—stories about how he would drive to Springfield in a Ford car; and if he didn't have enough money for a hotel room, he'd sleep in the car. The last time he did this, he was over on one side of the room repeating these anecdotes about the old days.[70]

Far and wide virtually everyone who could form an opinion had one about Paul Powell. But none captured the essence of Powell in fewer words than C. L. McCormick, a Vienna Republican, legislator, and friend of Powell. In 1959, McCormick stated: "Powell comes from Johnson County, whose steep hills necessitate wearing thick heeled shoes. Sniping at Powell's heels won't hurt him a bit."[71]

3

The Pinnacle: Mr. Speaker

DEMOCRATS SIMPLY WERE NOT PREPARED FOR BEING IN CONTROL OF Illinois government when Franklin Roosevelt swept them into office in 1933. For most of the first third of the century, Republicans had dominated politics in Springfield and Chicago. Since 1900 only one Democrat, Edward F. Dunne from 1913 to 1917, had served as governor, and then mostly because the Republicans split over the presidential candidacy of Theodore Roosevelt.

Until 1933, Democrats held a majority in the House only once, in 1913. In the Senate, Democrats had a majority once, and another time the parties tied. In the 1920s, Republicans ran amuck with large majorities in both houses, carrying elections with Big Bill Thompson as mayor of Chicago and Len Small in the governor's seat. In the legislature, Republicans rarely had to consider Democrats seriously.[1]

This despair of the Democratic party dated from the Civil War and affected national politics as well as Illinois. Only two Democrats, Grover Cleveland and Woodrow Wilson, served as president before 1932. To voters, Republicanism meant the party of union, the party of Lincoln and victory over the disgraced confederacy. To the same voters, the Democratic party meant failure, defeat, and a general disconnect with urban people. This carried into the twentieth century.

Republicans dominated the urban centers, received the labor and business votes, and counted blacks among the party's loyal supporters. Meanwhile, Democrats represented the countryside, particularly the rural south and west. The plight of Democrats in Illinois was shown in meager results: From the Civil War to 1932 Democrats elected only three U.S. senators, two governors, three attorneys general, two secretaries of state, and two auditors of public accounts.

Then came the Roosevelt revolution. For three legislative sessions in the 1930s—1933–34, 1935–36, and 1937–38—Democrats turned the tables with large majorities in the state House, bringing heydays rarely seen before. So unprepared were the Democrats that during those three sessions, no single leader emerged to take charge and command the troops. Unable to cope with success, Democrats wasted an opportunity to dominate public policy and build for the future.

In those three sessions, Democrats elected three different Speakers. Arthur Roe, from Fayette County, which included Vandalia, served as Speaker in the 1933–34 session, after the landslide victories of Roosevelt and Henry Horner in 1932. Democrats then elected John P. Devine, from Lee County in northern Illinois, due west of Chicago, as Speaker in 1935–36. He had entered the legislature in the 1913–14 session, and the 1935–36 term was his last. House Democrats then elected the third different Speaker in three terms, Louie E. Lewis, who served the 1937–38 term.

Lewis's election brought the Speakership enticingly close to Paul Powell's district. Lewis lived in Franklin County, just two counties north of Powell's home. Lewis had been in the legislature only since the Roosevelt years, but he had shown leadership qualities necessary to get the votes. The lone session as Speaker for Lewis was his last in the legislature, too. In 1938, he won election as state treasurer, and in 1940 he ran as a candidate for lieutenant governor but lost.

If Democrats had maintained a majority in the House for the 1939–40 session, yet a fourth different Speaker would have been named. Instead, Republicans returned to a House majority that they kept for ten years. While this churning of the Speakership hurt the Democratic party in Springfield, ironically it helped the Democrat from Johnson County. Powell quickly moved to fill the vacuum.

For legislators with the power twinkle in their eyes, the position of Speaker is unequaled, although those who have served in the Senate would argue that the position of Senate president is as desirable. The Speaker and president are, with minor differences, kings of their respective hills, and together they constitute an often unbeatable combination. In the Senate, the president serves both as presiding officer and majority leader of the ruling party. The Speaker, who is in the rostrum most of the time, delegates the majority leader role. In each case the leadership team, headed by the president or Speaker, runs the chamber's business, schedules bills for consideration, makes committee assignments, and controls the agenda. With only slight differences, the president and Speaker are similar positions of strength, with the slight differences making for mostly academic arguments. Almost any legislator would happily serve as either.

Minority party leaders in each chamber play a much less significant role, unless the partisan membership count is close. Then, minority leadership can mean the difference on controversial bills and contentious issues. Minority leaders are consulted as a matter of courtesy by the majority authorities, but rarely do they have a significant voice in affairs of the legislature. They do have authority to make committee assignments of minority party members and mostly are in waiting for the next opportunity to serve in majority leadership.

In anticipation of the day when Democrats would once again rule the House, Powell watched and learned. After nearly ten years in the House, he became minority whip—the person responsible for rounding up party votes and keeping members in line when pressure builds—in the 1945–46 session. As the person charged with keeping the party faithful mobilized in spite of the weak position in vote count, Powell learned the importance of building coalitions and working with Republicans and Chicago Democrats.

Powell became minority leader—the top Democratic party leadership position in the House—for the 1947–48 session, and he also established a reputation for hard work in behalf of downstate Democratic candidates. In 1948 he ran the downstate party campaign for candidates from the top of the ticket to the bottom, knowing full well that helping successful candidates would ensure his position as House leader. He used the campaign to tune up his partisan rhetoric, and when Democrats swept the ticket across the state, he had just the right words for the partisans. Democrats had taken the House by a 79 to 74 majority, and Powell warmed to the subject with an eye on Speaker.

About a month after the election, Democrats gathered in Springfield to celebrate the victory, and Powell addressed a group hungry for a taste of Springfield power. At that time he coined the phrase that rings to this day as his primary contribution to all-time Illinois political phrases. In the partisan fervor of that event Powell said, "I smell the meat a-cookin.'"[2]

Powell rang the bell with Democratic officials and workers around the state. They had risen again, and he urged them on. After a decade of political suffering at the hands of Republicans—make that four decades—the party stood rejuvenated. In the partisan flavor of the moment, it was payback time; the spoils belonged to Powell and the victors. In that context, Powell's words rang as clear as the chilled December air. Adding interpretation to the phrase, *Chicago Sun-Times* reporter Milburn P. Akers wrote that with the new administration in charge, Powell "expected the meat to be sliced in generous portions and passed to deserving Democrats."

Powell's critics, most notably the *St. Louis Post-Dispatch*, jumped on his words immediately. In a lengthy editorial entitled "The Danger in Paul Powell," the liberal Democratic-leaning editorial page smarted openly over the partisanship by Powell.[3] After observing that Powell had the inside track for Speaker, the editorial said, "By some of his own words, Mr. Powell has come mighty close to disqualifying himself for this important office."

The paper recounted Powell's legislative career and leadership positions, then took him to task for a lackluster performance. "He has managed to serve 14 years at Springfield without identifying himself in the public mind with progressive or forward-looking causes of measures. He is essentially a patronage politician. He sees state government almost entirely in terms of making the precinct committeeman happy." Powell probably agreed, for producing patronage during Republican days counted as a major achievement in southern Illinois.

The *Post-Dispatch* argument with Powell turned mostly on the impact his partisanship might have on the administration of the paper's favorite, Gov.-elect Adlai E. Stevenson. "He can ruin the legislative program of the Stevenson Administration and ruin it before it gets a good start," the editorial said. There was more on the Stevenson subject: "If Mr. Powell thinks that the Stevenson victory was a partisan Democratic victory he has completely misread the returns. The reason the Democratic Governor-elect won by the largest plurality in Illinois history, 572,000, is that many thousands of Republicans voted for him. They voted for Stevenson because they were sick and tired of the partisanship, the patronage and the corruption under Gov. Green."

Before suggesting to readers that Powell might not be worthy of the Speakership, the paper added: "If the Stevenson Administration is going to fulfill its promise, Illinois will require a Speaker in 1949 who understands what the people voted for on Nov. 2. More than that, he will have to be a Speaker who will roll up his sleeves and work hard to bring that vision of the voters to reality. The Democrats in the House should look over their membership and see whether they may not do better than take a leader who seems only to 'smell the meat a-cookin.' The least they should do is find out precisely where he stands on fundamental issues."

The criticism did not appear to slow Powell's partisan rhetoric, either. At another Democratic meeting late in December, Powell took on the Republicans again, although he backed away after initial press reports. The reports quoted him as saying, "People that know me know that if I had my way the Republicans wouldn't be on the payroll at all—they wouldn't even be breathing."[4] Powell claimed that cheers from the faithful drowned out a clarifying statement that followed: "I believe in the two-party system, and I certainly don't wish Republicans harm—even though I like to beat them in every election." A reporter who attended the meeting said that with all the noise, reporters might have missed the last part of the quote.

As the vote for Speaker neared, it became obvious that Powell had the votes, although Governor-elect Stevenson refused to endorse him. The Chicago press acknowledged Powell's ascension and generally approved. George Tagge, longtime reporter and columnist for the *Tribune*, wrote on the eve of the vote: "Friends of the speaker-designate point out that he has developed amazingly during the last few years. Once a hill-billy orator of more boldness than skill, he has become one of the leading spokesmen of his party."[5]

In the end, Powell did not need the governor's support, although the lack of it made cooperation between the two more difficult. The governor's concern about appearing too friendly with a southern Illinois Democrat had assured everyone that Powell would not be too friendly. On Wednesday, January 5, 1949, Paul Powell from Vienna received eighty Democratic votes for Speaker, and took the gavel as one of the most important officials in the state.[6] When he stepped down from the legislature at the end of the 1963–64 session, Powell had prevailed in leadership roles longer than any other Democratic representative in the twentieth century, and arguably he had made an impact on state public policy unrivaled by a single House member since the Civil War.

Powell enjoyed the spoils of victory to the fullest. Immediately after being elected Speaker, he joined other state Democratic dignitaries for the journey to Washington, D.C., for the inauguration of Harry S. Truman. Before leaving Illinois, Powell made one of his first appearances as Speaker before a political crowd in Livingston County. Singing a somewhat more moderate tune, he said the first duty of all "good Democrats" is to offer Governor-elect Stevenson "qualified men" for appointments. "If we all do that we will go to town with Stevenson and give Illinois the best administration in its history."[7]

On May 31, with barely a month left in the legislative session, *Chicago Daily News* writer George Thiem took stock of Powell's impact as Speaker with a decidedly friendly analysis of job performance: "Powell is a popular presiding officer and has been acclaimed by the Republican side for his fairness. . . . A skillful politician and ardent Democrat, Powell rules firmly and bangs the gavel often to maintain order. . . . He works hard at his job as speaker."[8]

As an example of Powell's work ethic, Thiem noted that he and staff stayed in Springfield on a Friday to work while most of the legislators were at home for the Memorial Day weekend. Thiem knew, as did any correspondent in Springfield, that most legislators spent only a couple of days in the capital on average during the session. If Powell worked just a regular work week, he put in more time than most members.

Earlier in the article, Thiem had mentioned criticism of the "do-nothing legislature." Powell responded that the General Assembly to that point had doubled its production over the same time period in the previous session. Twenty-five percent more bills had been introduced, Powell said, and the governor had approved twice as many. Actually, while it appeared that nothing much had happened up to May 31, the groundwork had been laid for June, traditionally the most productive month of the session. Legislative leadership had weeded out the bills destined for oblivion, leaving the remainder for serious consideration and bargaining.

Political divisions in the legislature assured that Stevenson's program, even if approved by the Democratic House, would meet with disruption in the Republican-controlled Senate. Nonetheless, most observers gave Stevenson good, if not great, marks for getting many items on his list through the legislature. Powell provided support in the House and worked closely and well with Stevenson's floor leader, Rep. Jimmy Ryan of Chicago. At the session's end, Stevenson praised Democratic leadership, including, specifically, the Speaker.

Stevenson came to the governorship determined to pass legislation establishing a constitutional convention—con-con for short—which would have been the first since 1870. He spent much of his energy with the legislature, up to May, on the plan, only to see it fail on two close votes in the House. According to Stevenson's biographer, the proposal failed mainly because the governor would not make a deal for votes with a group of representatives from the west side of Chicago, called the West Side Bloc.[9]

The deal this handful of representatives offered to Stevenson included their votes for con-con if the governor dropped his quest for anticrime legislation. Stevenson had campaigned in 1948 on a strong anticrime plank, promising to lead in cleaning up infestations of organized crime in Chicago and downstate. In 1950 he turned the state police loose in an effort to deter gambling in the southern half of Illinois. Later, in a speech to the American Bar Association, the governor lamented compromising local police jurisdiction but defended his action as part of an antigambling crusade.[10] There was no way he could gracefully accept the West Side Bloc offer. Consequently, both con-con and the anticrime measures failed. Nevertheless, Powell voted for con-con both times it came to the House and otherwise rallied Democratic votes for it.[11]

As a compromise, Republicans agreed to pass legislation calling for a public vote on what was called the Gateway Amendment. It allowed three constitutional amendments to be passed by the legislature and sent to the public, instead of just one at a time, as the 1870 constitution prescribed. While barely half a loaf when compared to a full-blown constitutional convention, this change received Stevenson's blessing, and it passed both houses. The public approved it at the general election of 1950. The importance of the Gateway Amendment to the politics of the House of Representatives and the future of Paul Powell became evident early in the administration of Republican Governor Stratton.[12]

The West Side Bloc also surfaced again in Powell's career and played a role in coalitions he put together on controversial bills. Bloc members did Powell large favors. Although they nominally carried the label of Republicans, they were Democrats tied closely to the Chicago machine. As such, they helped Powell when votes were close.

The bloc's importance to Illinois politics probably has been exaggerated, but on some occasions when a few votes made a difference on major legislation—often anticrime proposals or establishing anticrime commissions—the bloc made its voice known for a trade. Regardless of partisan flavor, they always were Chicagoans, and their tradeoffs and deals almost always had some connection to their pocketbooks. Journalists insinuated the bloc had close ties to the Chicago crime syndicate, although they failed to make direct connections. The bloc later played a key role in one of Powell's historic victories.

Conventional wisdom at the time of Stevenson's governorship (and in retrospect) is that Stevenson needed another term to fully understand the politics of Springfield and make things work his way. Certainly his lack of knowledge about the capital, the legislature, and realities of election politics made him dependent on Paul Powell and others who had more loyalty to a Democratic administration than to Stevenson.

After Stevenson's death, his son Adlai III spoke to a biographer about his father's unused potential and the ways of Springfield: "The Governor is the most powerful man in the state of Illinois. I mean favors, patronage, press, all the rest. He didn't use it to remake the party and change things at the grass roots. There's a great opportunity there for any Governor—to get patronage into the hands of his friends, to get better candidates and a better legislature. If he had been a politician he'd have been more than a match for the Eddie Barretts and Paul Powells. He was improving government at the top on the theory that it would trickle down. But you've got to start from the bottom up, too. He was learning, and learning fast, when his own term expired."[13] Adlai III made unsuccessful runs at governor in 1982 and 1986, barely losing to James Thompson the first time.

Powell's term as Speaker came and went in a flash. Because the legislature met only in the first year of a biennium, by July 1, 1949, Powell's term as Speaker ended, as far as legislating public policy. Looking back it had similarities to many legislative sessions before and since. In terms of Powell's future, his personal wealth, and the relationship with Democrat and Republican friends in the legislature, this session held special meaning.

Those interested in making it possible to have pari-mutuel betting at an expanded number of harness races succeeded beyond their wildest dreams. House Bill 1104 passed the House and Senate without a whimper, and Stevenson signed it. In terms of bills that created personal wealth and huge returns to the state of Illinois, there is not much to compare with it in modern legislative times. The aftermath, including profits made on stock in Chicago Downs, is an epic tale of dividing up the profits on one of the state's most lucrative and popular sports.

Among other accomplishments during the session, Powell and other southern Illinois legislators held firm for passage of a bill creating a separate board of trustees for Southern Illinois University, then still a small teachers college in Carbondale.[14] Powell had to use his Speaker muscle to quiet objections from supporters of the University of Illinois, but he showed how effective he could be fighting in the clinches. That single bill may have done more to create the second largest higher education institution in the state than any single bill passed during Powell's tenure in Springfield.

Dwight Eisenhower's huge victory over Stevenson for president in 1952 swept Republicans at all levels of government into office, ending the Democratic euphoria in a very short two years. Stratton, a familiar face in Illinois public office and in Springfield, captured the governorship, and Republicans controlled both the House and Senate. Powell stepped down from the Speakership but retained his party's minority leader position for both the 1951–52 and 1953–54 sessions.

Sitting on the front edge of the 1950s decade, few could have predicted that the last ten years of Powell's legislative career would bring turmoil, revolution, reshaping of regional politics, and riches. The decade also turned out to have many surprises—some might characterize them as earthshaking—for the future of state government.

In the truest political sense, Stratton had been around. It showed on his resume, and it showed in his relationship with the legislature. Republican or not, he had many friends among Democrats—including Powell—and he shared downstate sentiments with those who held increasing suspicions about Chicago Democrats. Stratton had never served a day in the legislature, but he had direct dealings with it, beginning in 1922, when his father, William J. Stratton, became Illinois secretary of state for one term.

Governor Stratton, a resident of Grundy County, just south of Chicago, served as state treasurer from 1943 to 1945 and again from 1951 to 1953, until just before he took over as governor. Stratton went to the U.S. House of Representatives from 1941 to 1943 and again from 1947 to 1949.[15] When he became governor, Stratton was a youthful thirty-eight years old, the boy wonder of Illinois Republicanism, and presumably the personification of the state's future.

Two changes occurred during Stratton's first term as governor that shaped Illinois politics generally and legislative politics specifically. Both changes had extraordinary influence on the career of Powell. One was reapportionment of the legislature, the first in fifty years. The second was the election of Richard J. Daley as mayor of Chicago in 1955.

Reapportionment legislation had been around the General Assembly as long as anyone could remember.[16] Various political factions had tried without success since the last reapportionment in 1901 to gain enough support for updating geographic representation and changing the outdated constitution. Rural interests beat back any attempt at reform, and state and federal courts declined to order change. As recently as the Stevenson administration, reform forces tried valiantly to put a constitutional convention before the voters. In a compromise, Stevenson settled for the Gateway Amendment. That legislation and the positive vote of the citizens in 1950 opened a door that could not be closed.

As early as the turn of the century, Illinois had become an urban state. But the 1870 constitution, with its rural emphasis, remained in tact, and it prescribed a legislative system that reflected nineteenth-century agrarian lifestyles and suspicions. The constitution called for fifty-one districts, with three representatives and one senator from each. Cook County, with more than half the state's population in 1950, had nineteen districts, which meant it had 37 percent of the legislative representation.

Reapportionment—which would give more seats to Chicago and Cook County—presented a clear threat to downstate domination of the legislature, regardless of party. Republicans controlled the northern half of the state outside Chicago, along with some suburbs, and Democrats prevailed in the southern half. None of them wanted to give control to Chicago and Cook County.

The shift of population in the half century since reapportionment meant population losses in many parts of the state, while metropolitan areas along Lake Michigan and in the vicinity of such cities as Peoria, East St. Louis, and Alton had gained greatly. More than five million persons in the Chicago metropolitan area elected twenty-one senators and sixty-three representatives, while less than three million persons elsewhere elected thirty senators and ninety representatives. Unfair, yes, but in politics fairness is rarely a foundation for change.

Many downstaters, clinging to old fears, presumed liberal and pro-labor laws would soon pass if Chicago took control. For decades that had been enough to preserve the status quo. Although Democrats from southern Illinois often teamed with Chicago Democrats on legislation, they were not prepared to give the city control on its own.

Stratton, a downstate Republican, knew the odds against reapportionment. He had a Speaker in Republican Warren Wood and a minority leader in Paul Powell, who opposed changing the legislative lineup. In order to get serious consideration of a change, the plan had to "take care" of current legislators.[17] That meant providing large enough increases in numbers to protect incumbents and leaving one of the two chambers of the legislature essentially unchanged. The only chance the proposal had of going to the electorate was to spread the pain in all directions. Downstate had to give up its dominance, but Chicago could get only part of what it wanted.

The compromise that received approval, subject to a citizen vote, increased senatorial districts to fifty-eight and representative districts to fifty-nine, giving Cook County twenty-four Senate districts and thirty representative districts. With that change, Cook County had 41 percent of the Senate districts and just a fraction over 50 percent of the House districts. The plan also called for new reapportionment after the 1960 census. If not a level playing field, at least the plan recognized the population shifts of half a century. Furthermore, by increasing the number of districts, incumbents felt less threatened.

The legislature of 1953 put the amendment on the ballot in 1954, and after popular approval, redistricting occurred in 1955. The first election under reapportionment occurred in 1956, still during the high point of Republican strength across the state. The dramatic turn in the fortunes of downstate Democrats is revealed in the numbers after the election of 1954 before reapportionment and the election of 1956 after reapportionment.

After the 1954 election, Democrats held seventy-four seats in the House, thirty-eight from downstate, which placed 51 percent of the Democrats outside Cook County. After the election of 1956, with an expanded House,

Democrats held eighty-three seats, of which thirty-four were downstate, or about 41 percent outside Cook County. The face of politics in the House had changed, and Powell's stature among Democrats would never be the same.

Reinforcing the drama, one other legislative item passed in 1955 to the cheers of reformers. A personnel code and a new Department of Personnel, with potential for great impact on patronage in state government, passed with support of the prominent people who had opposed reapportionment in the House: Speaker Wood, Powell, and Republican leader Reed F. Cutler. All the leaders, and Governor Stratton, feared what this might do to the use of state employees as political soldiers, and that explains why the code did not go into effect until 1957, after the election of 1956.[18]

If not enough to scare downstate Democrats and Republicans already in a state of shock, the Chicago mayoral election of 1955 provided the knock-out punch. Richard J. Daley, who had served in the legislature and then as an administrator on Governor Stevenson's team, romped to victory over his opponent. The man who gave new meaning to the word *power* in Chicago for the next twenty years knew the importance of control in Springfield, too.

Daley served just one term in the state House, 1937–38, as a disciple of machine boss Kelly, after being elected as a write-in candidate. Then Daley ran for the Senate, won, and served two terms until 1946. In 1941 he became Senate minority leader, serving as Mayor Kelly's man in Springfield. One biographer of the mayor wrote, "Daley quickly established a solid reputation as a hardworking, effective state senator, prompting the silk-stocking legislative Voters League to observe that he 'has made rather an outstanding record for a new member.'"[19]

By all accounts, Daley spent his time working in Springfield or staying in his hotel room, while other legislators devoted themselves to poker games, off-track betting, alcohol, and party girls. One writer called Daley a "Roman Catholic Puritan in Babylon." Pete Akers, in a 1945 political column, described Daley as "probably the best exhibit of the hard-working, decent, honest organization politician that the Kelly machine can produce."

Governor Stevenson made a few truly political appointments to his cabinet in 1949, and one went to Daley as director of revenue. Stevenson gave special attention to this position because he had pledged during the campaign to find ways of returning more revenue to local governments. Because Daley had been Cook County comptroller, he knew the ways of local government financing and the state's controls. At this time, Daley was on the move politically in the Cook County machine. Eventually he would be named county Democratic chairman, before being elected mayor in 1955.

Akers thought the Daley appointment by Stevenson deserved applause: "Daley, still a comparatively young man, has come to exemplify the best in politics. . . . If Adlai Stevenson can induce a few more men of Daley's unique qualifications—ability, political experience and integrity—to associate themselves with him for the next four years he will do much to assure the success of his administration."[20]

The story of Daley's takeover of Chicago and Cook County politics is legend. His grasp for power in Springfield is less chronicled but significant, too, for the political history of the state. With almost twenty years experience in the ways of Springfield, Daley knew the importance of public policy to the prosperity of Chicago and the significance of prosperity to his future. Daley knew if he wavered the slightest in his first term as mayor, others in the wings would push him aside or depreciate his control. Consequently, Daley established a guiding principle for Springfield operations: He demanded total loyalty and expected his soldiers to subordinate their own ideology to the interests of the machine.

Abner Mikva, who came to the legislature in 1957 and sometimes voted with Daley and many times against him, described the mayor's hold this way: "In Springfield it was total commitment to the party line. Daley kept an absolute close watch on everything that happened in Springfield. He knew the league. He served down there. He knew how it functions. The party leaders in both houses were in daily contact with him and held weekly meetings. He knew every major piece of legislation. He had his finger on it. There were very, very few free votes." Mikva added that those who tried to break away from the Daley orbit "were just never heard of again politically." Mikva explained, "You've got to go along with the program."[21]

Those who wanted to be independents but also wanted the benefits of the machine caused Daley the most discomfort, according to Mikva. "Those were the people that Daley used to be angry with, who wanted to be held as independents by the IVI [Independent Voters of Illinois] and newspaper editorials, but who wanted some jobs for a few deserving constituents besides. Nothing would make him angrier than those who supped at his table and then didn't want to pay the price."

The Daley pressure on Democrats in the House, along with reapportionment, moved Powell out of a leadership position for the first time since 1945. For two sessions, 1955–56 and 1957–58, Daley and Chicago called the shots. Daley designated Joseph De La Cour—who began his House career in the 1947–48 session and served in the House until the 1963–64 term, when he was elected to the Senate—as minority leader. A Chicago loyalist, De La

Cour had little of the skill or background of Powell, and he certainly did not have the debts owed by Republicans and downstate Democrats that had kept Powell in leadership for ten years. Both were Democrats, but that about covered the similarities.

After being dislodged, Powell had every reason to be unhappy, and he blamed Daley and the Chicago interests for his unseating.[22] He had no choice but to wait for the first opportunity to elect a Speaker. Daley waited too. That opportunity for both came after the 1958 off-year election, which restored the House to a Democratic majority, 91 to 86. Democrats prepared to elect a Speaker in January 1959.

Powell wasted no time after the election. As longtime Democratic legislator Corneal Davis recalled: "[Powell] went over to see Stratton. And he made a deal. . . . I don't know what he promised."[23] Whatever he promised worked. Stratton went to work for Powell's election, knowing his effort would draw the venom of Daley. Stratton's biographer believes the governor wanted to build a record so that he could run for a third term in 1960, and the only way to do that was to make a deal with Powell.

Daley's choice for Speaker was De La Cour, who hardly impressed anyone or dazzled them with legislative skills. But he had good friends in high places. Among them was William J. "Botchy" Connors, first elected to the state Senate as an agent of the Kelly machine in the session of 1933–34. Connors, a crusty old Chicago pol, had worked shoulder to shoulder with the young Daley and eventually became the mayor's Senate lieutenant. He took De La Cour under his wing and groomed him for leadership.

That may have counted with Daley and Botchy, but for the handful of independent Chicago Democrats elected during the 1950s, there had to be someone better. "Tony Scariano tried to get someone other than De La Cour chosen, but he couldn't get anyone to run," Abner Mikva remembered. In the end Mikva voted the Daley line, "holding my nose all the way," Mikva said.[24]

When 177 House members gathered in Springfield the first week of January, De La Cour had fifty-four votes of the eighty-nine needed for the Speakership—the Daley loyalists. Downstate Democrats numbered thirty-seven. Powell said later, "With only 37 votes downstate you know you haven't got a change to get elected—it's cut and dried."[25] By painting Daley as an outsider trying to control the legislature and raising fear that Chicago dominance would severely curtail downstate power, Powell held thirty of the votes until the last. A day before the vote for Speaker, Powell bolted the regular Democratic caucus and took his band of supporters to a site near the state fair grounds for a "rump" caucus session.

"It was the first time I ever boycotted the regular Democratic caucus," he admitted. By tradition, if Powell had appeared at the regular caucus he would have been bound by the decisions of the group. Meanwhile, at the Republican caucus, members agreed to vote for Powell on the second ballot.[26]

The House floor rocked and seethed on January 8, 1959.[27] On the first ballot, De La Cour received fifty-nine votes, which included five downstaters. Among those breaking away from Powell was Rep. Sam Shapiro from Kankakee, who became lieutenant governor in 1960 and ascended to the governorship when Gov. Otto Kerner accepted appointment to a federal judgeship. Powell never forgot Shapiro's "betrayal."

Powell received thirty-one votes, and Rep. Warren L. Wood, the Republican leader, received fifty-nine, including the vote of Powell. De La Cour received fifty-nine. As agreed on the second ballot—Stratton had asked Republicans to shift after the first ballot—Wood dropped out of the race, giving fellow Republicans the signal to vote for Powell. De La Cour took the floor to plead with Republicans not to take advantage of the Democratic split.

On the second ballot, De La Cour ended up with 59 votes (he did not vote), and Powell received 116, including 32 downstate Democrats. As the Associated Press reported, "It was a political coup unequaled in the Illinois legislature since 1915, when Republicans then the majority party, banded together with Democrats to elect a presiding House officer." Powell put his own spin on it. "What happened today lets the 177 members of the House know that they can elect a Speaker without interference from some outsider, somebody who's not a member." Guess who? Relaxing at the Speaker's desk on the floor after the vote, Powell told the press, "What happened today is good for the people of the whole state. And it serves notice it could happen again."

In a few days, Daley made one more run at Powell before completely folding his cards, this time in an attempt to nullify the Speaker's authority regarding the appointment of committees and committee chairmen. Daley loyalist Rep. William G. Clark offered a bill to curb Speaker powers, and Powell brought it straight to the floor, where he declared, "We might just as well find out now who is going to be boss of this House as well later on." He could have ruled the measure out of order and killed it outright, but Powell again knew who had the votes. Judging the outcome successfully, he did not vote himself. The bill died 127 to 36.[28]

A tiny subplot played out in the aftermath of the vote, as Daley Democrats threatened to destroy the Speakership of Powell by curtailing his powers. Mikva took the floor to plead for peace, saying, "We elected a speaker and now we have to work with him." Apparently Mikva, who Powell had shunned previously, impressed the Speaker, and Powell summoned Mikva to a private meeting.[29] "He called me into his office and said he would see that I got good committees from him," Mikva recalls. No way. "He welched on that deal because soon thereafter he and Daley cut a deal. I was on the outside again."

Powell's response to Daley's effort to strip him of authority prompted this final admonishment to his fellow Democrats: "I want to say this to some of the members on my side of the aisle. If they want to wash dirty linen in public, I'll take the floor to help them. It's always been my belief you wash your dirty linen among yourselves, not in the newspapers or on the floor of this House. And I have a good memory."

Before many weeks passed, Daley regained his composure, Powell again declared the fight over, and the two buried the hatchet. Powell made a show of naming Clark of Chicago as majority leader, and his friend from Anna, Clyde Choate, as majority whip. Powell and Chicago interests had their disagreements afterward, but rarely did they "wash the dirty linen" in public. Daley knew how to play hard to win and how to compromise when he lost. In the years ahead, Powell reaped a number of personal favors from the mayor and gave back a few, too.

Of course, many in state government denied Powell and Stratton had made any deals on future legislation. Nevertheless, on the single most important legislative item of the session—an increase of one half cent in the sales tax—they worked together to pass one of the most politically explosive issues for members of a legislative body. Again, looking for any coalition that would work, Powell knitted a nearly solid Republican minority with just the right number of downstate Democrats to push the vote total barely over the minimum needed for passage.[30]

House debate took nearly four hours, during which Republican minority leader Warren Wood passionately spoke in behalf of the tax, noting that much of the money would go for needed state education programs. He argued that Democrats had to accept the increase or chaos would result because there were no other tax bills available to pay for schools. Clark, speaking for the Chicago interests, painted a tortured picture of tax burdens on families and women at home trying to make food budget money stretch. "I don't know why the corporations and big business shouldn't be expected to support government, and the housewives are," Clark said.

The situation was made for Powell. He first criticized Republicans for not passing a tax program that did not depend on the sales tax: "I'll make as much political capital as I can in 1960 against the other side on this issue. But this bill is needed." Then he turned on the Democrats, with another oblique reference to Mayor Daley: "No one man or 10 men have got all the brains in this party or this House." Finally, having condemned the politics of it all, Powell made the pitch for education money. He wanted the increase only to assure aid to state schools: "Anytime I vote to spend money, I'll vote to raise it, and anyone who doesn't has something missing somewhere."[31]

Powell took twelve other downstate Democrats with him, including Choate and close associates Curly Harris and Leo Pfeffer. Six downstate Republicans abandoned the party-line vote, but with eighty GOP members voting yes, the bill passed with three votes to spare, 92 to 79. Seventy-three Democrats voted against the increase.[32]

Regardless of the increase for state schools, a cluster of liberal Democrats voted no. Scariano voiced his protest against the tax with a speech in the Democratic caucus, full of barbs aimed specifically at Powell: "I remember I made Paul Powell so mad he walked out; the first time that anybody's ever walked out of a caucus that anybody could remember."[33] As he remembered his speech, Scariano said: "You're punishing poor people in the state and you're taxing milk and bread on the poor people's table by increasing the sales tax. And you're doing it for your good friend, Bill Stratton, with whom you've always gotten along. . . . You're betraying the very people of your district. You did it only because this guy made you speaker."

The Speakership contest had its political implications for the 1960 statewide election. Before the 1959 legislative session, political speculation centered mostly on Mayor Daley as a prospect to seek the governorship in 1960. He never said he wouldn't run, and he never said he would. Much of the talk may simply have been flattery, and Powell indulged in that to some extent on the statewide stump. No political fool, Powell knew that Daley would decide who heads the 1960 Democratic slate for state offices, and Powell had no intention of appearing to be disloyal.

Powell did his best in speeches across the state to suggest various downstate Democrats for slating by the mayor, and he paid publicized visits to the mayor's office to talk politics. Powell's strongest recommendation was in behalf of friend Choate, who he proposed as a candidate for secretary of state. When Choate did not make the mayor's favored list, Powell backed off. Democrats did exceptionally well in Illinois in the 1960 election, the year that Daley delivered the state's electoral votes for John F. Kennedy's victory by a hairline margin. With one exception—secretary of state—Democrats won all state offices.

The mayor's candidate for governor, Otto Kerner, beat back an attempt by Governor Stratton for a third term. Kerner, who had served as a Cook County judge for six years before 1960, had a distinguished military career in World War II and as a reserve general officer. A handsome man with a chiseled profile and the dignity of royalty, Kerner had politics deep in his background. His father, Otto, served as state attorney general from 1933 to 1938, when he received an appointment to the U.S. Court of Appeals. His wife was the daughter of Anton Cermak, once mayor of Chicago and father of the modern day Chicago political machine.

Powell did not know much about Kerner at a personal level, but he knew that Kerner paid his dues to Mayor Daley. The closest Powell came to recommending anyone for the governorship before Daley designated Kerner was to mention the name of Edward J. Barrett, who had succeeded as a statewide candidate for secretary of state, auditor, and treasurer since 1930 and maintained a tight relationship with downstate Democrats. While Barrett became a trusted servant of Daley in city and county governmental affairs, he never again was slated for state office.

Among all the Democratic candidates, Powell did not like the choice for lieutenant governor, Sam Shapiro, because of political differences on downstate-Chicago issues. A resident of Kankakee with a legislative career that started in 1947, Shapiro developed more loyalties to Daley and Chicago than to Powell and downstate. Other elected officials knew Powell, and they respected each other. Michael J. Howlett, a political operative in Chicago and an executive with Sun Steel, stepped in as state auditor, and Joseph Lohman, a Chicago Democrat, gained reelection as state treasurer. William Clark, who carried Daley's spear in the House, was elected attorney general. As Powell must have observed with disappointment, not a single Democrat with true-blue downstate credentials was elected to statewide office in 1960.

After the 1960 election, Powell knew his days were numbered as a force in Democratic politics unless he pulled one more legislative miracle, got a statewide elective position, or both. He found the Speakership in 1959 invigorating, and for at least one more House term he had ruled the roost, although sharing that honor increasingly with Daley and his representatives. He did not need extraordinary vision to see that future Democratic controlled legislatures would serve Chicago interests primarily.

Incredibly, he got one more chance for glory after the 1960 election. In spite of Democratic successes at the presidential and state levels, Republicans held a one-vote plurality, 89 to 88, in the House of Representatives. Republicans also controlled the Senate by a margin of 31 to 27, still close enough for deal-making. Soon after the election, Powell went to Chicago for meetings the press characterized as secret but obviously having to do with the Speakership. "All I need is 89 votes," Powell told a newsman. Powell already had Republicans on the alert. William E. Pollack, Republican of Chicago and a candidate for Speaker, warned that a move for Powell "would be a great danger to the two-party system. . . . It would be a grab for power by the Democrats to grab the speaker."[34]

Powell, the Democrats, and Chicago Republicans had made their deal by the time officials convened the House officially on Wednesday, January 5. As prescribed by law, the secretary of state, in this case Republican Charles F. Carpentier, was to convene the House until a Speaker was chosen by a majority of those in attendance. Republicans knew what had happened when five of their total of eighty-nine failed to answer the roll call.

All eighty-eight members of the Democratic delegation took their seats after being sworn in. Three of the five Republicans who failed to show were Peter J. Miller, Walter "Babe" McAvoy, and August "Augie" J. Ruff, all employees of the Metropolitan Sanitary District in Chicago, which Daley's appointments controlled. The three reported in as ill. Michael Z. Zlatnick, who said he protested Pollack's chances of being Speaker because Pollack had campaigned for Zlatnick's opponent, stayed away, and John P. Manning of Rochelle failed to show because of a serious illness.

Manning and Zlatnick appeared not to be part of the agreement to elect Powell. The three sanitary district employees had a previous reputation for not always going along with Republican interests. Among state politicians, the three were part of the West Side Bloc. Abner Mikva, who dealt with the bloc in the House, called them "crooks." He added, "The West Side Bloc could be bought off, and they stayed bought."[35]

Anthony Scariano noted the absentee Republicans and summed it up this way: "Powell made a play for the speakership and got some Republicans to vote for him, Babe McAvoy, Peter Miller and Augie Ruff. All he needed was three votes and he got the three votes. . . . He could go to the Chicago Republicans and demand that three Republicans vote for him. And they did, three Republicans who held jobs controlled by the Cook County Democrats. I suppose there was some Democratic control that played its part there, too. So those three made it possible to capture the speakership for Paul Powell that year."[36]

Five votes short of a majority, Republicans needed to make a dramatic move to thwart Powell's election. Immediately after the roll call, Pollack proposed that the House recess until a later date, and Carpentier declared the motion passed on a voice vote. The House erupted with Democrats yelling

"No, no" and demanding a roll call. Republicans stalked out of the House chamber with Carpentier, ignoring the shouts. The eighty-eight Democrats calmed down, remained in the chamber, then convened the House and voted to elect Powell as Speaker, 88 to 0. The House of Democrats then passed a resolution calling for a joint session with the Senate to canvass the November vote. A canvass had to be conducted before the constitutional officers—governor, auditor, attorney general, secretary of state, treasurer—could be sworn into office at ceremonies scheduled for the following Monday. The Republican Senate, refusing to acknowledge the Democratic House, adjourned without a joint meeting.

Chaos is probably too strong a word for the atmosphere in Springfield, but it came close. The following day, Thursday, Carpentier, Pollack, and Republican Atty. Gen. William Guild filed suit in Sangamon Circuit Court claiming that Powell had illegally seized the Speakership and asked the court to declare the election void. Powell dismissed the suit as a "juvenile action based obviously on party politics." Republicans contended that after the recess, a quorum of the House was not present—eighty-nine votes being a majority—and Powell could not be elected legally. Democrats contended that there was a quorum in the House and that they rightfully elected Powell.

On Friday, with no resolution in sight, Powell said, "I was elected speaker, and I am speaker." His lawyers said they were studying the suit. Carpentier had a different take: "It is my opinion that Mayor Daley and Governor-elect Kerner know all about it and could put a stop to it." He went on to say that he "didn't hear" the shouts of Democrats for a roll call vote on Wednesday. Powell's answer to that improbability: "If he didn't hear them—he'd better have his driver's license revoked because he could never pass the examination."

By Saturday, nervousness had set in with state officials who had sent fifteen thousand invitations to Illinois citizens for the inauguration ceremonies and the inaugural ball on Monday. Press rumors on Saturday presumed a compromise would be hammered out among the principals, and sure enough, on Saturday, Powell and Carpentier issued a joint statement that the House would be convened Monday and would proceed to elect a Speaker. Pollack would be allowed to make a statement in behalf of the Republicans, and if all went well, the inauguration could proceed on schedule. Everyone knew that the Republicans could not get a majority there Monday and that Powell would be elected.

Carpentier convened the House Monday as scheduled. All eighty-eight Democrats answered the roll call, and only two Republicans answered as present. Ruff and McAvoy showed up to vote, while Miller remained in Chicago, reportedly in a hospital. Powell received the eighty-eight Democratic votes, and one vote from McAvoy, which gave him the needed eighty-nine and the Speakership. After the vote, all other Republicans came to the floor of the House.

The final official vote for Speaker gave eighty-nine votes to Powell and eighty-five to Pollack. Besides the hospitalized Miller, Manning remained too ill to attend, and Zlatnick still protested Pollack's candidacy and refused to vote. Afterward, the House and Senate held their joint canvass meeting, and the inaugural ceremony began forty-five minutes late.

Powell had achieved the impossible. Election of a Speaker from the minority party had never happened in the entire 142-year history of the Illinois General Assembly.

House members Scariano and Mikva, who voted for Powell, did not think much of the event and put their own slant on Powell's dealings with the West Side Bloc. Mikva said the upset victory must have given Powell partisan satisfaction, but that was not the way the system should work: "You pay a price for it in the long run. The system works better where the expectations (Republican majority) are fulfilled." About Powell's dealings with the bloc, Mikva said, "They were both crooks."[37] Scariano called Powell "the spiritual, the physical, the intellectual and every other kind of a leader of the West Side Bloc. . . . Who is the West Side Bloc? You know. Paul Powell and his crowd from downstate. . . . Powell had 15 to 18 votes from that area [in Chicago] he could count on. . . . The West Side Bloc was Paul Powell's motley group."[38]

Ten days after the election, Republican House leaders asked Powell not to give choice committee assignments to those who helped him become Speaker. Powell said he planned to name the four—including Zlatnick—to committees on the basis of their seniority. "You can kick them in the teeth if you want to, but I'm going to name them to committees as I would any other representative," Powell retorted.[39] Scariano gave this another explanation: "Now I'm told that the Republicans were mad and they were going to visit reprisals. I never saw anything visited on those three people by the Republicans that ever amounted to anything. . . . I suppose that the Republicans who were in the legislature understood their plight and probably sympathized with them."

Powell rarely let anything get the best of him, and no sooner had he tucked away the Speakership for what most certainly would be the last time, he encouraged speculation that he would consider running against incumbent U.S. Senator Everett Dirksen, who almost everyone expected to seek a third term in 1962. Nevertheless, Dirksen's poor health—an ulcer and a heart ailment—caused some of his advisers and his wife to urge retirement. Dirksen never gave it serious consideration, although rumors rumbled across Illinois and Democrats took heart with the prospect of an open Senate race.

All they needed, Democrats argued, was a good candidate. Dirksen's margins of victory rarely overwhelmed opponents, and Democrats certainly had enough strength in Chicago and elsewhere to threaten his incumbency. However, wishful thinking never beat Ev Dirksen.

By May, news articles suggested a Powell candidacy. Looking back over Mayor Daley's tenure and at his record of slatings of statewide candidates, a pattern emerges that puts such media blitzes in perspective. Daley often paid compliments to potential candidates but then ignored media candidates and appointed those who fit his expectations of extreme loyalty to Daley and the party and repayment for favors done. A candidate could look perfect by other standards, but if he failed on any one of those two, he did not have a chance. That is what occurred in 1962 with Powell.

On May 9 Powell held his biennial legislative dinner in Springfield, a traditional bash that brought all the state's top Democrats to his turf. Mayor Daley appeared and said all the right things about Powell.[40] Mainly, the mayor said, Powell "earned the right to represent the state on a national level—on the floor of the United States Senate." Powell knew the game. He told reporters he did not consider that an endorsement. He then said that his candidacy for the Senate could occur under "certain conditions." Although he declined to identify the conditions, they became evident later in the year.

Powell wanted President Kennedy to make a public endorsement and a personal commitment to campaign in Illinois before he agreed to run. Powell knew that unless a Democratic candidate smoked Kennedy out from the beginning that Dirksen would benefit from any hesitation at the White House. He also knew what everyone in Washington, D.C., suspected: that Kennedy preferred to have Dirksen in the Senate as minority leader to any of the more conservative and uncooperative possibilities. That could make all the difference to Kennedy's legislative program and his chances at reelection in 1964. Kennedy would gladly sacrifice the Democrats in Illinois for bigger returns. Democrats also suspected that Daley liked Dirksen.[41]

Knowing that, Powell made his case for Kennedy's support early enough to test direction of the political winds. In August, Powell headed a delegation of southern Illinois officials—including John Stelle—to the White House for a meeting with the president, and while he said afterward that no senatorial politics had been discussed, opportunities clearly were present for discussions with White House advisers to Kennedy. Asked about the discussions and his interest in running against Dirksen, Powell said, "I'm happy where I am" but that he would be a candidate if Democratic leaders "decide I am the best man." He added: "I'm a politician. I take orders. But we have plenty of good men to run against Dirksen."[42]

The cat and mouse game continued into September. Powell said he needed both a pledge of active support and at least four campaign swings through the state from Kennedy. He said that promise would be necessary even if he received the blessing of Mayor Daley and Governor Kerner: "If I couldn't get it, I would have to tell the governor and the mayor I would not be available." Powell might as well have withdrawn as a candidate at that point. To put the president on the spot in such a manner indicated that he had been unable to get the promise privately and simply provided Powell cover for a later announcement that he would not be a candidate. Meanwhile, Dirksen ended speculation about his health and his intentions by announcing for reelection.

When the slatemakers of the party met in Chicago to name a candidate, Daley chose none of the names that had been batted around for months. He selected U.S. Rep. Sidney Yates, a Chicago Democrat who passed the two tests with flying colors: No one had been more loyal to the mayor in Congress than Yates, and if elected, he could be counted on to continue as Daley's spear-carrier. Yates promised a vigorous campaign against Dirksen, and Daley and other Democrats in high places said Yates would be given a federal appointment if he lost. Dirksen won handily over Yates.[43] Kennedy made only one campaign trip to Chicago for Yates, and he canceled a planned campaign trip through the state and hurried back to Washington. Powell had dodged the Daley sacrifice.

4

Secretary of Trouble

POWELL NEEDED A NEW JOB. HE HAD SERVED FOR THIRTY YEARS IN the legislature and had racked up all the power, accolades, and high positions one could imagine in a political career.

More importantly, while he could continue to be elected to the House from his southern Illinois district for as long as he wanted, Springfield had changed. When the Democrats prevailed, that meant Chicago and Mayor Daley had control. Increasingly, Powell's Democrats and friendly Republicans left the legislature, and his leverage slipped. The future did not appear terribly exciting.

For years Powell had looked everywhere for an opportunity to run for a statewide office. He had sent signals to Daley in every way imaginable. He placed himself in the running for U.S. Senate and governor. He never mentioned lesser positions, but presumably he had an open mind. He needed to catch the eye of Daley to get it done—Daley, who had not exactly been a bosom buddy of Powell; Daley, who had plenty of candidates for state positions without bringing along the political baggage that Powell had accumulated; Daley, who rarely went out of his way to reward downstaters with high office.

To an outsider, the options did not look encouraging for Powell. Actually, Powell had been more attentive than headlines would indicate. In both the 1959 and 1961 sessions, when Powell served as speaker, he found common ground with the mayor's legislative agenda. He had accommodated the powerful Chicago Democrat, and he had cultivated those who whispered to the mayor. Expectedly, when campaigning began in 1963 leading up to the party slatemakers' meetings in January 1964, there was a field of contenders for the secretary of state position.

On the unlikely side were State Insurance Director Richard Hershey of Taylorville and Associate Circuit Judge Richard Scholz of Quincy. More of a competitor for Powell was State Sen. Alan Dixon from Belleville, who had friends among the mayor's Chicago associates but had no statewide exposure. Daley had no legitimate electable alternative to Powell.[1]

The Republican picture for the 1964 elections was unclear as the Democrats prepared to name its slate. Charles F. Carpentier, completing his third term as secretary of state, had built a support system across the state that many believed would take him to the governor's office. Charles H. Percy, an industrialist who had not sought public office before, had announced his intention to run against the incumbent, Kerner. Also in the wings was William J. Scott, elected to a first term as treasurer in 1962. All state races took an unpredictable turn in January, when Carpentier was stricken with a heart attack. He lingered for a while and then died on April 3. Subsequently, Percy and Scott slugged it out for the privilege of contending Kerner, and Percy prevailed.[2]

While Powell got his shot at secretary of state, the path already had been cleared of political obstacles. After Carpentier's death, the position had been filled on an interim basis with an appointment by Governor Kerner, which had the blessing of Daley. Kerner appointed his executive assistant, William H. Chamberlain, to fill the unexpired term. Chamberlain had no track record in elective politics, and he had been chosen only to do the dirty work and get the office ready for a newly elected secretary.[3] As ordered, Chamberlain swept the patronage-rich office clean of Republicans. Having completed his task, Chamberlain was elected as circuit judge in Springfield in 1965.

Carpentier had been secretary of state since 1953. Before that, Eddie Barrett of Chicago served two terms as secretary of state, beginning in 1945. Republicans, in shock over Carpentier's death, still were anxious to regain the office with the most extensive network of patronage workers in the state.

They chose Elmer J. Hoffman of Wheaton for the 1964 run.[4] Hoffman, a successful politician from the Republican suburban stronghold of DuPage County, was three years older than Powell. Twice he served as sheriff of DuPage County, and he ran successfully for state treasurer in 1952. He laid out two years, then returned to serve as treasurer from 1957 to 1959. He served in the U.S. Congress from suburban Chicago from 1959 to 1965 and gained extensive statewide election exposure.

Even though he received the party slatemakers' nod easily, Powell saw how the past could haunt his future. During slating deliberations, Martin Gleason, who represented DuPage and Will Counties, supported Dixon and loudly proclaimed that Powell would weaken the ticket. Gleason told reporters that Powell would be "a load." Gleason specifically mentioned Powell's racetrack stock holdings. The criticism brought this rebuttal from

Powell: "I've never known it was illegal for a man to be in business." He said Gleason "is not dry behind the ears yet [politically]." He added, "As I told him, they've been trying for 12 years to find something wrong with it [Chicago Downs stock]. The only thing they've found is that the critics don't have any of it."[5]

Many of the state's major daily newspapers found the choice of Powell or Hoffman uninviting. They had nothing in particular against Hoffman, and they had no reason to believe Powell would be any worse in the position than those who held it before. There had been a thought in some quarters of the state that the secretary of state's position had no public policy responsibility and was mostly an administrative position. Therefore, the argument went, it should not be an elective job but should be filled by appointment of the governor. This approach rarely got much attention, but in editorials before the election, the idea surfaced. The Lindsay-Schaub newspapers, publishing in Carbondale, East St. Louis, Champaign-Urbana, and Decatur, ducked the issue of Powell versus Hoffman with an editorial that endorsed neither:

> Rep. Powell has been an effective legislator in many ways, and has served three terms as Speaker of the Illinois House. Under his administration the secretary of state's office would be simply a patronage arm of the Democratic party. Moreover, the folksy Rep. Powell is quite unable to see any conflict of interest in his ownership of race track stock and his strong championship of the legislative interests of the race track industry. Congressman Hoffman has a dreary record in Congress and a high rate of absenteeism, owing to his penchant for playing courthouse politics in Illinois.
>
> The fact that voters of Illinois must choose between these two candidates for secretary of state is a good argument for making this office an appointive, non-patronage post under the governor.[6]

Other papers, including the *Chicago Sun-Times*, took the same route and refused to endorse either of the two. The *Sun-Times* said the two were county courthouse-type politicians of the old school who would use the position to build a personal political machine.

Powell and other Democrats on the ticket rolled by the Republican opposition on the coattails of President Lyndon Johnson's landslide victory. Kerner led the way, defeating Percy by a margin of 179,299 votes, or 51.9 percent of those voting. Democrats also kept the attorney general, lieutenant governor, and state auditor positions. Powell won easily over Hoffman by a margin of 488,555, which constituted 55.4 percent of the vote. Powell won the contest in Cook County and beat his Republican opponent downstate, as well. Hoffman defeated Powell in Johnson County 2,043 to 1,930.[7]

Now with a workforce of 2,400 people, authority over automobile and truck licensing, and responsibility for all the state's buildings and facilities, Powell had broken away from the politics of southern Illinois. He had, at last, sought and found acceptance on a scope he did not have even as Speaker of the House. Still, with his newfound position and statewide voter preference, Powell could not shake headlines and news stories that raised questions about the people he hired, the business he conducted, and the odor of impropriety.

Were the stories just nagging minor matters that his critics jumped on and magnified out of proportion to the facts, or did these tales provide a picture of a politician in over his head? The answers were inconclusive while he lived. For sure, Powell had stepped outside his cozy southern Illinois district squarely into the light of statewide watchdogs.

In his first four-year term, Powell had almost a scrape of consequence each year, but 1965 qualified as the winner in volume news coverage. Before his first full year in office passed, Powell had at least three public episodes involving his past practices and activities. None of the incidents threatened to unseat Powell, but together they brought to light questions about Powell's sense of propriety and his fitness to serve a broader constituency.

Powell had a tough summer in 1965. It began with information leaked to the press about an investigation of money paid to Powell by racetrack pal Sam Wiedrick for "finder's fees." The *Chicago Daily News*, among other papers, attempted to tie the payment in 1961 of a rumored $8,000 to Powell, who then was Speaker of the House. Reports said Powell received the payoff for killing a bill that would have increased revenues to the state general fund from racetracks.[8] The investigation was conducted by the Illinois Crime Commission, which included some legislators as members.

The 1961 bill in question was House Bill 693, sponsored by Rep. Abner Mikva. It would have increased the state's share of thoroughbred racing proceeds. Mikva's cosponsorship of a similar bill would have increased the take from harness racing. The thoroughbred bill died after a long and bitter debate in the House, during which Powell left the Speaker's chair to lead the fight against House Bill 693 on the floor. He succeeded in reversing an earlier committee vote in favor of the bill. The harness racing bill died in committee.

In 1965 the Crime Commission actually had conducted a more extensive investigation but voted 5 to 4 not to release the information. Powell, naturally, denied the finder's fee had anything to do with legislation.[9] A more elaborate explanation of the financial arrangement with Wiedrick surfaced in 1969, when the charges of the Crime Commission again arose.

The story rattled around the state for several weeks, including articles that Wiedrick had told the Crime Commission of longer term payments to Powell. That brought the headlines up to $70,000 in consulting fees for Powell. Through it all, Powell stuck to his often-repeated response to conflict of interest charges: "There's nothing in the law that has anything to say against a person making money. This income has kept me free from bribes or acting in any way in conflict of office."[10]

While that story spoke to Powell's actions before he became secretary of state, articles appeared at the same time in the *Daily News* about his budget requests and spending habits in the statewide office he had held less than six months. The *Daily News* noted that taxpayers footed Powell's bills for lodging at the St. Nicholas Hotel and the Conrad Hilton in Chicago; that his budget sought an additional three hundred patronage jobs; that he had hired longtime Republican friends, one of whom—Walter McAvoy—had helped him be elected Speaker in 1961; and so on.[11] Maybe those issues were news to the *Daily News*, but Powell had been engaged in such activities for nearly thirty years.

While these stories caused an increase in the snicker status of Powell, one bombshell exploded late in June and carried through the remainder of the summer. Tape recordings reportedly made from April to June by wiretapping a telephone and bugging a hotel room used by lobbyists for currency exchange interests fell into the hands of the Sangamon County state's attorney. The tapes, turned over to the prosecutor by reporters of *Chicago's American*, contained conversation about bribes of legislators to influence currency exchange legislation. The recordings mentioned Powell prominently.[12]

Powell was not quoted nor was his voice on the recordings. He was mentioned along with the names of twenty-four state senators, thirty-seven state representatives, five state departmental officers, two Chicago ward committeemen, and a former committeeman. The lobbyists who spoke on the tapes made it clear that while Powell no longer sat in the legislature, he still played a major role in the fate of legislation. Powell commented on the reports: "I'm sleeping good and my conscience is clear."[13]

The tapes provided no indictable information regarding Powell's actions but offered just enough verbiage to enhance his reputation for deal-making. The tapes gave Chicago reporters an opportunity to resurrect his past and speculate about his wealth. *Chicago's American*, for example, said, "Beneath Powell's veneered image of a crusty, folksy country boy is the inner-workings of a master politician, twice voted the state's outstanding legislator by the Springfield press corps." The paper added, "Known as the keenest political 'horse-trader' in the legislature, Powell also fancies the four-footed variety and holds highly profitable shares in harness race tracks in Illinois."[14] All words that Powell must have relished.

The story lingered, the state's attorney conducted an investigation, and bills were introduced in the legislature at the end of the session that would have broken new ground in state ethics laws. Rep. Adlai E. Stevenson III received notice for introducing some of the more aggressive legislation, but the probes and bills died in the Illinois summer heat.[15] When 1965 ended, it seemed that hardly a day had passed without Powell's name in the headlines. In 1966 that impression continued.

Powell regretted the day he hired Frank (Porky) Porcaro as a state investigator attached to the secretary of state's office. Actually, he did not hire Porcaro after his election in 1964, but the man who became Powell's number two person in the office did. Charles Smith—long associated with Chicago politics, Eddie Barrett, and Charles Carpentier—moved into Powell's office as chief of staff at the beginning. By March 1966, he had followed Porcaro out the door.[16]

Before service with Powell, Porcaro had been a lobbyist in Springfield and was a former employee of the Springfield sanitary district. He and Smith were associates. He also had a criminal record about which Powell apparently had known. Porcaro pleaded guilty in Chicago criminal court in 1958 to accepting $1,450 from men who said they gave him money for his pledge to get them easy jobs with the county highway department. He served seventy-eight days of a ninety-day sentence.[17]

The earliest indication of trouble with Porcaro occurred in February 1966, during a controversial raid on the campus of the University of Illinois, after which sixty students were charged with altering driver's licenses. This apparently was an attempt to stop the practice of altering driver's licenses for use as identification cards to purchase beer and liquor. Beyond that issue, Porcaro's behavior as an employee had been challenged. He later was accused of stealing money from the state by falsifying expense accounts. As these issues became public, Porcaro resigned as Powell's investigator in March. Powell called him a "Judas." Within a few months, Porcaro was convicted of theft and bigamy and faced a jail term of one to five years.[18]

In September, newspapers reported that Porcaro had told of bribery, corruption, and gangster influences in state government, including the secretary of state's office. Porcaro made the charges in a two-hour taped conversation with Edmund J. Kucharski, undersheriff of Cook County. Kucharski's boss, Sheriff Richard B. Ogilvie, turned transcripts over to Cook County State's Atty. Daniel P. Ward, a Democrat.[19] Immediately the issue boiled down to Republicans Ogilvie and Kucharski against Chicago and Springfield Democrats. Fallout from the involvement of Ogilvie and Kucharski tainted the future relationship with Powell.

After Kucharski and Ogilvie displayed the tapes, Porcaro denied making them, which muddied the already unclear water. In the disputed tapes, however, specific occurrences and names of individuals were reported and presumably implicated people associated with the auto license business.

The case got messy before it came to an end, with Powell unscathed. Grand juries in Springfield, DuPage County, and Cook County heard from Powell—and Porcaro—in mid-October. Grand jury testimony and appearances are protected from disclosure, and Powell played it straight. He volunteered to testify, before being subpoenaed, and received immunity from prosecution. Leaving the sessions, he said only that he answered all the questions. Up to his old quips, Powell responded to one reporter who asked if he had testified before a grand jury previously: "One time when your newspaper thought there was a race track scandal I went before the grand jury. It wound up with members of the jury wanting to know from me where they could buy race track stock."[20]

By 1966 Nicholas Ciaccio had taken the position of chief administrative assistant and close adviser to Powell. According to newspaper accounts, agents of the FBI had observed longtime reputed mob figure Momo "Sam" Giancana of Chicago in Mexico in a car with an Illinois license tag. Upon checking with the secretary of state's office, agents learned that files in Powell's office relating to the license number—PG 5000—had been misplaced or lost and could not be found. Agents reported this to Ciaccio and Powell in May, and the secretary said he would investigate and clear up any problems. By September, the FBI had no report from Powell. The first newspaper report of the affair surfaced September 8 in Chicago newspapers, leaving the impression that Giancana had been issued the license under mysterious circumstances.[21]

Within a week of the reports, Powell and Ciaccio called a press conference in Springfield to explain the unusual circumstances of the missing license application. Powell said the missing application had been found and would be turned over to the FBI. Meanwhile, he said, the license plates had been registered under the names of a Chicago theatrical corporation. Ciaccio said he had not handled the application. He added: "When you get this all washed up, it's a case where a couple of applications weren't handled properly and this can happen in an office as big as ours. I am not infallible."[22] Ciaccio wrote Powell a memo in which he said he found no conspiracy to issue the plates without fees or without appropriate records.

Taking the offensive, Powell charged that a certain segment "of the public press is trying to throw a blanket on all citizens of Italian ancestry. If his name had been Ogilvie or Cain instead of Ciaccio, there would have been no story." Richard Ogilvie was then Cook County Board of Supervisors chairman. Richard S. Cain, a former Cook County deputy sheriff when Ogilvie was sheriff, was associated with the car, the license plates, and Giancana in Mexico.[23]

Blaring headlines subsided as 1967 arrived and political writers speculated about Powell's intentions for another run in 1968, particularly after all the news of his first term. Shortly after his wife, Daisy, died in April 1967, Powell's comments about a campaign appeared in the Springfield newspaper column written by reporter Gene Callahan. Powell left no doubt about his fitness and interest in seeking reelection: "I'm like all other candidates, and if my health is good and things are normal I will be a candidate on my record so we can finish what we have started. There's no one in the statehouse who puts in more hours than I do. The doctor says my health is in perfect condition. I don't want to go out and wrestle with bears or anything, but I'm feeling real good."[24] At that time, reporters speculated Powell would be contested by State Sen. Donald Carpentier, son of the former secretary of state. Callahan's column also mentioned the Porcaro incident as something Powell would be questioned about frequently.

Powell soon committed to a second term, and the Democratic slatemakers made it official without quarrel. Republican challengers stepped forward, urged to some degree by newspaper editorial pages hoping that a challenger worthy of endorsement would surface. One such hope was Brian Duff, a suburban Republican associate of moderate Republicans such as Senator Percy and U.S. Rep. Donald Rumsfeld. Duff looked like a reformer, although he never had held public office. The *Chicago Sun-Times* leaned on Duff's youth (he was thirty-seven years old) and the promise of vigor in office to endorse him in the primary against Donald Carpentier.

Carpentier fought off the upstart Duff in the primary and prepared to battle a scarred and embattled Powell. Carpentier, the son of former secretary of state Charles Carpentier, served in the state Senate from East Moline and obviously hoped the still fresh memory of his father and a rebounding Republican party in the 1968 elections would propel him to victory over Powell.

Meanwhile, the Democratic party did not present a particularly strong slate of candidates, headed by Powell's nemesis Samuel Shapiro for governor. As the only downstaters on the ticket, Powell and Paul Simon, longtime opponents in the state legislator and about as opposite in their views of state government as two persons could be, found themselves thrown together on the stump.

Simon remembers Powell as a tireless campaigner, and they spent quite a lot of time together on the road. "We started a friendship," Simon says. "Some of the state ticket never did anything. We had a meeting of candidates at the Democratic national convention, and they said bring your schedule. Well Paul and I had long commitments. The other candidates, they had hardly anything. Powell, [Mike] Howlett and I were the only three Democrats elected."[25]

Predictably, Carpentier and the Republican party attacked Powell's record. One full-page advertisement used in papers across the state displayed headlines from Powell's tenure as secretary of state: "Powell to Face Cook Grand Jury," "Powell's Latest Caper Adds to Dem Woes," "Powell's Police—and Terror in the Night." The party headline declared, "What a Way to Run the People's Business!" Powell tried the high road, citing how he administered the secretary of state's office.

Generally speaking, newspaper editorials lumped Powell and Carpentier together and gave neither much of an advantage. The *Chicago Daily News* wrote: "This would have been the perfect occasion for the Republicans to put up a real winner against the Vienna Gallus-snapper. So they ran State Sen. Donald D. Carpentier. Schooled in the same wheeler-dealer traditions as Powell, Carpentier would only assure more of what Illinois has been putting up with from Powell."[26] The paper refused to endorse either.

While the state and nation watched a duel for president between Richard M. Nixon and Hubert Humphrey in an atmosphere of street riots and Vietnam War rhetoric, a predictable pattern emerged in the Illinois race. The split vote put a Republican, Richard Ogilvie, in the governor's mansion but a Democrat, Simon, in as lieutenant governor. The only other Democrats to win on a statewide basis were Powell and Howlett. Republicans elected with Ogilvie included Scott as attorney general.

The population's distress over two candidates for secretary of state cast as peas in a pod showed in the final numbers, too. Powell won by the skin of his teeth, with a plurality of only 55,029 votes out of 4,452,707 votes cast. He took nearly 55 percent of the Cook County vote but only 47 percent downstate. Republicans increased their margin for Powell's opponent in Johnson County to 59.2 percent from 51.4 in 1964.[27]

Back in the saddle for a second four-year term, Powell had survived his Republican opponent, the disinterest of newspaper editorial pages, and the damaging headlines of four years as secretary of state—and proved again that he could survive the best shots of his detractors.

5

A Helping Hand for SIU

IT MIGHT BE SAID THAT PAUL POWELL AND SOUTHERN ILLINOIS UNI-
versity grew up together, in spite of the fact that he did not attend a single day at any college and that there was no special allegiance to higher education in his background. The two stories certainly parallel each other: SIU
from lowly teachers college to multi-versity; Powell from local glad-handing
politician to Speaker of the House. All in less than a lifetime.

When Powell started his climb in the legislative ranks in the 1930s and
early 1940s, southern Illinois had just one institution of higher education,
the "normal" or teachers college at Carbondale. For much of that time, the
school had a few hundred students and few buildings.

Leo Brown, a legend for his work in behalf of SIU and a successful Carbondale physician, graduated from the teachers college in 1932 in a class of
180 students.[1] Mel Lockard, a native of Cobden and contemporary of Powell who later became a trustee of SIU, recalls the school more like a community college or just a step beyond high school. Those who completed
schooling in two years, as did Lockard, received an automatic teachers certificate without taking an examination.[2]

In a campaign statement to the *Southern Illinoisan* in 1958, Powell put his
own perspective on Southern Illinois State Normal University in the days of
Brown and Lockard. He said that in 1935, the year he went to the Illinois legislature, the university's appropriation was $663,900. For the 1955–57 bien-
nium, twenty years later, SIU received $20,342,426.[3]

Since 1867 the higher education system in Illinois had featured the University of Illinois as the crown jewel and sole state university, with five
teacher education schools taking up the rear.[4] When it came to state money
for higher education, the U of I received the cream, and the five other school
took the leftovers. This situation continued until after World War II without
serious challenge. The returning veterans, the GI Bill, and national prosperity dramatically changed the demand situation for higher education, and
with it came challenges from the lesser colleges to the continuing status of
the U of I. The "others" wanted more of the resources.

In 1945 Southern Illinois Normal University hired a new president, Chester F. Lay. The runner-up in that search was Delyte Wesley Morris, a speech teacher with a Ph.D.[5] Morris presented modest credentials for a top administrative post at a small college. He graduated with a bachelor's degree from Park College in Parkville, Missouri, in 1928. He added a master's degree and then received a doctorate in speech from the University of Iowa in 1936. He taught speech for a few years at Indiana State Teachers College in Terre Haute. More important than his professional credentials and experience to Brown and other supporters was that Morris was born and reared near Xenia in southern Illinois's Clay County, and their instincts said Morris could be the Messiah.

For the outspoken Brown, the decision to hire Lay and overlook Morris cost the school precious time in its growth cycle. Lay's tenure ended in 1948, however, and the teachers college board, with Brown a member, began looking for a new president. Brown remembers that he wanted Morris from the outset, and the board agreed. By this time, Morris had joined the faculty at Ohio State University in Columbus. "I remember we called Morris in Maine where he was building a privy on his aunt's holdings. We offered him a salary of $16,000 a year, and he took it."[6] No one ever doubted the payoff on that investment.

The Morris era at Southern began with his installation in 1948, just months before the Powell era as Speaker of the House began in Springfield. Coincidentally, Morris stepped down as president of SIU in 1970, the same year Powell died.

By the time Morris arrived, contact already had been made with Powell by Brown and Orville Alexander, a political science professor at the teachers college and Lions Club associate. "I was president of the alumni association when I first met Powell," Brown recalls. "I said to Alexander that we ought to go down to Vienna and meet him, because he could be a big help to us. We sold Southern as best we could with Powell and he listened. Later he told some friends, 'I like Brown. He cusses so good and all the time.'"[7] They hit it off. More importantly, perhaps, Brown had seized on Powell's southern Illinois pride and his desire for a reputation as a benefactor of SIU. "Powell could just as well have turned to the U of I or some other institution," Brown said. "It would have fit his image of a statewide political figure. Instead, Powell devoted his entire higher education interest to SIU."

The team that propelled Southern into a major university had begun to assemble: Morris, a masterful salesman and public relations wizard; serious and devoted volunteers, such as Brown and later many others; and Powell, first among many supportive legislators. In his first year as president, Morris went right to work with techniques for which he became famous.[8] Beyond his own deep commitment to Southern, Morris reached out to all manner of support group to help with decision makers. David Rendleman, a graduate of Southern and a physician who returned to Carbondale, was a sophomore when Morris organized his first student lobbying group to make the trip to Springfield to speak for the annual appropriation.

"We walked into Powell's office and there he was behind a mahogany desk in a place of grandeur," Rendleman—whose brother John would become notorious because of his associations with Powell—recalled. "Powell looked at us and said, 'I'll tell you one thing—tell that fellow Morris that he won't be getting $35 million—he's going to get $10 million which is three times more than he ever got before.'"[9] That's about the way it turned out.

Another major proposal before the session of 1949–50 concerned the future of Southern as a separate university with its own board of trustees. Slowly, the school had made progress in working free of the state teachers college board, which in turn was responsible to the state Department of Registration and Education. Two years previously, the school had declared itself a general university with the right to confer a liberal arts degree. Powell had tried to establish that designation in a bill he submitted in 1943, which failed to pass.

Even with a "university" designation, the school was governed by the state teachers college board. Now supporters of the university launched a major campaign to make the separation final and put the school in the hands of its own board of trustees.[10] As with most efforts of SIU to break away in those years, the idea met with substantial opposition in the legislature.

The principal opposition came from two quarters: friends of the University of Illinois and Gov. Adlai Stevenson, both of which actually may have been the same. The issue brought out all the old ideas about higher education and some new ones, as a bill introduced by Sen. R. G. Crisenberry of Murphysboro began its journey in Springfield. In the Senate it faced opposition from Sen. Everett Peters of St. Joseph, the patron saint of the U of I in legislative halls. In the House, another of the University of Illinois's servants, Rep. Ora D. Dillavou, a Republican from Urbana, tried a mixture of ideas directed at stopping the separate board movement. Senator Crisenberry managed to get his bill approved by the Senate, but the House slowed down the process.[11]

Powell, the first Democratic Speaker of the House since 1937, worked quietly behind the scenes, while others made headlines with various proposals. He brought the state Legislative Budget Commission to SIU in April to tour the campus. He helped arrange a meeting of President Morris and U of I President George D. Stoddard, designed to bury the higher education hatchet. Powell kept up contact with aides to Governor Stevenson on compromise proposals.

At a critical moment in Springfield, there were three major proposals under consideration:

• A separate board of trustees for SIU
• A separate board of trustees for SIU, subject to a two-year trial
• Operate SIU as a branch of the U of I

The governor expressed doubts about granting autonomy to SIU without a broader master plan for higher education. SIU wanted almost anything but to be under the wing of the U of I. The U of I preferred the status quo. The compromise proposal that finally received House approval and a signature by the governor granted the autonomy, with the two-year provision for a study of higher education.[12] The governor saved face; SIU supporters rejoiced. The U of I licked its wounds and prepared to fight another year.

Leo Brown, who lobbied tirelessly for this bill, ranks its passage as a milestone in SIU history. He also remembers how Powell came to the rescue of SIU and the proposal at a moment-of-truth meeting with the University of Illinois:

> The drive to get a separate board of trustees became a furor and all the leaders of the area at a fever pitched pace began bombarding all of the legislators and soon open opposition came, principally from the University of Illinois. . . . Similarly the jealous four other teachers colleges united with the University of Illinois and it became an extremely difficult matter to achieve a separate board of trustees. . . . The principal force to achieve this was established by Paul Powell of Vienna. I was present when he shook his fist in the face of the president of the University of Illinois Board of Trustees and the President of the university and stated, "Goddamit I will not call your god damn [appropriations] bill unless Southern Illinois University at Carbondale gets its separate board of trustees and begins to get a piece of the pie."[13]

Brown paid tribute to all the volunteers, letters, telephone calls, telegrams, and the usual devices used to pressure the legislators. But Brown, who became a member of the first board of trustees, leaves no doubt who should get the final credit: "As always the so-called 'pig cutting' is always done by someone in a position to call the shots; that person was Paul Powell. Let the record show that this is the way it was."

While Powell held considerable leverage as Speaker of the House and seldom hesitated to use it, he had positioned himself carefully for those times when others might hold the leadership reins. This forward thinking benefited SIU when in 1945 Powell became a member of the Legislative Budgetary Commission, which represented the legislative point of view on the state budget in consultation with the governor's office.[14] Powell remained a member of that commission as long as he served in the legislature. In those councils many of the financial deals were cut that ended up in appropriations legislation. Without support of the commission, no budget bills went anywhere. Consequently, the commission had much to say about carving up the higher education pie.

Powell found the University of Illinois to be well represented on the commission in the person of Senator Peters. During the growth period of the 1950s and 1960s, Peters served much of the time as chair of the commission. If the University of Illinois were to give any ground at all to SIU, Peters had to be a part of the deals. In many instances Peters had the political muscle to get what he wanted with little effort. Powell's presence on the commission and in Democratic party leadership in the House changed the balance of power but did not take it away from Peters or the U of I.

William Grindle, a Democrat senator from Williamson County for five legislative sessions at the time of SIU's biggest growth, explained the Peters-Powell dynamic this way: "Senator Peters was always opposed to southern Illinois raising itself up by its bootstraps. But with Peters up there in the Senate and Paul Powell from down in Vienna in our district, who was generally either Speaker of the House or a leader there, we used to strike a happy medium and we could get things done. . . . This game of politics is strictly a horsetrader's game; it's a game of compromise."[15]

Alan Dixon, who began a long and distinguished career in public office as a member of the state legislature in 1951, remembers the years of grappling between Powell and Peters, over many issues: "Paul got things for SIU, and then gave things for the University of Illinois, in deals with Peters. They were kin folks—a Republican conservative and a southern Illinois Democrat, and they made a lot of deals together. Paul took care of SIU because it would help the region, but he had a lot of agendas and that was just one."[16]

Not everyone had such an elevated opinion of Powell and Peters. Anthony Scariano, with whom Dixon sided on many issues over the years, characterized the motivation this way: "Whatever he [Powell] did for Southern Illinois University was only because . . . he helped to build it with appropriations. And Peters helped to build the University of Illinois with appropriations. But they got a quid pro quo. It wasn't that they were interested in higher education. 'How many more jobs does this give you in my area? How many more favors can I do for people in my area?'"[17]

If SIU were to grow, an essential element had to be the SIU president. With a dynamic, forceful, visionary leader, the politicians could do their work efficiently. Delyte Morris filled the bill. He relentlessly pursued the idea of SIU as a major university, second only to the University of Illinois. Tirelessly, Morris promoted the school, developed new plans and ideas, pleaded with decision makers, pointed out the shortcomings of Southern's physical plant, and reminded everyone of the explosion in attendance.

From those days of a few hundred students primarily from nearby communities, SIU enrollment blossomed to 4,364 in 1954, more than any of the other four former teachers colleges—Eastern, Western, Northern, and Illinois State. In those days southern Illinois students made up 80 percent of enrollment, but in the 1960s student growth came increasingly from northern Illinois. In the fall of 1959 enrollment hit 11,374.[18] In the fall of 1968 SIU had two campuses with combined enrollments of about 35,000.

Growth looked good to those outside the university, but in the classrooms, among those on faculty, and among people directly connected to the daily work, growth brought misery and anxiety and demonstrated how appropriations barely kept up with student demand and faculty salaries. Prof. David Kenney, writing in his memoir, describes life inside: "There were never enough classes in those days to meet the demand. Each fall there was a scramble by department heads and deans to hire qualified people to do the teaching to serve unexpected enrollments. Providing classrooms was a difficult task."

He goes on to say: "In the community there were inadequate facilities for food service, recreation, and parking, aside from the housing that was in demand. It was a 'boomtown' time. . . . The unforeseen increases in enrollment year after year had not been taken into account in budget estimates and appropriations, so each year saw the need for supplemental authorizations."[19] Such was the reason, then, for Morris's pleas for buildings, operating funds, and salaries.

Those who have sung Morris's praises are legion. Grindle said: "Delyte Morris was one of the best, you know, and his wife was the most gracious person that I ever met. She was really a doll as far as I'm concerned. . . . Dr. Morris deserved a greater part of the credit for making SIU the great university that it is today." Rep. James Holloway, who served from nearby Randolph County, echoed the praise: "In my opinion I hope that history will show Delyte Morris was really the father of Southern Illinois University. We owe him a great debt of gratitude for his farsightedness and his dedication in the building of a great university."[20]

Morris, an energetic man with a dignified presence, might have turned off some people of southern Illinois, but he knew the landscape and won people over with his dedication to southern Illinois and the school. Those present during the growth years remember how different Powell and Morris seemed but how effectively they worked together. Leo Brown explains: "Delyte Morris liked Powell—you had to like him. Morris realized he was necessary.[21] David Rendleman saw the arrangement from the other side: "Powell saw in Morris a real leader. He had a certain contempt for educated people, and he scoffed at Morris some of the time. But they worked together."[22]

But Powell rarely gave an inch when it came to claiming his share of credit. Rendleman remembers another time—while he served on the student legislative committee—when they invited Gov. Adlai E. Stevenson to attend an open house on campus. Stevenson called at the last minute and said that he couldn't come but that he had asked Powell to appear and make the speech. "When Powell got up to talk, he read a telegram from Stevenson and then said, 'Those words were from the Governor—these words now are from Paul Powell.'"[23]

As much as Powell wanted a major university in Carbondale, he also saw the political benefit to being a champion of SIU and higher education. Prior to his first run for election as secretary of state in 1964, Powell had the Legislative Council prepare a paper titled "Legislation Benefiting Southern Illinois."[24] Specifically the study dealt with the 1957 legislative session, but more generally it wrestled with the concept that legislation could be sorted out for impact on a regional basis. It specifically cited legislative assistance to SIU as one of the identifiable regional benefits. In one paragraph, the council summary struck at the heart of SIU resource impact on the region:

Economic advantage for Southern Illinois may likewise spring from the increased appropriations to Southern Illinois University. That institution is constantly expanding its leadership activities in developing the many potentialities of the southern end of the state. The increased funds available to the university will enable it to carry out more adequately its many programs devoted to improving the economic and social life of Southern Illinois. The total Southern Illinois University appropriation in the 1955–57 biennium totaled about $21,000,000, while for the 1957–59 biennium SIU appropriations were increased almost a third, to about $31,000,000.

Leo Brown remembers the practicalities of working with Powell on the growth of SIU: "We all realized that Powell was a necessity, including Morris." Reflecting on his dealings with Powell, Brown said, "He had a high set of rules for everybody, but not himself."[25]

Paul Simon, who during the growth years represented Madison County in the legislature and later represented southern Illinois in Congress, is not sure of Powell's motivations: "It was clear he was championing the SIU cause. Another thing, it was great political cover for him in terms he could go back to the people in Johnson County and say he was a champion of the university. And at that point it helped the region economically. . . . He was an effective legislator and he proved it for SIU."[26]

Before Morris's tenure had progressed far, another key person joined the team. John S. Rendleman, a native of southern Illinois and a graduate of SIU and then the University of Illinois College of Law, had returned to home ground with his law degree to practice among friends. Morris hired him in 1951 as acting university counsel and lobbyist, with the title of assistant professor of government.[27]

Leo Brown called Rendleman and Powell "partners in crime," meaning, he said, that "they worked closely together for SIU. Rendleman rendered a lot of service to SIU." Lockard, whose wife and Rendleman were cousins, added: "He was one of the smartest boys we ever had in the organization. He was a good lawyer and a good lobbyist." His work for SIU first brought him in contact with Powell.

Representative Holloway gave Rendleman a lion's share of credit for SIU's good fortune: "I probably knew John Rendleman better than I did Delyte Morris. John Rendleman was Delyte's right hand man. John was the one who actually got the work done. It was Delyte who set things in motion but John carried them forward to completion. The two made a wonderful combination and to be quite frank about it we haven't had such leadership at SIU since. They were people that you really don't replace."[28]

The team now assembled analyzed the legislative successes of the University of Illinois. In addition to Senator Peters, a graduate of Illinois in 1918, the legislature was full of graduates of the university, and alumni of the U of I held positions of power and authority throughout the state. At one time during the 1950s when Republicans controlled both the Senate and House, Dillavou served as chair of the House Appropriations Committee, giving the U of I a significant advantage over SIU interests. U of I grads contributed a lot of money to campaigns, and they made a lot of noise in behalf of the university. The university also had its lobbying directly with legislators down to a fine point. An example was the annual visitation at the University of Illinois, conducted by the school's lobbyists.

Rep. Paul J. Randolph, a Republican from Cook County who began his career in the legislature in 1945–46, described the U of I party: "After the session they would come over and pick us up if you didn't have a car and drive us over, or arrange for transportation. They put us up at the Illini Union. I never missed them. They were good get-togethers. They were mainly just luncheons and dinners, some tours, and mainly the deans coming in and speaking, or the president, the coach and so on. . . . We always had a party at the Champaign Country Club. They were good entertainers." He remembered the lobbyist parties at the Sangamo Club in Springfield, too. The U of I team threw good parties.[29]

Grindle recalled those good times as well: "Yes, we went over there and then we had dinner in the evening. And our families were invited. I took my wife to a couple of those. They were always very gracious at the University of Illinois. Of course that's understandable, that's a kind of a lobbying deal. University of Illinois had one of the greatest lobby teams I've ever seen."[30] The challenge for Morris, Powell, Rendleman, Brown, Clyde Choate, and other key players was how to become as effective as the U of I with less history and less time. The objective was not to invent new ways of lobbying but to do a better job.

While Brown did not have a corner on volunteer lobbying in behalf of SIU, his commitment is typical of how the team overcame the U of I advantage. He recalled: "I could do a day's work, leave Carbondale, drive to Springfield in a couple of hours and hit the bars by evening buying drinks for politicians."[31] Morris was indefatigable. His schedule reveals a steady daily diet of speeches, meetings, conversations, trips to meet important people and decision makers, and tours of the SIU campus, a la the U of I. Those who met with him and listened to his unending facts and figures remember him as a "super salesman." The SIU effort impressed legislators such as Grindle: "The only one better than them [U of I] I always thought was Southern Illinois University, which was close to home you know. But I think SIU learned from the University of Illinois and finally caught up with them almost."[32]

In Springfield the magic required putting together effective coalitions that would help Southern Illinois University without punishing the University of Illinois. The master craftsman of coalitions in the halcyon years of SIU was Powell. The Democrats of southern Illinois had learned well that a coalition with Democrats from Cook County could often carry the day on major legislation. It helped that Republicans from southern Illinois frequently sided with their regional partners, and in Chicago those who called themselves Republicans actually were Democrats. Carved that way, the legislative carcass looked different than strictly along the lines of partisan labels. On SIU matters the cooperative position with Chicago worked beautifully, for SIU and for Chicago.

In the most practical interpretation, here is how the cooperation looked from the viewpoint in Chicago. The interests controlled by Mayor Richard Daley were willing to give the Democrats from southern Illinois whatever they wanted. Doing so created no problems for Chicagoans, and if it helped Democrats win elections downstate, so much the better. Southern Illinois Democrats had come to accept this tradeoff, and if that meant a quid pro quo for Chicago, it didn't affect anybody in their districts. Powell knew exactly how to activate this arrangement for the benefit of his favorite subjects. It had worked miracles for the racetrack business in Illinois.

In retrospect the successes of SIU seemed secure each step along the way. At the time, however, the battles were hard fought, and success came in some instances only after repeated efforts. SIU's desire to offer an engineering degree program is an example. SIU's engineering school plan surfaced in the 1950s during a time when Republicans controlled the House and Senate and the governor's office.

Also, University of Illinois interests maintained a watchful presence in both bodies, and the Republican party leadership leaned toward the university. At the same time, Powell had his party differences with Mayor Richard Daley and fell out of a leadership position in the sessions of 1955 and 1957. The engineering school issue became a test of SIU's relentless progress and the U of I's stubborn streak.

Senator Crisenberry championed the engineering school in Springfield for the first time in the 1953 session. The U of I and its allies stopped it cold in 1953 and 1955, but SIU came back again in 1957, armed for the battle.[33]

With facts and figures and with expert witnesses to testify before legislative committees, SIU ran head-on into a U of I wall once again in 1957, but this time Southern took the fight to the senior institution. The university argued effectively that one engineering school was more economical and more efficient in producing graduates than having engineering programs at several smaller schools. The U of I engineering dean showed up to argue the cause, with the blessing of President David Henry.

SIU countered with Morris and SIU board chair John Wham, claiming an extreme need for engineering students to meet downstate need. Twice

SIU tried to get its engineering bill out of the Senate education committee only to have tie votes. On the third attempt, the U of I, having called for a show of strength from its alumni across the state, killed the measure 9 to 5.[34]

Friends and officials of SIU made a last-minute appeal to Governor Stratton, but the U of I had won and Stratton could not change the outcome. In spite of this episode, Stratton remained one of SIU's strongest supporters, especially when its growth could be related to helping the economic picture in southern Illinois.

Angry over the U of I tactics, Senator Crisenberry stated: "The University of Illinois has from the beginning opposed every bill to liberalize Southern. I feel the University of Illinois would like to see all higher education controlled on one campus." In the war of words, President Henry called it just a "difference of opinion." He added, "The University of Illinois has the greatest of good will for the development of Southern Illinois University."[35]

Again, in 1959, with Powell as Speaker, SIU supporters tried for the engineering program, only to fail. Republicans, led by Senator Peters, simply withheld the votes and the bill died.

For the sixth consecutive biennium, SIU came back in 1961. With Powell as Speaker and with some luck and major help from Mayor Daley, the bill passed. In lifting the restriction on an engineering school, the legislature also lifted restrictions on all other professional programs such as law, medicine, dental, and architecture. Senator Grindle, at the center of the battle in 1961, acknowledged that it could not have happened without the weight of Powell as Speaker of the House.[36]

An analysis in the *Chicago Tribune* explained the outcome: "The main base of SIU at Carbondale is booming. Both houses of the legislature have approved bills permitting the establishment of a school of engineering there. Passage of the legislation resulted from a deal under which supporters of the University of Illinois at Urbana traded votes with SIU backers in return for pledges to defeat a bill setting up a new state board of education to regulate competition among the state's six universities."[37] Once the engineering school matter was settled, barriers against other professional programs—such as medicine—fell, and SIU soon had all the offerings of a major university.

While the engineering school became a frustration for SIU, the university's growth in other arenas continued without serious delay. In 1957 SIU had success in its pursuit of operational and capital funds. In a letter dated July 24, 1957, SIU Trustees Chair John P. Wham and President Morris wrote to thank Powell: "Funds were provided to add additional staff members so sorely needed in a university whose enrollment had doubled in a four-year period and where the prospects of additional hundreds of students each year are now being estimated."[38]

Also during the late 1950s, momentum had developed for a second SIU campus to serve the student population of the St. Louis area and southwestern Illinois. The breakthrough came with approval by voters statewide in 1960 of a $195,000,000 bond issue for construction projects. SIU received $53,000,000 for both campuses, with $25,000,000 for the campus at Edwardsville. This huge step forward to accommodate growth for SIU came on Paul Powell's watch as Speaker of the House in the period 1959 to 1962.[39] Powell's associate and prize political student, John Rendleman, who had moved to the top echelon of SIU officials by the early 1960s, became the first chancellor of the Edwardsville campus in 1968.

Powell remained an ardent supporter of SIU to the end of his legislative days in 1964 and thereafter as secretary of state. But he, along with many elected officials, lost faith in the campus leadership and in the mission of SIU during student riots that began in 1968 and lasted into 1970. During the campus turmoil, which led to the resignation of Morris as president, Powell confided in Rendleman and others that he could not continue as a supporter. As a final statement of disappointment in SIU, Powell changed his will in the fall of 1969 to eliminate a $50,000 bequest to the SIU foundation.[40]

Paul and Daisy Powell at a rare public appearance of the couple. (Courtesy of the Illinois State Historical Library)

Formal photograph of Powell from the 1941–42 legislative session. (Courtesy of the Johnson County Genealogical and Historical Society, Vienna, Illinois)

Powell (*far right*) campaigns with President Harry S. Truman through southern Illinois in 1948. (Courtesy of the Johnson County Genealogical and Historical Society, Vienna, Illinois)

Speaker of the House Powell receives gavel at the podium from Secretary of State Edward J. Barrett in 1949. (Courtesy of the Johnson County Genealogical and Historical Society, Vienna, Illinois)

Gov. Adlai E. Stevenson (*right*) and Powell at a political dinner. (Courtesy of the Illinois State Historical Library)

Powell is applauded by William G. Stratton, Illinois governor (1953–61), at a Kiwanis Club event. (Courtesy of the Illinois State Historical Library)

From left: Mrs. Margaret Hensey, Paul Powell, and Marilyn Towle. (Courtesy of the Illinois State Historical Library)

From left: John S. Rendleman, Clyde Choate (side to camera), Paul Powell, and Delyte Morris, after an Illinois Budgetary Commission subcommittee meeting at Southern Illinois University, Edwardsville campus, April 17, 1964. (Courtesy of the Illinois State Historical Library)

Paul Powell and his driver, Emil Saccaro, pose in front of the official secretary of state car in 1969. (Courtesy of Mrs. Emil Saccaro)

Nicholas Ciaccio (*left*) and Powell at a press conference on the Giancana license plate matter in 1967. (Courtesy of the Illinois State Historical Library)

From left: Paul Simon, Paul Powell, William G. Clark, Samuel Shapiro, Michael Howlett, and Frank Lorenz, Democratic candidates for statewide office in 1968. (Courtesy of the Illinois State Historical Library)

Mayor Richard J. Daley (*right*) confers with Powell with at the 1968 Democratic National Convention in Chicago. (Courtesy of the Illinois State Historical Library)

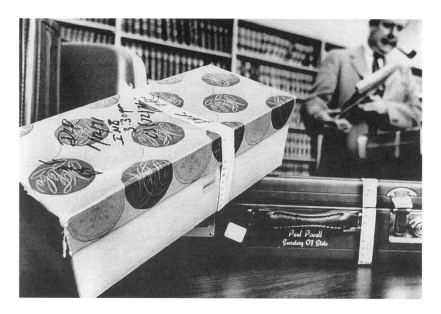

Famous shoe box, photographed in 1975, that allegedly contained about $150,000 and was retained as evidence in a grand jury investigation. (UPI/Corbis-Bettman)

6
Off to the Races

HORSE RACING IS AS MUCH A PART OF ILLINOIS HISTORY AS THE CIVIL War, Chicago mayors, and floods. There is hardly a region in the state that has not experienced horse racing at some level, from county fairs, where the racing of choice is harness, to Chicago, where thoroughbred racing has prospered.

Add to that the business and pleasure of breeding and races for the thrill of the sport, and you have ingredients that have tied all geographic areas of the state together since 1940. As much or more than any other issue, horse racing cuts across social, cultural, business, and political differences to merge diverse interests from the gentle, rolling hill country of deep southern Illinois to the urban clank of Chicago.

Although horse breeding and racing for sport are an integral part of downstate Illinois history, Chicago is where people go to the track and bet the ponies in large numbers. Except for tracks in the East St. Louis area, pari-mutuel action has been in the greater Chicago area and has generated the money to drive the sport.

Bridging this gap between the love and purity of the sport and the reality of huge amounts of money have been the Illinois state legislature and governor's office, the sources of support, strength, and power plays that have made racing more than just the sport of kings. Horse racing has made people wealthy and certain portions of state government flush. Without the determination of lawmakers, racing would be a minor attraction and modest business.

For more than 150 years, Illinois has been a national leader in harness racing.[1] The sport, which dates to colonial times in the eastern United States, first appeared in Chicago in 1845. Thereafter dozens of ovals for harness racing popped up from Waukegan to Decatur to Jacksonville and Springfield. By 1869 there were twenty-eight tracks operating outside Chicago. Over those years, dozens of Illinois horses were national leaders in harness racing. No place in the state, or in the nation for that matter, developed as outstanding a reputation for harness racing as the track at Du Quoin, where for many years the ultimate in harness racing—the Hambletonian—was run, and the Hayes family bred horses on its ranch.

Late in the 1800s, thoroughbred racing took hold, thanks in large part to the promotional activities of Gen. Philip Sheridan, the distinguished cavalry leader of the Civil War and a resident of Illinois at that time. In the early 1800s, Sheridan organized and became first president of the Washington Park Jockey Club. He and his wife participated frequently in a Chicago social life that was tightly connected to horse racing.

The modern era of horse racing in Illinois, meaning the beginning of pari-mutuel betting, began with the passage of the Illinois Horse Racing Act of 1927. While the act allowed for betting on thoroughbred races, it did not permit wagering on harness racing. Furthermore, the law restricted pari-mutuel development by declaring that no association could apply for and receive racing dates unless a track existed.[2]

Stories, maybe apocryphal, abound about shenanigans during consideration by the legislature of pari-mutuel betting in 1927, but eyewitnesses to payoffs are hard to find. Among prominent rumors was a story told by John W. Fribley of Pana, who served in the state Senate from 1935 to 1952.[3] Fribley knew Hayden Davis, a substantial owner of a refinery in Pana and associated with the Abraham Lincoln Hotel in Springfield. Davis told Fribley that during consideration of the legislation, influential promoters associated with the Kentucky Derby came to Springfield to lobby for the bill.

Fribley, quoting Davis, said: "They rented a suite in the southeast corner of the top floor of the Abraham Lincoln Hotel and they had a black bag they wanted placed in the hotel safe, and Davis said, 'Has that got valuables in it?' The answer was 'yes very substantial.' So Hayden Davis had it taken over to the First National Bank and put in a big lockbox. After the pari-mutuel law was passed, supposedly the powers that be received an approximately $180,000 payoff."

The 1927 law also established a racing commission as the governing body for thoroughbred racing, but no such governing body was necessary for harness racing because betting was prohibited and harness races were restricted to noncommercial locations. In 1941 the commission became the Illinois Racing Board.

The breakthrough for pari-mutuel betting on harness races occurred in 1945. For years harness racing had been associated with downstate county fairs and the state fair in Springfield. They were showcases for horses bred in central and southern Illinois and were popular attractions for fair-goers. The horses raced for prizes, but there was no pari-mutuel betting, and prizes were modest. Some state legislators strongly opposed pari-mutuel betting at county fairs and similar downstate events because they thought betting would make harness racing less of a sport.

Charles W. Clabaugh of Champaign, who served thirty-six years in the legislature ending in 1975, expressed the anti-pari-mutuel position: "I was sorry to see the Du Quoin fair go to pari-mutuels. I guess it got to the place where they had to compete for the patronage of the people they appealed to, but it always seemed a kind of a good breath of fresh country air to go down there and not be bothered with [betting]. Because I find that the people, generally speaking, that attend racing at the tracks don't go to watch the horses run. They could care less who won except the one they're betting on. And I think it's a sport that, like baseball and football, a great deal of the sport has gone out of it to business."[4]

Betting may not have meant much to county fair track patrons, if Clabaugh is to be believed, but it was a different story for horse owners. They could race their horses for larger purses in states that permitted betting on harness races, while Illinois fairs got the leftovers, often barely mustering a handful of decent horses for a race. Officials, breeders and state officials, including John Stelle and Paul Powell, serving his first term in Democratic House leadership, produced an agreement in 1945 that allowed limited pari-mutuel betting on harness racing. Most of the groundwork on the legislation came from the hand of Rep. Henry T. Knauf, called "Heinie" by his friends.[5]

Knauf owned Siskiyou Farm near his hometown of Ladd, Illinois. He had an established reputation in the harness racing world, giving him the credentials for writing the harness racing bill of 1945. He was listed among the top six breeders of standard bred horses in the United States. Before election as representative, Knauf had driven horses at county fairs.

The Harness Racing Act permitted the first pari-mutuel betting but prohibited harness racing meetings at pari-mutuel tracks in July and August, when county fairs flourished. With those limitations, the Illinois Harness Racing Act passed, establishing a harness racing commission.[6] Almost immediately, two tracks opened to harness racing in the Chicago area. They were Suburban Downs and Maywood Park. The Harness Racing Act also protected county fairs, promoted Illinois breeding, and continued a near monopoly in pari-mutuel betting for thoroughbred tracks. As everyone learned later, unbridled harness race expansion was just a legislative session or two away.

Once pari-mutuel betting was allowed on a limited basis, horse racing of all kinds in Illinois exploded. By all measurements, as the state opened up harness racing, the numbers shot off like a rocket. The popularity of thoroughbred racing continued, and those crowds grew as well; but harness racing, when eventually able to race in the summer and at nights, outpaced thoroughbred racing. The sport became an economic engine that attracted people of power and money. The concentration of racing dates was in the Chicago area, matching the expanding and spreading economy of that region.

Politically, the growth paralleled perfectly the tenure of Paul Powell as leader of the Democratic party outside of Chicago. In those twenty years from 1945 to 1965, horse racing became the hottest sport in Illinois.

In that time period of Powell's reign, days of harness racing in Illinois increased from 90 in 1946 to 235 in 1963. The number of races tripled; purses totaled $447,450 in 1946 and $4,448,614 in 1963. Total attendance at harness races shot from 388,065 in 1946 to 2,289,922 in 1963. For the same time period, thoroughbred racing numbers were impressive, too. The total purses doubled; the number of days of racing increased by 30 percent.

You get a limited view of what happened looking at thoroughbreds and harness racing separately. When combined, the numbers for thoroughbred and harness racing together are impressive. The total mutuel handle for both—the amount wagered—rose from $205,619,228 in 1946 to $344,712,055 in 1963, near the end of Powell's legislative career.[7]

The attraction of horse racing to those who promoted and invested in it is understandable after assessing the flow of dollars. There was money to be made and dividends to be paid. All of this, and there was absolutely no cost to state government. Racing sought and received no public money. All that the racing people requested were meeting dates from the governing boards and an attentive and watchful number of elected officials in the state legislature to make sure revenue from racing was used to maintain and promote the sport across the state.

The benefits to the state of Illinois are shown in figures from 1962 and 1963, about fifteen years after the Illinois Harness Racing Act. In 1963, the state of Illinois took in almost $25,000,000 from horse racing, a true bonanza. Of that amount about $.95 of every dollar was earmarked for six special funds.[8] The hard-pressed general fund of the state, which could barely be balanced every biennium, received just $1,410,676 of that $25,000,000 in 1963. Legislators not aligned with horse racing tried valiantly to raid the racing treasury and put more dollars in the general fund, but Powell and his friends stopped each attempt.

The six special funds that received the bulk of racetrack money also had healthy surpluses over which many state officials drooled. They were as follows:

- Service Recognition Fund: Veterans of World War II and the Korean conflict were paid state bonuses from a bond issue that was being retired at the rate of $12,500,000 a year by this fund. In 1962, the fund had a balance of $23,497,912, and in 1963 it received $11,770,664.
- Agriculture Premium Fund: This fund gave grants in aid to the state and county fairs. In 1963 this fund received $8,103,926, about six times more than went to the state's general fund.
- Illinois Fund for Illinois Colts: This money was used for harness racing purses at the Illinois State Fair. In 1962 the fair appropriated about $394,000 for the purses, and in 1963 the take for this fund amounted to $564,230. This fund was created in 1951 by the legislature and received one half of one percent of the total betting at harness tracks where pari-mutuels operated.
- Illinois Bred Thoroughbreds Fund: The money was used for flat track racing purses and stakes at county fairs and the race tracks licensed by the state racing board. In 1963 the amount received was $785,517, and the amount appropriated in 1962 for purses and stakes totaled $657,000.
- Veterans' Rehabilitation Fund: Money for this fund came from uncashed winning pari-mutuel tickets. This fund began immediately after World War II.
- Fair and Exposition Fund: This money was used in part to retire building bonds for McCormick Place in Chicago. In 1963 it received $2,300,000. While this expenditure of horse racing proceeds met with profound displeasure among downstate legislators who did not share Powell's enthusiasm for racing, two legislators who supported using horse racing money to retire these bonds discussed their reasons.

Clabaugh said: "They [Chicago] got absolutely nothing from the fair fund in the way that the fairs did in the other counties. And so I thought if that was the kind of thing that the Chicago members wanted, to the extent that the Chicago members reflect the thoughts of their people—well, there just was not at that time any apparent way of giving Cook County people a share. And I was for it."[9]

State Sen. Elbert Smith of Decatur recalled that sharing with Chicago was not popular with the fair boards in his district: "They counted on a good deal of this money to run their fairs. And they still got a good deal of it. But the idea that we cut and divide some of it up with Chicago was unpopular. Well, I was for it. I supported it. I couldn't think it was fair to not give to Chicago a portion of this fund."[10]

On his way to being conferred with the title of "the state's most powerful booster of horse racing," Powell combined forces with a handful of wealthy, influential, and politically connected power brokers. They ranged from friendly southern Illinois colleagues such as Clyde Lee and Clyde Choate to the highest elected officials of the state and those in politics and business in Chicago. They had much in common. They had money or access to money. They did not let partisan politics interfere with a good deal. They understood the connection between business, sport, and state government. They liked to make money and wield power.

Although many others powered the growth, Powell's contribution to harness racing cannot be exaggerated. Those associated with the sport knew of his value and recognized it. In 1981, when the Illinois Harness Horseman's Association elected him to its Hall of Fame, the IHHA summarized Powell's place in history as "without question . . . the strongest, most influential and greatest elected representative ever to bless harness racing in the annals of state governments in the United States."[11]

One man, arguably more than all the others, helped Powell reach that pinnacle. He was Irwin S. (Big Sam) Wiedrick.[12] Powell aligned himself with any number of deal makers over his adult life but none who lined his pockets and those of his legion with more cash than Wiedrick. This ex-convict from the eastern United States became the pied piper of harness racing and took some of the most powerful men in Illinois along with him on a twenty-year ride. The story of how he and Powell worked together is the story of how harness racing was launched on the fast track to riches.

As much as Powell, John Stelle, and their political friends knew about horse racing, what they really knew was the politics of horse racing and racing at the county fairs. They were fascinated by the sport, but that did not make them smart about it. For an understanding of the sport and how to organize, invest, and promote it, they looked to Wiedrick. From the days when the legislature allowed betting on harness racing in the mid-1940s until Powell's death, they worked as a team, bringing knowledge of racing together with the opportunism of politics at the state level. A true accounting of the money they raised and the cut they took for themselves will never be known. But estimating it in the millions is a good place to start.

Wiedrick's nickname "Big Sam" reflected his size (six feet tall and three hundred pounds). It described his personality as well. He filled the room and got everyone's attention. Big Sam started his sports organization career in Rochester, New York, where he was controlling owner of the Rochester International League Baseball Club. It was his acquisition of the club that got him in trouble. He gained sports operations knowledge and skills with the club, but he also acquired a prison record that dogged him across the country to Illinois.[13]

Authorities arrested Wiedrick on January 29, 1927, for grand larceny in the alleged defrauding of his benefactor, Mrs. Agnes E. Miles of Rochester. The deal involved $100,000 in Eastman Kodak stock that Wiedrick used to purchase the ball club while he was acting as Mrs. Miles's fiduciary agent. Convicted a year after the arrest, Wiedrick served twenty-seven months in prison. Upon release he pleaded guilty to an old charge of fraud in which he was accused of failing to pay more than $10,000 in amusement ticket taxes in 1926 and 1927. In 1932 he paid a $1,000 fine in the case.

From New York, Wiedrick headed to Michigan, where in 1944 he teamed with New York investors to start the Northville Downs Association, a harness racetrack in the Detroit area. However, his prison record caught up with him, and the Michigan Racing Board barred him from participating in harness racing in the state.

Unable to work his trade in Michigan, Wiedrick moved to Illinois, where he put his racing knowledge to work in the days immediately after passage of the state law that allowed pari-mutuel betting at harness tracks. He became acquainted with Stelle, Powell, and their friends from central and southern Illinois and with William H. Johnston Sr., who ran Sportsman's Park, a thoroughbred track in Cicero, just outside Chicago. Johnston and his son, William H. Johnston Jr., became longtime racing associates of Powell.

Over twenty or more years, Wiedrick moved in and out of various racing operations, occasionally drawing attention in news accounts because of his prison record and the press's propensity to link racing with the criminal element. Illinois racing law did not permit an ex-con to have operating control of a racetrack, so Wiedrick made his way mainly as a consultant, and a well paid consultant, too. The Wiedrick-Powell partnership worked beautifully and made them plenty of money. They shared consulting fees, took large stock positions in new racing ventures, brought their political friends to the action, and enjoyed the fruits of the racing world. At one time or another over the two decades, they were deeply involved in Cahokia Downs (thoroughbred), Egyptian Trotting, Fox Valley Trotting, Mississippi Valley Trotting, Suburban Downs, Maywood, Chicago Downs, and Sportsman's Park, just to name the most prominent ventures.

Wiedrick launched his career in Illinois by managing and promoting the first harness race meeting in 1946 at Maywood Park in suburban Chicago.[14] His active management at Maywood ended in 1949. Through the relationship, he received a significant stake of ownership in Maywood, which he later sold for modest profit. However, he maintained a longtime consulting relationship with the operation.

Although the Harness Racing Act of 1945 opened the door to pari-mutuel betting, the major breakthrough for Wiedrick, Powell, and many others interested in harness racing investing occurred in 1949. With the political leadership of Powell—who was serving his first term as Speaker of the House—the legislature passed a bill allowing pari-mutuel harness racing at nights in July and August.

As a result of this law, Powell and Wiedrick bought huge equity stakes for pennies per share in Chicago Downs, the first and most prominent harness organization formed immediately after passage. Wiedrick, who served briefly as general manager of Chicago Downs, bought 15,580 shares of stock in the name of his wife Kathreen, and Powell bought 16,900 shares in the name of his wife Daisy.[15] The payoff was immediate and huge. Stockholders in Chicago Downs received profits on their original investment of 4,000 percent in the first four years.

Powell and Wiedrick had their hands in horse breeding, too, as revealed in Powell's tax returns and correspondence. Four people who tied together the legislature, horse breeding, harness racing, and Sportsman's Park were partners in breeding horses for stakes races in the 1950s.[16] They were Powell, Wiedrick, Hugo Bennett, auditor of Sportsman's Park, and Carl H. Preihs of Pana, a Democrat, who served with Powell in the House. The Kefauver Committee revealed, in 1950 and 1951, that Bennett had loaned $80,000 to his friend Paul Ricca, onetime boss of the Chicago crime syndicate.[17]

In one letter to his partners on February 21, 1953, Preihs wrote: "I have expended a considerable amount of money in the care of our horses and it will require some further six months care and keep until the Stake race which I believe we should point them to. . . . We will have to start them at a few county fairs so as to qualify them for the big race and after that, I would suggest taking them to the pari-mutuel meets to earn some money."[18] Powell's 1952 tax return showed the partnership sold a horse for $3,000, and Powell earned a net capital gain of $478.13. The partnership lasted only a few years and served mostly as a playful venture and a tax write-off.

The Powell-Wiedrick relationship did not stop with harness racing. Thoroughbred opportunities arose, too. In 1953, when central and southern Illinois investors formed Cahokia Downs racetrack near East St. Louis for thoroughbred racing, Wiedrick again was prominently involved with his friends Stelle, Rep. Clyde Lee of Mt. Vernon, Rep. Preihs, and many political people. They hired Wiedrick to promote the track, which included selling stock.

Soon after, however, investors fretted over Wiedrick's notoriety in the Chicago Downs case (he had to step down as manager of the track) and feared that they would be embarrassed by public disclosure.[19] Wiedrick concluded his promotional duties but remained a shareholder.

Wiedrick had no reason to worry about his ouster at Cahokia Downs. He had harness racing opportunities at tracks in the Chicago area. Through a longtime association with Louis M. Jacobs of Buffalo, New York, president of Sportservice, a highly successful concessionaire at sporting locations, Wiedrick cut himself in for a nice piece of action at Maywood.

After Wiedrick brought Jacobs in as concessionaire, Maywood agreed to pay Wiedrick a percentage of the concession take. No such agreement ever was discovered at Cahokia Downs, but when Wiedrick bowed out, his friend Jacobs invested in the track and also took over concessions. Later, when reform-minded members joined the Illinois Racing Board in the early 1970s, they succeeded in getting Sportservice out of all Illinois associations because of concerns about reports of corruption.[20]

Wiedrick's other involvements included a consulting arrangement paying him $20,000 a year at Chicago Downs; and at one time he held 6,839 shares of Fox Valley Trotting Club, Inc. In 1959 he managed the Aurora Downs harness racing meeting for 10 percent of the net take, and he received 5 percent of the gross from sale of food and beverages during meetings of Suburban Downs, Egyptian Trotting, and Maywood Park. A shareholders list for Egyptian Downs from 1963 showed Wiedrick with 5,500 shares. Powell held 6,750 shares at that time.

The centerpiece of harness racing action from 1950 to Powell's death in 1970 was passage of legislation in 1949. Those interested in racing and those interested in preserving quality racing for fairs across the state realized that the 1945 Harness Racing Act was incomplete and needed to be broadened for all interests to benefit. The election in 1948 of a Democratic majority in the state House of Representatives and Powell's election as Speaker provided the perfect setting for reconstructive surgery on the Harness Racing Act. The interests had their man in charge.

Little is left to guesswork in a legislative session. While there may be unpredictable moments and even some nuisance bills introduced, the leadership controls the agenda and introductions of bills that are destined for passage. Rarely does anything major occur without the party in power giving its blessing or taking a role in the outcome. At the same time, legislative success takes more than just a dominant speaker. Passage of a bill in 1949 required organization, timing, and political agility.

Outside the legislature, there were opportunists waiting, too. Among those was William H. Johnston, a wealthy racing investor and promoter who had been successful in Florida operations and with his Sportsman's Park facility in Cicero, and his sidekick Wiedrick. They had common interests in getting the legislature to lift restrictions on harness racing so that Johnston could book his track for harness activities each year after the thoroughbred racing meetings. In the plan that unfolded, Johnston and Wiedrick timed the incorporation of a harness racing entity with anticipated legislative action. With the session ending about July 1, the track could be open for business later in the month.

Another element critical to success of this venture was the powerful county fair lobby, well represented among downstate legislators of both parties. Any harness racing bill needed this support and had to provide further protections and benefits for Illinois horse breeders and the fairs. Also, successfully moving a bill through the legislature required cooperation from Republicans who controlled the Senate.

The earliest known organized discussion of a harness racing bill occurred in January 1949 at a meeting of the Illinois Agricultural Association of County Fairs.[21] Leaders of the organization acknowledged among themselves that the long-held position prohibiting pari-mutuel harness racing from July through September had backfired. In a statement issued in 1951 at the height of newspaper exposure of the 1949 bill consideration, the association recognized "the fallacy of exempting harness horse racing at pari-mutuel tracks from the third Monday of July until the last day of August." The association called for further discussions among fair organizations about a legislative remedy. Heinie Knauf took the legislative lead and brought Speaker Powell and his southern Illinois friends into the discussions.

The legislative group sought a further blessing from the fair organization at a March meeting in Springfield. Representatives from all fairs holding harness racing—there were about thirty—gathered with influential politicians and horse racing promoters. Familiar names included Wiedrick and legislators Powell and Clyde Lee. Wiedrick assured fair officials that lifting the prohibition would ensure the success of harness racing for fairs. He explained that during the months of July, August, and September, there would be a pool of one thousand horses at the tracks, which would guarantee a sufficient supply to fill all races with at least five quality horses.[22]

The March summit meeting concurred on two pieces of legislation: one to wipe out the summer harness racing prohibition and the other to provide an additional $1,000 to each county fair from pari-mutuel tracks for harness racing premiums and horse shows. Official minutes of the meeting state that

Powell "assured those present that this bill would have priority in being presented to the legislators." Two years later an explanation by the association went out of its way to declare, "We specifically state that such legislation was not recommended to be passed by the Honorable Henry Knauf nor the Honorable Paul Powell, but that the request for such legislation came from the representatives of the County Fair Associations."[23]

There were a few curious activities related to the proposed bills before they were introduced late in May, just a month before adjournment. An early version of the harness racing bill included absolution for ex-convicts associated with the sport. Obviously aimed at allowing Wiedrick to operate with a free hand, it created a furor. The final version did not contain the white wash, causing Wiedrick to say, "It doesn't mean that much to me and I don't think the law is constitutional anyway with that in it and I am going to stand on my record."[24]

A curious letter dated April 13, 1949, to Powell from James S. Kearns, Chicago public relations official, urged passage of the bill, which had not even been introduced.[25] Kearns joined Johnston and Wiedrick in organizing Chicago Downs, the first track to take advantage of the law lifting the summer prohibition.

On May 27, about five weeks from the end of the biennial legislation session in 1949, House Bill 1104, dealing with the harness act prohibition, was introduced and referred to the House Agriculture Committee. Also introduced was House Bill 756, which increased the take for fairs by $1,000. Later it was claimed that the bills had been introduced quietly and well after the session was under way, thus giving claim to them being "sneaky bills." Given the preparation for the bill and the number of people involved, *sneaky* is hardly appropriate. However, there was virtually no newspaper coverage of the subject.

A look at the principal sponsors—there were three—of the House bill reveals the fine hand of Speaker Powell. All were close to him and the fair interests. The sponsors were Rep. Clyde Lee, a Democrat of Mt. Vernon; Rep. Clifford C. Hunter, a Republican from Taylorville; and Rep. W. P. Westbrook, a Republican from Harrisburg.[26]

Lee served a distinguished career in the state House of Representatives, beginning with the 1939–40 term and ending with the 1971–72 session. After that first term, he entered World War II and did not return to the legislature until the election of 1946. An effective behind-the-scenes worker and party loyalist, Lee became a legislative and business partner of Powell through much of their Springfield service.

Their friendship arose from a shared interest in county fairs and the Illinois state fair. Lee explained: "I never knew Paul very well the first few sessions. But after I got into the county fair here, he was in the County Fair Association at Vienna and also Metropolis, and we worked together and that was really the beginning of our friendship was in the fairs."[27]

That constituency of fair boosters and promoters, springing mostly from central and southern Illinois and not following any straight political party lines, worked for Powell and Lee as an effective coalition on legislation of all kinds. Lee went on to say: "The fair at Vienna I think sort of ran out about the time that I got into the fair business. I don't think it continued. But he [Powell] was interested in the fair at Metropolis and the fellow who was president of it, Paul Miller, was a good friend of his and it was in his legislative district so he took an interest in the fair down there."

In a public statement about his own interest in helping county fairs, Powell said it began with his father Thomas, who was a director of the Johnson County Fair: "I took my father's stock over. . . . My interest was that I lived with those people, I am in political office and it doesn't hurt to be connected with people connected with county fairs, promoting them."[28]

Lee's interests in breeding, harness racing, making the county fairs strong, and support for the state fair in Springfield, paralleled and even exceeded Powell. While Powell spent more time on leadership affairs, Lee devoted his attention to the associations that made for effective legislative activity. He accepted management and officer responsibilities in several racing ventures and kept in close contact with Powell on matters of track business. They were both deeply involved in Cahokia Downs near East St. Louis, in Egyptian Downs, and in Mississippi Downs. They corresponded over matters of lease negotiations and profits.

Lee became another set of eyes and ears for Powell. Shortly after World War II, Governor Stevenson appointed Lee to the State Fair Advisory Board, where he kept watch over operations and contacts with the legislature. The two became known for their ability to promote harness racing and explain its virtues. Discussing his racing connections, Lee told about a trip Powell and he made to a meeting in Indiana: "One time Powell and I went to Indianapolis and talked to their state group over there. Powell did most of the talking, but I talked a little bit and introduced Powell to the group. That was in the afternoon as I recall, then we went to their banquet."

The Powell-Lee appearance had been promoted by a writer for the *Harness Horse* magazine, which was published in Indianapolis. Having seen what Lee and Powell had done in Illinois, the writer arranged for the visit. Lee explained: "So he promoted us coming over there. And I remember they had the governor make the speech that night at the banquet. I can't think of his name, but he made it clear to the group that he would never sign a pari-mutuel bill for Indiana." Powell and Lee laughed about the episode, as it was clear the governor believed they had come to the meeting to promote gambling. "He was an outstanding governor and very righteous, and he would have no part of gambling in Indiana."[29]

Together, they worked Illinois governors as well. After the election of Richard Ogilvie in 1968, Lee recalled attending a reception in Springfield honoring *Chicago Tribune* reporter Bob Howard on his retirement: "Powell introduced me to Governor Ogilvie. And I invited him to come to Washington Park [in Chicago] the night that we raced the Hambletonian Preview. This was a race for the three-year-old trotters that were going to race in the big Hambletonian at Du Quoin in September. He told me to write him a letter, giving dates and so forth, and he would let me know if he could make it. He replied before long and advised me that he could attend. We invited the members of the Illinois Racing Board, representatives from the other tracks, along with the outstanding horsemen in Illinois. And we had the governor present the trophy to the winning horse."[30]

Lee's name on a horse racing bill signaled that Powell had blessed it and had turned it over to his good friend to rally support. When Powell served as Speaker or as minority leader and had control over key committee assignments, he always put Lee where it counted the most. Except for 1949, Lee often served as chairman of the Agriculture Committee, to which all race-track and fairs bills were referred. Lee eventually became a major beneficiary of investments and profits from thoroughbred and harness racing.

Lee and Powell also became business partners in ventures related to horse racing. Lee, faced with needing business opportunities outside the legislature in order to earn a living, started an insurance agency business in Mt. Vernon: "It seemed to me that would be the kind of business that I could handle and also be in politics. I could have an office downtown where I could see my constituents instead of them having to come to my house. I knew a lot of people and I felt like I could build up a pretty good insurance agency."

Lee had been inspired to enter the insurance business by J. Will Howell, a legislator from nearby West Frankfort. Powell pursued a similar nonlegislative business, although he never made it a major income-producing sideline. Powell wrote insurance policies for racetracks with which he was associated—including Cahokia Downs—and placed the business through Lee's agency directly to insurance companies.

Another sponsor of House Bill 1104, Republican W. B. Westbrook, was from Harrisburg, in the same legislative district as Powell. Westbrook's career in the House covered twelve years beginning in the 1943–44 session.[31] He surfaced again in 1951 newspaper revelations of politically influenced hirings at Sportsman's Park. He had a long association with county fairs in deep southern Illinois.

Representative Hunter's legislative career included just three terms in the House starting with 1947–48, but his interest in county fairs was lengthy. He ran the Christian County fair operation and also served from the same district as one of the primary horse breeders and racing promoters of that time, Carl H. Preihs of Pana.

Later questioned about his sponsorship of the bill, Hunter, then an employee of the state treasurer's office, said he viewed the issue from his perspective as an activist in county fair work:

> I understood the pari-mutuel track people originally proposed the bill and I was cool toward it at first. I was afraid that if the pari-mutuel tracks operated in late July and August they would draw horses away from our county fair meets. I called a meeting of track representatives and county fair people and the track men pointed out that if they had more racing days there would be more tax income to the state, which meant more state aid to county fairs as provided by law. Also the pari-mutuel people promised that if we would support the bill they would make horses available as needed for the county fair races. That won me over to the bill and I helped sponsor it.[32]

Another position necessary to passage of the harness bill was chairmanship of the House Agriculture Committee. Knauf filled that position in 1949. Powell referred all bills involving horse racing to the committee for first consideration. Nothing got through without the approval of Chairman Knauf. A fixture in the House since his first session of 1935–36 (the first session for Powell, too), Knauf in 1949 served as president of the U.S. Trotting Association. Fribley said of Knauf: "At that time there weren't too many breeding farms in Illinois. [One was] Heinie Knauf, who was quite a promoter, because he had some pretty good stallions, too."[33]

The House seemed secure. Republicans controlled the Senate, so Powell needed a nonpartisan approach to get the bill through. Chairman of the Senate Agriculture Committee Simon Lantz, a Republican from Woodford County, east of Peoria, liked the idea, but he wanted a Democrat to do the work. Powell's agents chose Fribley, whose first interest in politics occurred while he was a student at the University of Illinois. He was elected to the Senate in 1934 to fill a vacancy, and he continued to serve until defeated for reelection in 1952.

Talking about his involvement with the bill almost thirty years later, Fribley described his initial contact and involvement: "I didn't know anything about it [the bill] until, I think, Cliff Hunter . . . and a big old Dutchman who ran the Fayette County fair, and two fellows from the Cumberland County fair, or three, came up to see me and asked me to back such a bill and handle it when it came over to the Senate. Now, these men always treated me nice at their fairs. Senator Simon Lantz, who was chairman of the agriculture committee in the Senate, agreed to help me handle it."[34]

Fribley reacted to the contact much like others in the legislature who at first blush thought the bill would provide direct competition for the county fairs. Knauf's response to Fribley's concern sounded logical: "He told me that they very sincerely believed that the reason there were no horses available to the county fairs during the time they were racing was that the horses were all out of the state at mutuel tracks, particularly in the East." Fribley got the point when he recalled that his experience at county fairs was they frequently would have only two or three good horses, "and the rest were old pelters."[35]

The bill received a nice nudge along the way from Governor Stevenson in his budget report to the legislature. The governor's description put the proposal in a tax increase context: "An increase in the rate of tax on harness racing to bring it into conformance with that on running races is estimated to produce an additional $2.4 million."[36] The note did not mention the expansion of harness racing.

The bill moved quickly through the House, 117 to 0, after a 16 to 0 approval by the Agriculture Committee and went to the Senate on June 14. The Senate Agriculture Committee voted 11 to 0 in favor on June 21, and the full Senate approved the bill without dissent, 45 to 0, on June 27. Governor Stevenson signed it on July 1.[37] Subsequently, a number of members of the legislature looked back on those days and wondered how they missed what was happening. Sen. Elbert Smith told of his puzzlement. After a public brouhaha erupted later, Smith said: "Well, anyway after the story came out . . . I went home and looked at the Senate Journal and not only had I voted for that bill, but it was unanimous. We'd all voted for it."[38]

Following are the specific changes in the bill that opened harness racing to pari-mutuel betting in the populous areas of East St. Louis and Chicago:

• It allowed harness racing between April 15 and November 15 and eliminated prohibition from the third Monday in July to the last day of August, which had been preserved for county and state fair racing only.
• It eliminated prohibition on harness racing within five miles of any track licensed for the same date for horse racing on the flat. Racing on the flat no longer had exclusivity.

• It gave the Racing Commission authority to grant harness racing licenses to horse racing tracks where it served the best interests of the public and the sports. This broad authority made it possible to license harness racing under any circumstances.

In retrospect, many puzzled over Stevenson signing the bill, given his strong feelings about gambling. Among those with recollections of conversations during that time was William "Smokey" Downey, who served as assistant to Gov. William Stratton from 1952 to 1959. Before that he worked as a journalist covering Springfield, then in public relations for Stratton in 1946, and in Stratton's 1950 campaign for treasurer. He believed there was a specific political reason for Stevenson signing the bill: "Now the man who put that bill into effect was Stevenson. He was the one that signed it into law. And all the do-gooders and everybody that were talking, Stevenson was the man that's responsible. . . . And I know this, that Powell told him that all those people, all the county fairs in the state, they all wanted this because the bill would give the money that went from the harness racing mutuels into this agricultural premium fund. And there was nothing wrong with that. It helped the breeding of horses in the state both for harness and thoroughbreds."[39]

The political twist came from Powell to a governor who even then could see that he might want to run for election again in Illinois. Downey added: "And the only reason he [Stevenson] signed it, [was] Paul Powell. . . . He [Stevenson] was against it. And Powell said, I heard him tell it myself, 'You're thinking about running for governor again. Have you any other ideas of running for office? Every county fair in the state of Illinois, they'll all be against you because this is going to help them.' And Powell was right about it. And that's how mutuel harness racing went on in the state."

Meanwhile, at Sportsman's Park, Johnston and Wiedrick incorporated Chicago Downs on May 4. When passage of the bill seemed assured, they formed a trust dated June 25, with the two of them as trustees holding all the stock, variously reported at 100,000 shares.[40] A slightly different version of the Chicago Downs birth came from Kearns, the public relations counselor, who told the *Chicago Daily News* that the harness operation was started by Wiedrick, James Quinn, a commercial photographer, and Kearns. "We concluded that there was an opening for trotting races with pari-mutuel betting at Sportsman's Park, and also that such a meeting would keep the trotting stables in Illinois during the summer," Kearns said. Conferences were held with Speaker Powell about a suggested agreement by harness horse owners that good horses would be available for downstate fairs. Kearns said Powell wanted such an assurance before passing House Bill 1104. Kearns described Chicago Downs as a "shoe-string" operation that paid dividends only after successful meetings.[41] As legislation whisked through Springfield, they were poised for action. The first meeting of Chicago Downs at Sportsman's Park occurred on July 18.

The Chicago Downs story might have ended there were it not for a stock offering that could be correctly identified in the annals of Illinois politics and horse racing as "The 10-Cent Stock Payoff." Presumably the offering of stock in Chicago Downs at $.10 a share would not have caught anyone's attention except for two other matters: the choice of persons to whom the stock was offered and the sudden, large return on investment.

After passage and signing of House Bill 1104, founders of Chicago Downs had a busy summer. The first meeting in July was just one of the major activities. The other was offering of stock to at least forty carefully chosen people including friends, business associates, benefactors, and relatives of the two principals, Johnston and Wiedrick. The major players in creation of Chicago Downs and passage of the legislation received an opportunity to buy the largest number of shares. Daisy Powell, wife of Paul, became the single largest shareholder of Chicago Downs with 16,900 shares, for a payment of $1,690. The next largest block of shares, 15,580, went to Kathreen Wiedrick, wife of Big Sam, general manager of Chicago Downs. Johnston, owner of Sportsman's Park, did not take any of the shares personally, nor did his wife. But his children bought a total of 21,000 shares.[42]

There is no record of how many legislators were offered stock by Wiedrick and Johnston. Possibly some turned it down, although walking away from shares of stock at $.10 each would have been difficult. Many of those who purchased shares or had shares listed in the name of a close relative—as in the case of Powell—had made a difference in passage of the law in Springfield, although just one of the three sponsors of the bill in the House bought stock. That was Lee, who purchased 1,000 shares in the name of his wife, Berniece. The other seven legislators listed among initial stockholders were Democrats and Republicans from all over the state.

They were Rep. Reed F. Cutler, Republican legislative leader of Lewistown, 1,000 shares; Sen. Fribley, Democrat of Pana, who ran the bill through the Senate for Powell, 500; Anna Mae Harris, wife of Rep. Lloyd "Curly" Harris, Democrat of Granite City, a Powell ally, 100; Sen. Roland V. Libonati, Democrat of Chicago, 200; Sen. Everett Peters, Republican of St. Joseph and political benefactor of the University of Illinois, 1,000 shares; Sen. Frank Ryan,

Democrat of Chicago, 2,000; and Irene G. Ryan, wife of Rep. James J. Ryan, Democrat of Chicago and House majority leader in the 1949 session, 1,000.

Lost in the conversations of history are the reasons for specific amounts purchased or whether they were the original amounts offered. But one account of a legislator is on the record about who purchased stock, how the offer came about, and his reaction to later public disclosure. Fribley of Pana was shown on the original list of buyers with 500 shares:

> Along in August, about six or seven weeks later [after passage of the bill], during the state fair, I received a call from Rep. Henry Knauf and he wanted to see me. So I went up to the St. Nick Hotel and met with him and he told me some of his friends, including Paul Powell, were going to organize a corporation to operate a harness horse race track at Chicago with pari-mutuel betting—and lease Sportsman's Park, as I recall, and inasmuch as I'd helped out on the bill they wanted me to buy some stock. And the stock was only 10 cents a share and they wanted me to buy 2,000 shares. And I said, "Hell no. I don't want any part of it." Well, they said, we think this is going to go and you can make money at it. And, hell, I could have had 2,000 shares for 200 bucks. I finally agreed to go along with them, but like a damned idiot I only took 500 shares and gave him a check for $50.[43]

That was not Fribley's last experience with Chicago Downs stock: "About two or three months after that, Paul Powell or Henry Knauf called me and told me this outfit was going to rent Sportsman's Park, but they had to have $10,000 to guarantee payment of the light bill—it was night racing. And would I sign the note? Well there was about 15 or 20 people on the note, so I signed that note. And later on, Paul Powell—it wasn't three weeks I don't think, until he sent me a copy of the note with my name and other co-signers blacked out. . . . That was because the note was paid off or not used. . . . I never paid any more attention to it."

One state representative remembered brushing aside the purchase of Chicago Downs stock. Rep. Paul J. Randolph, a Republican from Chicago, began his career in Springfield in 1945 and served for thirty-two years. During the legislative session, Randolph had a bill that he wanted to discuss with Powell: "You always spoke to the speaker when you wanted your legislation, your bill, called or held. And I dropped into his office one morning. It was late, he was always late. I thought sure he was in there because the secretary nodded and said, 'Go right in.' And I walked in and there was this big fellow in there. And he said, 'Have a chair.' And I said, 'Thank you, I'll see you later.' And walked right around and walked right out. I wasn't having any of the 10-cent stock. . . . He was asking how many shares, 'How many shares

do you want? You're allowed this if you want it,' and so on. . . . He was signing up."[44] Randolph surely was referring to Wiedrick.

Newspapers in St. Louis later reported conversations with legislators and
wives who bought shares from Wiedrick. Powell said Daisy was "given the
opportunity" to buy stock by Wiedrick. However, in a lengthy explanation
written in 1951 for the *McLeansboro Times-Leader*, Powell gave this version:
"Representative Knauf suggested to me that I purchase stock in Chicago
Downs Association, which was then being offered at a very low figure. . . . He
further advised me that because of the location of this track and the transportation facilities, it should prove to be a good investment and on his advice
I advised my wife to purchase this stock."[45]

A slightly different story given in testimony in 1952 during a hearing of
the Illinois Harness Racing Commission started with the comment that his
first contact regarding stock in Chicago Downs was on opening night of the
track, July 18, 1949: "I was there the night the track opened; sat in the box
with Rep. Knauf, and he told me that Mr. Wiedrick had some stock. He said,
'don't know how much he will let you have, but I would like to see you, you
are always interested in fairs, would like to see you take a little stock if you
want to take the chance.' That is the first I knew the stock would be available.
. . . I came back to Springfield and called my wife on the telephone and asked
her how much money we had in the bank and told her what I was thinking
of doing and she took the roof off."[46] But they bought the stock. On another
occasion, Powell said his wife got the stock opportunity directly from Big
Sam Wiedrick.

Representative Harris of Granite City denied that the purchase of 100
shares by his wife had anything to do with passage of the bill: "Here is how
my wife happened to buy the stock: We were having dinner at the St.
Nicholas Hotel in Springfield some time after the 1949 session ended and
Sam Wiedrick of Chicago Downs happened to be at our table. He suggested
I invest in the track and I said I didn't have any money for that. My wife asked
him how much the stock was and he said 10 cents a share. She said she
couldn't go wrong on that and that she would take 100 shares. Later she sent
him her personal check and received a stock certificate. Of course we were
amazed when she got a $100 dividend. . . . We looked on the whole thing as
sort of a joke at first."[47]

Lee, whose wife bought 1,000 shares, said they were offered the stock by
Wiedrick in August 1949, when they attended Chicago Downs races in
Cicero: "Best investment I ever made. . . . If I'd have had any judgment I
could have bought more stock. But I thought that a hundred dollars was all
I could take a chance on."[48] Lee said his sponsorship of House Bill 1104 was

based on his interest in the success of county fair race meets and had no connection with a stock purchase.

Beyond the legislators, there were the curious investors, associates of Johnston, some names of star quality, and those with alleged ties to crime syndicate characters. Among the curious were Lucille E. Koval, secretary to and close friend of Powell during 1949, who bought 1,000 shares. She told newspapers that she bought the stock on recommendation of Powell.

Koval had become acquainted with Wiedrick "because he came in the speaker's office frequently during the session," but Powell had handled the purchase transaction, further implicating him in the action. "As far as the purchase being connected with passage of the legislation, I wouldn't know anything about that, but I doubt very much that there was a connection."[49]

Associates of Johnston included James B. Quinn, an original incorporator of Chicago Downs who received 4,050 shares, and Hugo Bennett, auditor for Sportsman's Park. The star quality names were associated with ownership and operations of the Chicago Cardinals professional football team. Charles W. Bidwill Jr. and William Bidwill, college-age sons of Charles Bidwill who owned the Cardinals, each received 3,000 shares. Ray C. Bennigsen of Winnetka, a former president of the Chicago Cardinals, bought 2,000 shares.[50]

One name on the list tied the Chicago Downs operation to the administration of Gov. Adlai E. Stevenson. That was James Mulroy, a distinguished Chicago journalist who won a Pulitzer Prize for reporting on the infamous Leopold and Loeb murder case while at the *Chicago Daily News*. A witty, hard-drinking Irishman, Mulroy had worked for several Chicago newspapers before joining Stevenson after his nomination for governor in 1948. On the candidate's small personal staff, Mulroy became a close and trusted adviser.[51] However, he did not tell the governor or any other staff people of his purchase of 1,000 shares after the governor signed the bill.

Hardly had the shareholders paid their fee and tucked away the certificates than the first dividend payment arrived. The first meeting of Chicago Downs in July 1949 paid handsomely because each share earned a dividend of $1, thus more than wiping out the initial investment. Newspapers reported that purchasers did not have to pay for the shares until the first dividend check arrived. For a shareholder who purchased 1,000 shares for $100, the first return in a matter of months was $1,000, or tenfold. For large shareholders such as Daisy Powell, the payoff amounted to $16,900. Needless to say, $16,900 in 1949 dollars put Powell in an exclusive income group.

The money did not stop flowing to the lucky shareholders. After another successful harness meeting in 1950, Chicago Downs paid a dividend of $.75 per share.

Powell's direct involvement in business affairs of Chicago Downs continued. Records reveal Powell recommended that certain members of the legislature—including one tied directly to sponsorship of House Bill 1104—be hired for work during the harness season at Chicago Downs. In 1951 he recommended the hiring of Leon M. Schuler, Democrat of Aurora, J. Harold Downey, Democrat from Joliet, and W. B. Westbrook, his legislative friend from Harrisburg, who was a cosponsor of House Bill 1104. He worked as a clerk at the Maywood and Aurora trotting tracks as well as at Chicago Downs.[52]

All these relationships and dividends continued as a course of business without uproar or disclosure until August 1951. On the heels of the Kefauver Committee report on organized crime, reporters for Chicago newspapers began nosing into affairs of Johnston and Sportsman's Park. The story tumbled out in a series of articles capturing page-one headlines across the state. The *Chicago Daily News* blurted to its readers: "Track Stock Paid 1650% in 2 Yrs.; Owners Listed."[53] Records of the Harness Racing Commission confirmed stock ownership in Chicago Downs, and reporters had an easy time of putting together the rest of the story.

Fribley tells of the swift reaction and his dilemma:

> The following year or so [after purchase of the stock] my wife and two kids and mother-in-law went out west. We went up to Lake Louise in western Canada for a short summer vacation and I got back—I hadn't read any papers except western papers—and here my secretary . . . had laid on my desk the *Chicago Daily News*, the *Chicago Tribune* and in black headlines they proclaimed that certain legislators were guilty of graft and accepting a payoff. And among those pictures was Senator John W. Fribley. . . . And goddam, it hit me like a ton of bricks. . . .
>
> And of course, a lot of people, in this area at least, thought I was a crooked s.o.b. Well, there was quite an investigation and I volunteered to be the first witness to appear before the Illinois Racing Commission. . . . I volunteered to be the first witness before that, and not ask for any immunity. And I told them the fact just like I am telling you. And hell, the only thing I am mad at is why in the dickens didn't I take 2,000 shares of stock? You see, that has been a bonanza.[54]

Newspaper accounts struck hardest at Stevenson aide Mulroy. Immediately he issued this statement:

> On the recommendation of a friend, Mr. Edward Fleming, now deceased, who was president of the Fleming Coal Corp., and operator of the Lincoln Fields racetrack and who urged me to take advantage of legitimate race track stock if it was offered to me, I made a very small investment through Speaker Paul Powell in the Chicago Downs Harness Racing Association. Powell told me that lights had been installed on a Chicago track and that the investment might be very worthwhile, or a dismal failure. This was in July, 1949. Until today, I did not know the names of any stockholders in the Chicago Downs venture. I have never been to the Chicago Downs race meets, know nothing about racing, and have never been approached by anyone in connection with the race track for a favor of any type.[55]

The revelation jolted Stevenson and his close associates. Writing years later, Stevenson's biographer, John Bartlow Martin, said the Mulroy affair "blemished the spotless Stevenson administration."[56] The *Chicago Sun-Times* editorialized, "Racetrack operators don't cut people into their profits without a reason" and "if Mulroy doesn't understand, he's not smart enough to be assistant to the governor." The *Daily News* said about Mulroy: "We feel the greatest surprise and regret that Gov. Stevenson's assistant, Jim Mulroy, should have been one of those who invested even a trivial $100 in Chicago Downs stock that has paid a mere $1,750. As for most of the others, it was about what you would expect."[57]

The *St. Louis Post-Dispatch* offered: "This is the very kind of inside tie-up between special interests and men in state government which Illinois voted against when it sent Adlai E. Stevenson into the governor's chair. . . . There is nothing at all to show that Gov. Stevenson had anything to do with his assistant's misstep but there is ample reason for him to make this crystal clear to the people of Illinois."[58]

Reacting at a press conference, Stevenson replied, "I have a very high personal regard for Mr. Mulroy, and I have no further comment whatever at this time about him." Privately, Stevenson lamented the episode in a letter to his friend Alicia Patterson: "Mulroy, the damn fool, put $100 in the Chicago Downs racetrack & of course told me nothing about it. Now there's hell to pay. . . . I haven't summoned the courage to fire him, and the hotter it gets the more embattled and stubborn he gets about resigning."

One of Stevenson's closest associates, Carl McGowan, took a practical political view of what had occurred: "Paul [Powell] was smart enough to figure out that he could get Mulroy involved—and it would be good to have him involved if it blew up. Paul Powell was an old fox."[59] Mulroy had done nothing illegal, but he had betrayed his boss and associates in a politically sensitive situation. He refused to sell the stock, and he paid the price. On November 2, 1951, Stevenson accepted Mulroy's resignation "because of ill health." Mulroy died a few months later.[60]

Confronted by news reports and the public record of the racing commission, Powell spoke candidly, acknowledging that Wiedrick had offered him the stock in 1949. He told the *Daily News*: "I know the newspapers can make this sound bad. I told Daisy that when we were offered a chance to buy. But I don't see anything wrong with it. I am interested in trotting racing and always have been, I have an interest in two county fairs, too—at Vienna and Metropolis. We bought in when harness racing was getting unpopular in Illinois because it was run by foreigners—men from the East. We haven't gotten rich, but we may some day and when we do, I'll quit politics."[61]

Powell offered these additional comments on his involvement in harness racing legislation:

I had helped pass the first harness racing bill early in the 1940s. In 1949 I worked with the late Henry Knauf to amend the bill. We changed it to allow trotting races during August. We wanted to keep the trotters in Illinois. At that time the three big trotting tracks—Maywood, Aurora and Fairmount—agreed to subsidize the county fairs if they lost money on the deal. We also agreed to appropriate $1,000 more to each county fair. I told them I wouldn't pass one bill if we didn't pass the other.

About a month after they started running at Sportsman's Park Wiedrick came to me and said, "You've done a lot for harness racing. We want some Illinois men in on this and we would like to have you."

Powell added that having Illinois investors "has kept the syndicate from moving in here like they did on the Roosevelt Raceway in New York."[62]

Not satisfied with the newspaper version of his comments, Powell mounted a defense of his actions on House Bill 1104 in his own district. He circulated to district newspapers a lengthy explanation as a letter to the editor, and many of them printed it. In the version published by the *McLeansboro Times-Leader*, Powell explained his actions, then counterattacked: "I have served the people of the 51st District for seventeen years to the best of my ability and have always voted for legislation beneficial to downstate, regardless of the wishes of some of the Chicago newspapers. I do not propose to have any metropolitan newspaper influence my vote in the Legislature against the best interests of the citizens of the 51st District who have bestowed upon me the honor of electing me as one of the Representatives."

Newspapers called for investigations, and there were inquiries by the racing boards, but nothing of consequence resulted. At a hearing by the Illinois Harness Racing Commission on January 29, 1952, chaired by Eugene Hayes of Du Quoin, the lineup of witnesses included those directly involved in House Bill 1104 and Chicago Downs: Fribley, Representative Cutler, Peters, Representative Harris, Lee, Powell, William H. Johnston, and Wiedrick.

There were calls for Governor Stevenson to initiate a state probe, but he declined: "I heard no objection to the [Chicago Downs] bill when it was passed and none since. It was very curious financing, but I don't know the details or practices in that industry. The stock was sold at a very low price, but whether it was sold as an inducement to pass the bill, I don't know." There was no interest in the governor's office, the legislature, or other official state agencies to probe the stock deal.

Regardless of the justifications, denials, and legitimate explanations, rumors and tales never ceased about what happened in the Chicago Downs episode. Journalists often were the sources of supposition, or even eyewitness accounts, of questionable dealings. William Downey covered statehouse activities and political campaigns leading up to his service with William Stratton in the 1950s. With maybe a bit of a partisan twist on happenings, Downey remembers the stock deal somewhat differently from the accounts of participants: "The story was that they get two hundred dollars cash for voting for the bill. I was not in the legislature working at that time. The story was it was 10 cents a share of stock or two hundred dollars cash. They'd give you [two thousand] shares of stock or two hundred dollars."[63]

While Downey's numbers do not work out with reports of actual stock purchases, nor does $200 seem much of a bribe, the smell lingered. Later newspaper accounts said that the original Chicago Downs dividend of $1 per share in 1949 was after a $.10 per share credit, which in effect paid for the stock, and that cash payments for the stock did not have to be made until the dividend checks arrived. At the worst, there was the promise of something for the votes. At best, the opportunity to buy came after the legislature acted. The fact remains that those who bought the stock for a song heard the melody play in healthy dividends for years to come.

For Powell the stock episode of 1949 to 1951 began a paying relationship with Chicago Downs that lasted until his death. Of all his investments in racetracks, nothing matched his personal take from the Sportsman's Park operation. Powell's stock holdings in Chicago Downs accounted for about two-thirds of the value of his total racetrack stock. Just as the original pay-off in stock could be attributed to Powell's relationship with Sam Wiedrick, so the continuing income stemmed from a deal cut with Wiedrick.

Powell and Wiedrick arranged a long-term fee-splitting deal starting in 1955.[64] Powell and Wiedrick said the arrangement began with contact from the Fox Valley Trotting Association, which raced at Maywood Park and was not profitable because of poor meeting dates. Fox Valley wanted to switch to dates that were open at Sportsman's Park. Wiedrick, then a consultant to Chicago Downs, considered Fox Valley a prime possibility for a rent paying tenant at Sportsman's Park, owned by William H. Johnston Sr.

Failing to persuade Johnston of the value of his idea, Wiedrick turned to Powell, knowing that Johnston admired Powell and appreciated the help that had been given Sportsman's Park by the legislator. Before interceding for Wiedrick, Powell cut an agreement for splitting Wiedrick's consulting fees. Afterward, Powell took the agreement seriously. He met with Johnston several times in Chicago and traveled to Jacksonville, Florida, for a session. He also met with the president of Fox Valley and began negotiations for a four-year lease. Finally, Powell brought all the parties together in a deal that made all of them money. The agreement permitted Fox Valley to race at Sportsman's Park, while Suburban Downs moved to fill the dates at Maywood.

Wiedrick told the Chicago Crime Commission, which conducted an investigation of the arrangements with Powell in 1965, that as long as Fox Valley raced at Sportsman's Park, he would receive a fee from Chicago Downs and in turn would split the fee with Powell. Between 1956 and 1963, Powell and Wiedrick divided equally $20,000 annually received by Wiedrick as management fees paid by Fox Valley to Chicago Downs. In 1964, Chicago Downs agreed to assume the obligation of paying the $10,000 to Powell. Wiedrick and Powell denied any political collusion or misuse of Powell's position as a legislative leader and state official.

From 1967 until his death, Powell received an annual payment of $20,000 for consulting with Chicago Downs. Powell explained what he did for the consulting funds in a document among his files that was labeled "Affidavit of Paul Powell." He may have prepared it for an inquiry into the arrangement in 1969. He said Chicago Downs paid expenses for two trips to Las Vegas and a trip to Florida. The document listed these services performed for Chicago Downs:

1. Powell, always active in Illinois state fair circles, promoted the interests of Chicago Downs at the fairs in 1964, 1965, and 1966 by persuading own-

ers and drivers of outstanding horses to race them at the Chicago Downs meetings.

2. When in Florida, Powell traveled to Pompano Park, Pompano Beach, Florida, on many occasions while that track held its trotting meeting. The purpose of the trips was to persuade the owners and drivers with good horses to race them at the Chicago Downs meeting the following summer.

3. Powell was constantly on the alert in 1964, 1965, and 1966 for any bills introduced in the Illinois legislature that might prove damaging to the interests of Chicago Downs in particular and harness racing in general. This, according to the document, meant Chicago Downs did not have to employ a paid lobbyist in Springfield. In effect, while he served as secretary of state, Powell was a lobbyist for Chicago Downs.

Asked what Powell did for the consulting fee, William Johnston Jr., then running Sportsman's Park, listed the following duties:

• Reading and interpreting any legislation before the state legislature that could affect horse racing operation
• Visiting the track whenever he is in Chicago to help with day-to-day decisions concerning operations and future improvements
• Coordinating racing at Sportsman's with racing at state and county fairs during meetings held each winter in Springfield and introducing Johnston to the fair chairman

Johnston added: "Mr. Powell has been in racing a long time. I don't think there's a horseman in the state he doesn't know. He also knows a lot about the legislature. He's a smart man. He earns his fee and he deserves it. Racing is big business and I can't know everything. We've been growing like mad, and it's partially because of the experience of men like Paul Powell. I'm glad to have his help."[65]

The arrangement broke no laws, and Powell claimed it resulted in no conflict with his elected state position. Powell commented: "I've been the consultant for three or four years, but I've been helping out for a long time. Since they're making a success out of harness racing, I decided I should get something for my time. I suggested they pay me direct."

True enough, Sportsman's Park had become one of the most successful racetracks in the state, and Powell had been a part of its financial growth. In the last year of his life, Powell received $55,300 in dividends from Chicago Downs and $20,000 for consulting.

In spite of overall good times for harness racing, the sport experienced turmoil with the growth. The competitive nature of harness racing led to casualties, unpleasantness, and occasional disturbing newspaper headlines. With various attempts to alter racetrack laws, the picture in the early 1960s rarely looked tranquil. Because Powell had a share of almost every harness racing operation, he naturally felt the impact on his workload and his pocketbook.

A sign of economic strain in racing occurred when a stalwart of the harness racing scene in Chicago, Maywood Park, stumbled financially after nearly sixteen years as a premier racing site. Started in 1946—Maywood had Illinois harness racing license no. 1—the track pioneered pari-mutuel betting.

One of the first operatives at Maywood was Wiedrick, who managed the operation and held a substantial ownership stake. The trouble in 1962 resulted in large part from minority shareholder lawsuits, which management settled out of court and which weakened the financial position. Plaintiffs charged management with fraud and misappropriation of corporate funds. With settlement, the charges never came to trial and undoubtedly saved the reputation of many associated with harness racing. Wiedrick, not a party to the lawsuit, sold his stock before the case surfaced publicly, cashing in 2,497 shares for about $4 a share.[66]

At the time of trouble, Maywood's tenants included Egyptian Trotting and Suburban Downs, another early harness racing organization. Egyptian, owned largely by downstate interests associated with Cahokia Downs and including large holdings by Powell and John Stelle, began harness meetings on the Cahokia Downs track in 1957. Management found customer response to be much less than expected, and with permission from the Harness Racing Board, Egyptian switched to meetings at Maywood Park in 1960. After four years of racing at Maywood, Egyptian Trotting followed the crowd to Washington Park and became a very profitable operation.

The move to Washington Park meant much more than just another home for Egyptian. It brought Egyptian in contact with one of the biggest names in Chicago racing circles. The controlling interest in Washington Park was held by Marjorie Lindheimer Everett, owner of Chicago Thoroughbred Enterprises, Inc., one of the best known and successful flat track operations in state history. Marjorie's father, Ben Lindheimer, CTE founder, died in 1960 after an extraordinary career as racing owner and developer. The two main parks run by Lindheimer were Arlington Park and Washington Park. Marjorie—or Marje as she was known—inherited her father's empire and began making changes almost immediately. Acquiring a piece of the fast growing harness racing business became one of her priorities.[67]

Everett knew her way around politics, and she knew the importance of politics to the success of horse racing. One of her most valuable contacts with the legislature came through the contractual agreement with Egyptian Trotting. Clyde Lee conducted most of the business affairs for Egyptian, and when the association signed a ten-year agreement with Everett to race at Washington Park, Lee became a close adviser, helping her with harness racing interests at Washington Park.

The involvement with Everett paid off for Lee by increasing his vast holdings of racetrack stock. "She made it available to me," he said later. "But I paid—actually not only me but a lot of the other members of the legislature. But I paid for my stock and there was no problem there. The only problem there might have been was the impropriety of a member of the legislature owning stock in a racetrack. But I got out of the legislature about the time I bought my stock in those organizations." He had owned stock in racetracks as early as 1949.

The politically astute Everett had her eye out for other political opportunities that would improve the profit potential for her track holdings. This ambition drew her to contact with the Illinois Racing Board and the Kerner administration in Springfield. In her quest for influence, she turned to William Miller, then chairman of the racing board, and Theodore Isaacs, a close associate of Governor Kerner.

These associations eventually led in 1962 to granting an option for 25 shares of stock in Chicago Thoroughbred Enterprises each to Kerner and Isaacs, with Miller as the go-between. Minor as that appeared, by 1966 Kerner and Isaacs had parlayed the holding into about $150,000 cash each in profits. Everett later testified in the federal trial of Kerner that Miller advised her to offer the stock because Kerner and Isaacs would be helpful to her interests.

The infamous Kerner trial in 1973, after which a jury convicted the former governor and sent him to prison, provided a shocking picture of racetrack politics in Springfield in 1962, when Powell was very much the legislature's prime racetrack advocate. Although at various times Kerner, Isaacs, and Miller denied Everett's account of what happened then, on the witness stand Everett turned on Miller with some of the most damning testimony presented at the Kerner trial:

- After her father's death, she formed Chicago Thoroughbred Enterprises as a holding company for her Arlington Park and Washington Park tracks and racing associations (jockey clubs). She said this was done at Miller's suggestion.

- Following Miller's advice, she contributed $45,000 to Kerner's 1960 campaign.
- Following Miller's advice in 1962, she executed a memo making 25 shares each of CTE stock, worth $1,000 each, available to Kerner and Isaacs. Everett said Miller told her Isaacs would be an important man in the Kerner administration.
- On two occasions, men she felt would be detrimental to racing were proposed for membership on the Illinois Racing Board. She conveyed her objections to Miller, and the appointments were not made.
- On at least two occasions, bills were introduced in the Illinois legislature to increase the state's share of racing revenues. On the first occasion, the bill died after testimony by Miller. On the second, a graduated scale increasing the state's take, proposed by Miller, was adopted.
- In 1966 Miller triggered deals that allowed Kerner and Isaacs to exercise their options to buy the 25 shares each of CTE. They backdated a promissory note to 1962 and paid interest on it. After a short time, she said, the stock was traded for 10,000 shares of Balmoral Jockey Club worth $30 a share, permitting Kerner and Isaacs to realize approximately $150,000 in profits each.

Everett had phenomenal success with the legislature, and we may know the reason why. One specific bill in the 1961 session, when Powell was Speaker, helped Everett enter the harness racing business with impact. Passed and signed by Kerner, it permitted her to switch all thoroughbred racing from Washington Park to Arlington Park, leaving the former open for harness racing. More importantly, the harness racing commission virtually assured Everett's success by awarding her a three-week racing meeting that started with one of the choice holidays, Labor Day.

Thomas Bradley, commission chairman, said about Everett entering the harness sport, "Washington Park has the potential to become one of the finest harness racing parks in America." Sponsorship of legislation followed a familiar pattern. In the Senate, for example, the principal sponsors included Sen. Arthur Bidwell, Republican from suburban River Forest; Sen. Daniel J. O'Brien, Democrat from Chicago; and Sen. Everett Peters, Republican from downstate St. Joseph. O'Brien and Peters held shares of stock in several racetrack operations with Powell.

Evidence exists of direct lobbying by Powell with Miller and other racing officials, demonstrating the coziness of politics and racetrack regulation. Powell never shrank from corresponding with the highest officials of the harness and thoroughbred racing governing boards, regardless of the position he held. The content of the letters almost always dealt with legislative politics and what Powell perceived as the best interests of horse racing.

Out of the Speakership, but not out of the business of protecting his racing interests in 1963, Powell peppered Miller and Thomas Bradley, chairman of the Illinois Harness Racing Commission, with letters regarding specific legislation. He identified the culprits in the legislature and spoke frankly about specific bills and how they either were defeated or needed to be defeated. There appeared to be no hesitancy to deal directly with the appointed officials or to address them as "Bill" and "Tom."

In a June 1963 letter to Miller, Powell referred to an amendment in the House by Rep. Abner Mikva "which would have reduced your appropriation a considerable sum. You will note that I moved to table his amendment which carried by a vote of 95–58. All those voting nay were voting against you and those who did not vote are certainly not friendly."[68] He recommended that Miller keep the roll call, along with others sent to him by Powell, "so as to refer to them when requests are made of you." Then he took after Sen. Alan Dixon of Belleville, who clearly had made Powell unhappy: "This damn Senator Dixon from Belleville voted against us in the Senate. . . . I gave him some passes to Cahokia after you mailed me your letter but I sure as hell will not give him any more." Powell concluded the letter by urging Miller to appear in Springfield against a "quarter horse bill because . . . this could cause some conflict if they try to race there if other racing is going on at Sportsman's."

A day later, Powell wrote Bradley, whose commission approved meeting dates for a number of racing organizations in which Powell held stock: "Enclosing copy of roll call on which you will note the members who voted to reduce your appropriation. I made a motion to table the amendment offered by Representative Mikva which would have reduced your appropriation. All voting nay were voting against you, those who did not vote certainly were also against you. You will note that I defeated him by a 90 to 50 vote. These names are worthwhile when they are writing in for passes and want extra favors and I feel they should be looked over carefully."[69]

During the same session, Powell kept busy writing influential members of the legislature, urging them to see racetrack issues as he did. His arguments were not new, but he made them forcefully and backed them up with specific references to published information. In a letter to Sen. Bidwell, he wrote: "I also want to call your attention to the May 6, 1963, issue of *Sports Illustrated*. On page 34 you will note that Dr. Albert Hammond, professor of philosophy at Johns Hopkins University says some favor an increase in the

[racetrack] take because they want the tax to discourage, inhibit and penalize betting. . . . Anyone who knows anything about racing knows that the bet-
tor is not dumb and if you take too much out of his dollar then he is going
to look for a bookie. . . . To increase the take more than it is now will lower
the betting at all tracks. In this instance both the state and the tracks would
suffer."[70]

Directing his attack to specific legislation proposed first in 1961 and again
in 1963 by Mikva, Powell noted the House had defeated the measure both
times, resoundingly: "I trust the above will prove valuable in defeating this
useless bill."

That was typical of Powell. He knew only one phrase when it came to legislation that attempted to lessen the take for racetracks: "Kill it." When legislators crossed him on racetrack legislation, he showed no mercy. Powell
had a number of ways to deal with these proposals, as revealed in legislation
introduced by Chicago Republican Walter Hoffelder that would have
increased the state tax on harness race betting. The representative wanted to
put more money—up to $3,000,000 in the 1961–62 biennium—into the state
general revenues.

Powell, in urging the House to defeat the measure, said it would cut down
track attendance and reduce, not increase, state revenue. The bill died, as did
other bills introduced to slice off a portion of track profits for use by the
state. When serving as Speaker, Powell killed these proposals by referring
them to the House Agriculture Committee, headed by his friend Clyde Lee.

From passage of the Illinois Harness Racing Act in 1945, to 1964, Powell's
final year in the state legislature, hardly a legislative session occurred without major racetrack legislation passed—or opposing bills stopped—by the
strong hand of Powell. In 1951, the legislature approved the Illinois Fund for
Illinois Colts, which provided money for stakes races at the state fair. In 1955,
legislation amended the racing law to provide that on days when the handle failed to reach $300,000, the state tax would be 4 percent instead of 6 per-
cent. This particularly benefited Cahokia Downs and Fairmount tracks in
the East St. Louis area, where daily handles often were less than $300,000.

In 1959, Powell and his friends passed House Bill 884, which added fifteen
days to the harness racing season. In defending the bill from attack by Rep.
Paul Simon of Madison County, Lee rolled out the economic arguments that
often carried the day in the legislature. He listed projects at the University of
Illinois and Southern Illinois University financed by revenues from horse
racing. He concluded the retort to Simon, saying, "I love horses and I enjoy
seeing them race, and just can't understand why the gentleman from Madi-

son is so set against horses, unless he was kicked or bitten by a horse when he was a boy."[71]

In 1961 Powell supported House Bill 618, which reduced license fees for racetracks, saving them nearly $450,000 annually. The bill passed 144 to 9 in the House.

These continuous efforts to shape racetrack legislation earned Powell the kind of endorsements that William S. Miller, chairman of the Illinois Racing Board, wrote during Powell's 1964 campaign for secretary of state:

Beginning with the 1955 session and continuing with the 1963 session of the legislature, Representative Paul Powell was the constant and unfailing aid to the Racing Board and Harness Commission regardless of the fact that during six of the nine years of that period the members of the Board and Commission were not predominantly of his political party. It can be said, therefore, that Representative Powell is a genuine friend of horse racing.

What does this mean? What have been the results?

(1) The Illinois Horse Racing Act was full of loopholes and defects, but today, it is a model for and applauded by the entire racing world.

(2) There were few breeding farms and Illinois-bred horses prior to 1958. Since then, however, Illinois ranks third in the nation in the Thoroughbred Breeding Industry.

(3) The total mutuel handle for harness racing in 1958 was approximately $51 million, but in 1964 the handle will be over $100 million. The total handle for flat racing in 1958 was approximately $200 million but in 1964, it will be over $269 million. Every racing plant in Illinois has been improved in the past six years.

Yes, Paul Powell has been an unrelenting friend of horse racing. I shall always be grateful.[72]

7

Cahokia Downs: In Search of a Parlay

L EGAL, ILLEGAL, IN THE OPEN, OR BEHIND CLOSED DOORS AND COVERED
windows, gambling in Illinois across from St. Louis is as easy as driving across a bridge. Go back to a time before there were bridges, and it was
the same story. Missourians ferried across the Mississippi to put down
money and gamble in Illinois. In East St. Louis, Collinsville, or Granite City,
gambling has flourished because the games were there, and the people came.

Beginning in the 1920s and lasting until the mid-1960s, the "take" of gambling fueled organized crime operations of the Shelton brothers and Frank
"Buster" Wortman and his associates in Missouri and Illinois. The four
Sheltons allegedly pocketed estimated annual profits of more than $1,000,000
in 1930.[1] The lust for illicit money corrupted police and compromised the
judiciary, because for the money to flow there had to be plentiful gambling
action. Today there is legal and illegal gambling on the East Side, and it may
always be so.

In the 1940s, one did not have to study history to understand the gambling ethic of the East Side of the St. Louis area and its importance to a business venture. Every kind of action—from craps games to bookie joints to
card games and numbers—thrived on the streets.[2] Even remnants of the
Capone syndicate in Chicago showed interest in the gambling potential of
the region and tried to muscle in.

Leading up to 1950, many gamblers chose to place illegal bets on horse
races at tracks across the nation. Horse players in East St. Louis, for example, could bet on races in New York through bookie joints near home that
were connected to track information sources by high-speed racing wires.
At one time in the 1940s, a Capone wire affiliate competed in the East St.
Louis area with a wire operated by Wortman.[3]

Wire operations received a virtual death blow in 1950–51, when the Senate committee investigating organized crime headed by Sen. Estes Kefauver
exposed the blatant operations and accused them of violating federal law.
The death warrant for track wires meant little to those who wanted to gamble. Gamblers simply turned to other bookies down the street. The urge to
gamble in Illinois never dimmed.

Cahokia Downs: In Search of a Parlay

The key to a continuous take from gambling in St. Clair or Madison Counties over the years has been the tolerance of the political environment. Although some interests contested this softness on gaming and, occasionally, municipal police toughened, the friendliness of public officials toward gambling made it possible for legal and illegal betting to exist, as well as other illegal ventures. Given the history, it is no surprise that pari-mutuel thoroughbred and harness racing near East St. Louis arose in the 1950s from political associations.

If you lived in the East St. Louis area all your life, as was the case with Dan McGlynn, East St. Louis attorney and longtime downstate Republican operative, you understood the realities of politics in St. Clair and Madison Counties. One rule of thumb was that although Republicans seldom were elected to any office in the region, the two parties long had agreed to bipartisan political leadership in St. Clair County.

There was, by understanding, only one objective—winning and dealing—and it had little to do with partisanship. Both parties shared in the patronage, fringe benefits, and political security that the arrangement offered. A Republican—such as McGlynn—had access to the full weight of the St. Clair County political organization, regardless of his partisan label. Outside of Chicago, this was the most potent political machine in Illinois.

Former Gov. John Stelle shared many common interests with Schaefer O'Neill, Alton attorney and state representative. When Stelle started his climb in state politics early in the 1930s, O'Neill represented Alton in the House. They went back years in downstate Democratic politics. As contemporaries they crossed paths in Springfield during the 1930s and 1940s, when they shared a common approach to the practicality of working with members of the Republican party. They also shared an interest in making money and horseracing. Stelle recognized O'Neill's strength in the Madison County political organization as quite similar to the clout of McGlynn in St. Clair County. Not much got done in St. Clair and Madison Counties without both of them being involved.

These relationships, and familiarity with the patterns of gambling, brought Stelle, McGlynn, and O'Neill together in the 1940s to discuss a thoroughbred racetrack operation in the heart of St. Clair County that would draw betting customers from the St. Louis market and also would hold the prospect of a future opportunity in harness racing.[4] McGlynn supposedly knew of available land in Centreville Township, between East St. Louis and Belleville, that could be obtained at a bargain, and all three knew countless people who would be interested in investing.

Not everyone qualified, however. The founders established specific criteria for involvement in the venture. They knew that developing a racetrack required political influence as well as business instincts. Therefore they wanted investors with blue chip political credentials and an ability to succeed in politics.

Paul Powell's name must have been at the top of that list. By the early 1950s, no one could propose a horseracing investment in southern Illinois that did not include Stelle and Powell. Although founding papers and documents carefully avoided use of his name, Powell purchased stock with the original group of investors, and his tax returns showed income from the track's first year of operations.[5]

In addition to the political influence of Stelle and Powell, they needed expertise in racetrack development. To attract investment dollars, they reached out to Big Sam Wiedrick, by that time deeply involved in harness racing ventures in the Chicago area. O'Neill and McGlynn and their local friends completed the political picture. The founders had all they needed to organize Cahokia Downs in 1953, with the goal to begin racing in 1954.

These business visionaries produced an intricate investment plan designed to accomplish very specific objectives:

• Bring powerful people and their money to the project
• Structure ownership to avoid potential embarrassment for elected officials
• Provide an opportunity to parlay thoroughbred and harness racing together on the same track, as permitted by the 1949 state law
• Make money

Initially, the founders sought about one hundred investors to invest $5,000 each in Cahokia Downs, Inc., a Delaware corporation. Of that amount, $1,500 purchased a single unit of a land trust, and $3,500 purchased 3,500 shares of common stock at $1 per share. The corporation originally issued 85 units of the land trust—fractional share ownership was permitted—and 500,000 shares of common stock available for public purchase. In order to retain control of operations, original shareholders reserved 357,000 of the common shares.[6] Regulations of the state Racing Board decreed that the names of persons holding common stock had to be made public. The land trust was another subject.

Under Illinois law, formation of a land trust for ownership of property that could be rented to a tenant had distinct advantages. First, beneficiaries of the trust were paid rental fees by the tenant and therefore had a secure income. Second, the law permitted the names of trustees to be kept secret.

In effect, Cahokia Downs, Inc., operator of the racetrack business, owned no land and was a tenant paying rent to the land trust.[7] Those who owned both common stock and a land trust share essentially paid themselves rent.

In time it became known that the real owners of Cahokia Downs were those who held land trust units, not the shareholders. In a 1963 investigation, *East St. Louis Journal* reporter Charles O. Stewart determined that common shareholders in Cahokia Downs had not received a single dollar in dividends in the first eight years of operations. However, land trust beneficiaries had received $7,200 per unit in that period, a nice return on the $1,500 investment.

To further complicate the picture—but also to further create personal income—original shareholders and land trust beneficiaries had one other investment opportunity. The corporation issued $1,400,000 in ten-year first mortgage bonds to construct the track and buildings. The corporation also issued $600,000 in nineteen-year debenture notes for operating expenses. Holders of the bonds received 6 percent interest per year; holders of debentures received 8 percent interest.[8] All bond and debenture holders were land trust beneficiaries.

The original Cahokia Land Trust agreement, dated July 1, 1953, named Schaefer O'Neill as trustee. He technically held the land in trust for the beneficiaries and managed it. The legal beneficiaries were the owners but otherwise were passive in terms of management of the assets or dealings with the tenants. The agreement was for twenty years. The original list of beneficiaries included Stelle and business people from Springfield and Alton.[9]

The importance of Stelle to the organization and continued operation of Cahokia Downs cannot be understated. He served as president from the earliest days until his death, and he spent countless hours promoting the track and working to make it profitable. The respect founders held for Stelle showed clearly in August 1962, about a month after Stelle's death, when voting trustees contacted owners of the Cahokia Voting Trust about an extension of the trust agreement. The trustees sought the extension in memory of Stelle.

In a letter signed by George Edward Day, Andrew Ryan, John A. Stelle, Schaefer O'Neill, and Dan McGlynn they recalled Stelle's commitment: "He loved the sport of thoroughbred racing from boyhood and into Cahokia in the past nine years he poured his constant efforts and time, all contributed personally, with no expense or charge to the track. . . . He sought in every way to keep the ownership and management of Cahokia on a high level. He believed the best way to assure this was through a Voting Trust."[10]

The secrecy surrounding Powell's involvement is surprising considering his ownership position and active involvement in management and political strategies. It was as if everyone conspired to keep him out of public view on matters of Cahokia Downs. Powell's name did show up when the state racing board made public the lists of common stockholders in 1971. There were not even many good guesses about his involvement, by the press or others.

Records reveal that Powell bought his first shares of common stock on July 8, 1954, at approximately the time Cahokia Downs began operations. He purchased 3,500 shares from George Edward Day, which indicates that he paid $5,000 along with other initial owners and that he presumably received at least 1 unit of the trust at that time. The same records show that he purchased 1,000 more shares of common stock in November 1954 and 57 shares shortly thereafter. He later bought 438 shares on June 29, 1962, and 875 shares on October 2, 1962.[11] The purchase of 875 shares coincided with his purchase of one-quarter trust unit for $4,500, placing the value at that time at $18,000 per unit. Each unit was valued at $20,000 upon his death. When his ownership became public knowledge after his death, Powell's total ownership of common shares was listed at 5,365.[12] All shares purchased by Powell before 1962 were originally issued either to Day or John Stelle, in effect concealing the ownership from the Illinois Racing Board.

Powell accumulated more than 1 unit of the trust, as did many individuals. Some of the original investors and insiders bought more than Powell, although many of them ended up in the hands of relatives. For example, when beneficiaries first became known in 1971, the survivors of Stelle owned 4.875 units; Day's family had accumulated 4 units. In the settlement of his estate, Powell's ownership included 2.625 units.[13]

The land trust concealed Powell's beneficiary position on the land, but his common stock shares should have been public knowledge, according to state racing board regulations. Instead, his ownership position remained secret, thanks to Stelle and Day, who maintained ownership of record for Powell's shares, while Powell took any profits and paid taxes on them. After Stelle's death in 1962, his son John A. Stelle and Day continued the friendly practice.[14] In a letter dated December 22, 1965, Powell wrote Day about missing records of his stock and trust transactions. He concluded with this paragraph: "I am in the process of making arrangements of having these shares [common stock] put in my name and am writing this letter . . . so that you will have something in your records which would give a basis for your paying this stock dividend to me as I will report it on my income tax and you will not have to report it on yours."[15]

Occasional units of the land trust came on the market and were snatched up immediately by insiders, but most of the initial beneficiaries kept their trust holdings and passed them on to relatives upon death. Few people wanted to sell out. Consequently, when the trust list became public, it was assumed that virtually all of the names had appeared on the original list, too. Judging from the list, founders of Cahokia Downs remained true to their standards of political ambitions and bipartisanship.

The beneficiary list in 1971 included Rep. Clyde Choate; William (Smokey) Downey, an aide to Gov. William Stratton; Dan Foley, East St. Louis city finance commissioner; East St. Louis Mayor Alvin Fields; Sam Wiedrick; State Sen. Everett Peters, Republican, and longtime Powell friend, who served with him on the powerful Legislative Budgetary Commission and showed up on various horseracing investment lists; Dan McGlynn; U.S. Rep. Mel Price; Francis Touchette, Centreville Township (home of Cahokia Downs) supervisor and political antagonist of Mayor Alvin Fields; Peter Rossiter, downstate Democratic patronage chief; Rep. Clyde Lee; and Edward Barrett, Chicago associate of Stelle and Powell dating back to the early 1930s.

When full disclosure of land trust holdings were made in 1971, the press made much of one land trust investor, Mrs. Janice L. Marsh, the daughter of Secretary of State John W. Lewis, a Republican, who was appointed to succeed Powell in October 1970.[16] She appeared as the owner of 1,157 shares of common stock in Cahokia Downs, Inc., and a full share of the trust. She also held 2,000 shares of Chicago Harness and 2,700 shares of Egyptian Trotting, both then conducting racing meetings in the Chicago area.

Under pressure with the disclosure, Lewis ducked press inquiries but finally issued a vague statement: "My daughter, Janice Lewis Marsh, has owned race track interests for over 10 years. Several years go she bought some additional interests to that which she originally had. . . . My daughter informs me that her income from her race track interests for the year 1970 was $7,365.64. The amount she owns would be like comparing a tea cup of water to Lake Michigan." If the amount of income were small, holders of stock often used that as a means of minimizing the importance of being a stockholder.

The Cahokia Downs charade with Lewis reflected a similar stock arrangement he had with Egyptian Trotting, the harness racing association linked tightly to Cahokia Downs investors. On the 1963 stockholders list for Egyptian Trotting, Lewis owned 2,700 shares, although the shares technically were held by his daughter. Later that year, Rep. Clyde Lee wrote Powell at the St. Nicholas Hotel: "We now show John Lewis stock in the name of his daughter, Mrs. Janice Marsh and suggest you call him and see if this is the way he wants it when we send in our list of stockholders for the [Harness Racing] Commission hearing."[17]

Mrs. Marsh could not have acquired the shares except through her father. Lewis's turmoil was an example of the dilemma faced by political leaders in high-profile political positions who wanted to participate in racing investment opportunities but did not want the public to know. The embarrassment factor for Lewis by 1971 was heightened by the death of Powell and exposure of his racing involvements and the impending investigation and trial of former Gov. Otto Kerner. Everyone who knew Lewis, knew that he and Powell had a close political relationship. While serving in the legislature, he had the reputation as a mainstay of a group of downstate Republican legislators regarded as friendly to racing interests. Eventually Lewis took responsibility for his action and admitted ownership. The declaration ended his political career.

Concealed ownership of the land trust drove newspaper reporters crazy. Over the years, there were countless newspaper guesses about names on the list and demands by editorial page articles to release the information. The threats did not work, however. While an occasional beneficiary became known or declared ownership publicly, when the list was made public for the first time in 1971, reporters and the public were stunned at names.

They reacted with articles in which they could hardly disguise their glee. One reporter who mined enough sources periodically to at least expose a small percentage of land trust beneficiaries was Stewart of the *East St. Louis Journal*. He wrote two extensive series of stories about Cahokia Downs, one in 1962 and a second in 1963, revealing the most known then about operations of Cahokia Downs. But he did not have proof that Powell held a major stock and trust position.

In his 1963 articles, Stewart revealed the identity of one original holder of the trust, common stock, and debentures, who sold off his interests in 1962. The disclosure gave a glimpse of the intentions of an investor, the holdings, and value. The investor was Jacob Bunn Jr. of Springfield, who at the time of establishing Cahokia Downs was a major stockholder in Sangamo Electric and was active in horse shows. Bunn's original investment amounted to $60,000, representing 1 unit in the land trust, 8,500 shares of Cahokia Downs, Inc., stock purchased at $1 a share, and $50,000 in 8 percent debenture notes. Bunn, talking to Stewart, confirmed that he sold his interests for about $330,000. He retained one-half interest in the Cahokia Downs trust in the name of his wife.

Bunn explained his reasons for selling: "I have long been identified with harness racing. That's why I invested in Cahokia Downs. I had hopes that Cahokia would work in night harness racing. Dates for harness race meetings were hard to acquire, so harness racing at Cahokia never did work out." As with many other land trust investors contacted by reporters through the years, Bunn said he didn't "have the vaguest idea who the other Land Trust investors are."

The beneficiaries may have enjoyed the experience, but operating a racetrack in St. Clair County turned out to be no bed of roses. The original rent deal with the land trust established 1 percent of the gross handle (the amount bet at the track) as rent each year. Until 1958, Cahokia Downs could not pay the rent, so the land trust agreed to cut annual rentals to one-half of 1 percent of gross handle. On the accrued rental debt, Cahokia Downs, Inc., paid 6 percent interest annually. Financial concerns plagued Cahokia Downs off and on until the track closed in 1979, making it a marginally profitable venture for common stockholders. Capital improvements to the facilities stretched budgets, and deteriorating social conditions in East St. Louis added to woes.

In the 1967 annual reports to stockholders, Day, who had taken over as president and director of racing, said: "It appears to us that economic conditions in this area are reasonably good. However, there is apprehension in the minds of people in this area because of the riotous conditions that exist throughout East St. Louis and surrounding territories. If this does not get out of hand, we feel we will have a good season. We have put forth every effort to make the public as comfortable as possible and the only thing that would affect us badly would be to have the above conditions exist—which are quite beyond our control."[18] After Powell's death, the track's financial ailments appeared periodically in print, usually to be denied by whomever was president.

The political and social environment in St. Clair County, particularly near East St. Louis (Cahokia Downs was actually in Alorton, a small community just outside the corporate limits of East St. Louis), presented a challenge to Cahokia Downs operations from the start. Because of its location and an investor list heavy with local political figures, Cahokia Downs management hired scores of patronage workers and small-time elected officials. The connections made efficiency difficult at the track. Eventually, hiring practices came under press scrutiny because of alleged links with crime elements in the St. Louis metropolitan area.[19] Powell's racetrack ventures, including

126

Cahokia Downs and Chicago Downs, included connections with ex-convicts and those rumored to be friendly with crime syndicate figures.

Making a profit at Cahokia Downs meant constantly promoting the track and working members of the legislature. For two decades, starting in the 1950s, the legislature considered a handful or more of serious proposals every session, some designed to expand horseracing and some designed to curtail activity. Powell depended on a legislative coalition to sort the issues and keep the racetracks safe. The coalition needed constant attention. The more freebies handed to elected officials, the more they asked for. The handouts included free passes to Cahokia Downs, providing horse stalls for friends, cocktail and dinner parties, patronage jobs at the track, and protection for those who had shares of stock but wanted their names concealed from public exposure.

The keepers of the favors at Cahokia Downs were Day and Powell. As general manager with deep roots in the state political system, Day knew the importance of legislative support, and he worked with Powell to maintain the highest level of good fun at Cahokia Downs. Together they arranged to bring busses of legislators to the track for cocktails or beer, food, and a night of racing. Powell made the plans in Springfield, and Day provided the busses and beer.

After the annual legislative party in May 1957, Day wrote to thank Powell for his work: "Just a few lines to let you know what a wonderful job you did in assembling members of the General Assembly for the buffet dinner and cocktails here at Cahokia Downs. As usual you came through with flying colors and I want to thank you and let you know how much I appreciated it. I hope everyone had a good time, and also hope that they had luck in the mutuels."[20] Warren Wood, longtime Republican legislator and Speaker of the House at that time, apparently had a successful evening. Day wrote: "When I get the photographs of Warren Wood with the winning horse and trainer I will send the three photographs to you and you can give them to whom you please."

A number of legislators sought stall space at Cahokia Downs for themselves or for friends. Turning down a legislator's request required serious preparation. On at least one occasion, Day pleaded with Powell to understand why he might have to deny the request of a legislator: "There is no one in the General Assembly that I would rather accommodate than yourself and I have always tried to meet every request that you have made of me with no questions asked, but the last two requests that you have made of me, one for

Homer Smith for five stalls, and one for Kenneth McCormick for three stalls have me in a terrible spot—let me outline my position to you."[21]

Day said he had 1,057 stalls at Cahokia Downs with 792 in use and 310 horses en route, due to arrive soon. Day wasn't sure what he would have to do: "I have had numerous requests from representatives and I have tried to do my best for each of them but I wish they would realize that I have a certain number of stalls and there is nothing I can do about it."

Day then reported on a difficult experience with Senator Fred J. Hart, a veteran Republican legislator from Streater: "He became very abusive because I did not have stalls for A. Troutt who has horses, four of them, who are absolutely no good and never will be able to run in the 60 days we are going to be in operation. He even inferred I was taking all out of state horses and no Illinois bred horses."[22] Day explained that he actually had more Illinois bred horses than required by law.

The connection of stalls and legislative votes is described clearly in correspondence from 1961 among Day, Powell, and their friend Clyde Choate. On March 7, Choate wrote Day saying that Rep. Joseph F. Fanta, a Democrat from Chicago, asked about obtaining three stalls and tack room for the coming meeting. He identified Fanta as "a personal friend of ours for several sessions now."[23] The owner of the horses was a personal friend of Fanta from Chicago.

Ten days later Powell wrote Day requesting four stalls for a Chicago man, as a favor to "my good friend" Rep. Hector A. Brouillet, "who has always voted with us and is certainly entitled to this favor." It turned out that the request was for the same person in Chicago, and Powell added a postscript: "This request was also made by Representative Fanta to Clyde Choate, so you will be taking care of two requests by filling this."[24]

The most frequent favor handed out to the most legislators was free passes to Cahokia Downs and treatment as a very important person at the track. While passes might seem less than significant gifts, they were in great demand, and Day and Powell carefully regulated the flow as a reward for loyalty to the horseracing cause. How the political reward system worked begins with a routine form letter from Day to a list of legislators in March 1961:

It won't be long before the thoroughbreds will start running at Cahokia Downs racetrack, and in going through files I note your name on my mailing list for passes. . . . It is our intention sometime early in May to have a dinner for the General Assembly here at Cahokia Downs and we would like for you to attend. We have had several dinners in the past and you can rest assured that we will exert every effort to make this a memorable event. . . . I am enclosing an envelope for your convenience in letting me know just where you like your passes sent.[25]

During the General Assembly of 1961, at which Powell served as Speaker, two pieces of legislation—bill numbers 195 and 618—designed to alter the original 1927 racing act and benefit racetracks, had been introduced. By March there were critical floor votes, and Powell kept score. When letters came back from legislators to Day requesting passes, he sent them to Powell for comment. The results reveal just how closely Powell watched the votes on racetrack legislation and how those related to the handouts of free passes.[26]

On the letter from Rep. Walter P. Hoffelder of Chicago asking for free passes, Powell wrote at the bottom, "Voted No on both 195 and 618." Those were the bill numbers of interest. A. Lincoln Stanfield, a Republican from Edgar County, wrote back with an address for the free passes. Powell wrote, "No Good—no on both." Republican Rep. Charles Clabaugh of Champaign, not a favorite of Powell, asked for his passes, and Powell wrote on the letter: "Voted no 195; did not vote on 618. Send no additional passes."

Rep. Gale Williams from Murphysboro asked for his passes, and Powell wrote to Day: "voted NO on both bills. Don't send any additional passes." One could always tell who had a favored position with Cahokia Downs officials. Lee, a stockholder, received a letter back from Day with this comment: "I believe I have always made it a point to take care of my good friends in the past and shall continue to do so in the future."[27]

No matter where one turned at Cahokia Downs, Powell left footprints, revealing again the attention he gave even the smallest details of management. Through much of his legislative career, Powell maintained a one-person insurance business that produced small amounts of income. The money never amounted to much, but total volume may not have meant much compared to control. Powell's correspondence indicates no hesitation to use his inside position for the business. In 1963, his last year in the legislature, Powell's files reveal extensive correspondence regarding the placement of insurance policies on Cahokia Downs, Inc., property and payment of commissions to him.[28]

Powell worked through Clement Noll of the Noll Insurance Agency in Alton to place some of the business. Noll was an original investor in Cahokia Downs Land Trust. When Noll placed a policy at the request of Powell, a commission was paid to Powell. Correspondence indicates he did business on a similar basis with the Earl W. Jackson Insurance Company in East St.

Louis and also received commission payments. Yet another agency with whom Powell did business was the Guy A. Wood Agency in Mt. Vernon. The commissions were small. For placement of one policy, Powell received $12.61. In 1964, Powell brokered Cahokia Downs policies with a commission paid through the Jackson Agency of $178.45.

A characteristic of Powell and his business associates was the continuous search for a parlay—the use of one venture to build another and another. Cahokia Downs presented a perfect example of this opportunity. The founders and investors in Cahokia Downs always had thought harness racing would be a natural winner at Cahokia Downs. They believed night harness racing at Cahokia Downs would bring the bettors to the track almost on a year-round basis, with virtually no competition in the metropolitan St. Louis area except Fairmount Park, down the road near Collinsville. The first attempt to fulfill that dream came with organization of Egyptian Trotting, an appropriate name for the number of southern Illinois investors.

A paper racetrack—insiders used that term for harness racing organizations that used an existing track for meetings—Egyptian Trotting began operations in the late fall of 1957, just about three years after the first races at Cahokia Downs.[29] Egyptian Trotting held its first meeting from October 14 to November 16. Revamped facilities at Cahokia Downs greeted bettors and race fans. The clubhouse was glass enclosed and heated, and the track was adjusted for the differences between races for trotters and thoroughbreds. The public face on the organization gave it a new look, and readers of newspaper articles would not have linked it with Cahokia Downs investors. The three top officers were Charles M. Waite of Mt. Vernon, president; Edward Cox, Fairfield, secretary; and William E. Freeman, Greenup, vice president. While identified as "well known to harness horsemen," they were not familiar to political reporters. Officers recruited Edwin T. Keller, an experienced harness track operator from Norway, Maine, to be general manager.

All that might have come under the heading of no news, except that Egyptian Trotting existed principally for the benefit of those who started Cahokia Downs and many would have been embarrassed by public disclosure of racetrack stock ownership. Egyptian Trotting had no land trust behind which to hide identities, and by rules of the Harness Racing Commission, all common stock shareholders names had to be made public. This obviously would have presented a problem for anyone except the clever political interests associated with Cahokia Downs. They had learned that the law permitted a legal owner of stock to sign over money to actual owners who paid the taxes and took the dividends and interest. Thus Paul Powell could own thousands of shares of common stock, have it held in the name of a friend such as John Stelle, and collect the income, without getting in trouble with the Internal Revenue Service.

In the association files from 1963, the list of public stockholders in Egyptian Trotting included many familiar names from the Cahokia Downs list and a number of people who preferred to remain anonymous owners.[30] Compared to the stockholders list of 1959, there were no additions or deletions. They were John A. Stelle, the son of John H., who had 8,750 shares, including 6,750 belonging to Paul Powell; Clyde Lee, 7,200 shares; Clement L. Noll, 7,087.5 shares, including 5,062.5 held for Sen. Paul A. Ziegler from White County; George Edward Day, 4,750 shares; Alvin G. Fields, 2,125 shares; Francis Fields, 1,250 shares; Leonard L. Levin, Chicago, 2,500, all belonging to State Sen. Dan Rostenkowski, who later became a U.S. Congressman and served prison time for misuses of government funds; Delbert Loos, Quincy, 1,350 held for Rep. H. B. Ihnen of Adams County; D. M. Madigan, Philo, 675 held for Rep. Leo Pfeffer, Champaign County; Dan McGlynn, East St. Louis, 2,612.5; and former Rep. James W. McRoberts, East St. Louis, GOP leader, 625.

Also, Schaefer O'Neill, longtime associate of Stelle and Powell and a founder of Cahokia Downs, held 14,275 shares, including 5,500 for Wiedrick, LaGrange Park, and 6,750 shares for Rep. Choate of Anna; Carl H. Preihs, Pana, former legislator, 6,750; John Sankey, Springfield, 1,350; John H. Stelle estate, 8,500; Russell T. Stelle, son of John H., 3,000; and Twin City Development Company of Champaign, 2,700 shares belonging to Everett Peters of Champaign. Mrs. Janice L. Marsh of Tuscola, daughter of Rep. John W. Lewis, held 2,700 shares for her father.

Powell's correspondence files for the early years of Egyptian operations reveal how much time and energy were spent concealing the names of investors who did not want the information disclosed or whom the association preferred to keep secret. While ownership of stock by elected officials did not violate any state laws, the embarrassment factor bothered anyone who had to face an electorate. Furthermore, Egyptian officials feared the Harness Racing Commission might penalize the association by awarding them unfavorable meeting dates if there was political embarrassment.

The potential legal ramifications of showing stock ownership in a name other than the person who held the certificates and collected the dividend obviously concerned Lee. He consulted George W. Howard, a Mt. Vernon attorney, for guidance. Howard explained that the person whose name is officially on the stock is called a nominee, and he must furnish full information to the IRS about the person who owns the stock and to whom the dividends are paid. He concluded, "Therefore, it would appear that the nominee would merely give the information and the actual owner would include it in his income tax return."[31]

In a July 26 letter to Lee, Powell wrote: "I will appreciate your having this stock issued in the name of John A. Stelle for 6,750 shares. I will also appreciate your sending the stock certificate to me instead of John A. Stelle so that I can then forward same to him for his endorsement."[32] In other words, the shares belonged to Powell and he took the dividends, but Stelle had his name on the certificates. That fall, much of the correspondence dealt with a handful of Egyptian shareholders who held elective office and how to list their certificates. An October 29 letter from Lee to Powell spelled out how the system worked and asked for Powell's help:

Dear Paul:

I am finally getting time to go over the stock and figure out what changes should be made.

I am enclosing sheets on [Rep. Clyde] Choate, [Sen. Dan] Rostenkowski, [Sen. Paul] Zeigler and [Rep. H. B.] Ihnen, which I believe are self-explanatory. However, call me on these if there are any questions.

I will contact [Sen. Ev] Peters and am now in the process of taking care of [Rep. Leo] Pfeffer's transfer. I have also written letters today to Geo. Edward Day, Dan McGlynn and Al Fields as all three of these fellows had their first stock put in one of the Keeley Brothers names.

We now show John Lewis stock in the name of his daughter, Mrs. Janice Marsh and suggest you call him and see if this is the way he wants it when we send in our list of stockholders for the [Racing] Commission hearing.

Also, the certificate issued to Robert Pool was first issued to Martin Keeley so I am writing direct to Bob about this. I will ask him to send in both of his certificates and issue one direct to him.

[Former Rep.] Carl Preihs has all of his stock in his name and I think this is the way he wants it but you might ask him about this if you want to. . . .

I still need to work out the Downey-Lou Mindling stock but will try to do some work on that this afternoon.

Your promptness on all this will be greatly appreciated. Call me if you need any information.

Best regards,

Clyde[33]

The attachments from Lee showed the holder of the certificate, the number of shares, and to whom the certificates were issued. For example, on Clyde L. Choate it showed he had two certificates for 4,250 shares issued to Martin Keeley and 2,500 shares issued to Choate. Lee added: "Certificate No. 35 and 112 have been endorsed in blank by Mr. Keeley. Certificate No. 72 was evidently made direct to Clyde and he should endorse it in blank. All three certificates should be surrendered and a new certificate for 6,750 shares will be issued to the person designated by Choate." On separate sheets, Lee showed all stock in the names of Rostenkowski, Ziegler, and Ihnen to be held by Martin Keeley.

In the early years, Egyptian struggled trying to attract Missouri customers. In the first eight months after opening, which included one meeting date, the organization showed a loss of $94,228.[34] This included many startup expenses, such as $20,057 for advertising and $14,190 for initial repairs and maintenance. The tremendous losses, however, caused Egyptian management to skip the 1958 racing season.

Harness racing on the Cahokia Downs track never worked for Egyptian, and operators began looking for an opportunity to race in the Chicago area. In 1959, Egyptian signed a lease for racing at Maywood Park, near Chicago, with an expiration date of 1962. That location provided the first profits, but more significant growth in dividends began with the move in 1962 to Washington Park.

In a letter dated December 21, 1963, Clyde Lee, serving Egyptian as secretary-treasurer, reported with glee to Powell on the association's financial condition: "When I was in Chicago last Wednesday I made investments at the First National Bank of Chicago in government securities as follows: $90,000 due on March 15, 1964, at 3.72%; $90,000 due on June 15, 1964, at 3.81%; $250,000 due on October 15, 1964, at 3.98%. It may be possible to invest a little more after the first of the year after all bills are paid. When we were struggling at Cahokia Downs in 1957 I never thought it would be possible to put $430,000 in a surplus account in the next six years. Did you?"[35]

8
Creating Cash His Way

MUCH HAS BEEN MADE OF THE FACT THAT PAUL POWELL AMASSED A small personal fortune of more than $3,000,000—in 1970 dollars— while never earning more than $30,000 in a single year from employment as a public official. Granted, Powell could not have generated such an estate on state salary alone. On the other hand, he did build a major part of his estate from intriguing sources and the frugal investment of cash flow.

Putting aside $800,000 in cash found in Powell's hotel suite and $538,573 in funds marked as campaign contributions, Powell had a personal estate of almost $2,000,000, a substantial sum for economic conditions of the 1970s.[1] An explanation, and some understanding, for this share of Powell's fortune is available from federal income tax returns found among his personal papers. The most complete picture of Powell's financial condition is provided by combining information from his estate filings and data from the tax returns.

Powell's papers include federal tax information from 1940 through 1969, along with miscellaneous tax documents. They disclose sources of income that provided Powell with cash well beyond what he spent maintaining his lifestyle. In fact, his reputation for being a tightwad with money suggests a personal inclination rather than a need. Powell had plentiful cash from racetrack ventures, farm income, an investment in a Vienna funeral home, a half interest in an apartment building, a regular payment every year from the company owned and operated by the John Stelle family, and a variety of miscellaneous business ventures.

The tax returns demonstrate how a state legislator with a modest annual income became a state official with a total annual take that reached $164,548 before taxes in 1969 and would have topped $200,000 if he had lived to the end of 1970. Powell's income level took several escalations over the years, coinciding with circumstances that provided infusions of income other than salaries.

In the period leading up to 1949, Powell's gross income ranged from just $1,312 (in 1944) to about $10,000. With racetrack dividends in 1949, Powell's income went to a new level ranging from $25,000 to $40,000 in the period leading up to 1960. Then, as cash from racetracks and other investments mounted, his income went to levels of the well-fixed. Powell earned a gross income of $64,634 in 1961, and it increased to $87,415 in 1964. In the years when he served as secretary of state, Powell's income reached more than $100,000 in each year. In 1967 he declared $160,537, and in his last full year of life, 1969, Powell's gross income totaled $164,548, including about $135,500 from sources other than salaries.

How accurate are his returns in accounting for income? There is every indication that Powell walked a cautious line with the Internal Revenue Service. That care may explain why he kept $800,000 or so in cash rather than in interest or dividend bearing investments. If that money came from sources that for obvious reasons could not be declared on his tax returns, then all the more reason to keep it out of sight of snoopy reporters and federal tax people. Powell knew of many examples where public people went to jail because they were untruthful on federal tax returns.

Powell's tax returns were carefully and professionally prepared and appear to be quite complete. In a handful of years, he filed amended returns to account for relatively small changes in income and deductible expenses, indicating intentions to keep things accurate even for minor variations. Rarely did the amendments change his taxable income by more than a few dollars.[2]

The bulk of Powell's income resulted from dividend, interest, and miscellaneous sources. Comparatively, his salary declarations were minuscule. When Powell entered the legislature, the annual salary was $2,500, or $5,000 for the biennium. Powell took the full $5,000 in some two-year terms—thus showing no income from the state in the second year—and in other terms he split the amount over the two years. After the mid-1940s, legislative salaries increased to $6,000 a biennium, and in 1953 the salary moved to $10,000 for two years. The legislature work paid $12,000 a biennium, until he left the legislature in 1965 and became secretary of state. To understand the relationship of his state salary to total income during times of growth, consider two examples, 1955 and 1964.

In 1955, the state paid Powell $5,000, and his tax return showed an adjusted gross income of $28,725. His income that year had not begun to reflect substantial racetrack investments, but even then 76 percent of his total income came from sources other than salaries. In 1964, Powell had a gross declared income of $87,415, with a state salary of $6,000. In that year his non-salary income, consisting almost entirely of dividend and interest income, accounted for 81 percent of the total. This pattern persisted throughout the years from 1950 to 1969, during which he became the beneficiary of substantial investments in racetrack operations that paid handsome dividends, and even his passbook savings were substantial.

When Powell died, the media focused on his stock holdings and their value, leaving much of the total story untold. For example, he held 6,750 shares of common stock in the Egyptian Trotting Association, Inc., a harness racing operation that he had much to do with forming. The estate valued the stock at $27,000. From the time that Egyptian Trotting first paid a dividend in 1963, through 1969, the stock paid Powell cash dividends of $91,124. Over that seven year period, he averaged $13,017 in dividends annually. In the last full year of his life, Egyptian Trotting paid $17,550, and it had increased every year.

Other than Powell's state salary, the longest continuous source of income was from a very small insurance brokerage business. Given the almost insignificant annual amounts, one wonders why he bothered to maintain his license and write any business. In only three of the years reflected by his tax returns did he earn more than $1,000 in commissions, and those occurred while he was secretary of state. The largest annual amount was $1,632. He always charged off most of the commission income in miscellaneous expenses, including car mileage. Most of the commissions earned resulted from policies written on racetracks in which he owned stock or in county fairs with which he had a long-standing involvement.

The returns revealed other long-term payments besides insurance. Without explanations, little can be determined other than the sources. In 1946 Powell received the first of annual salary payments from Arketex Ceramics, Inc., owned and operated by the family of John H. Stelle in Brazil, Indiana. That first payment to Powell was $900, and after the first year, it rarely varied from $1,800. There is no explanation for the payment or indication of what services Powell performed.[3] An additional benefit to Powell from the Arketex connection was that he wrote off travel expenses almost every year for visits in his home district and southern Illinois.

As an investor in Mansion View Motel in Springfield—located across the street from the governor's mansion—Powell received interest payments in the annual range of $800 for about ten years. Powell helped his investment along by insisting during his years as secretary of state that out-of-town employees of the secretary of state's office stay at the motel.[4]

One of the longest paying investments for the Powells came from a half interest in farm land in Alexander County, south of Vienna. In 1947, Powell and a Vienna friend, John M. Marlin, purchased 586 acres of land through the Farmers Home Administration and the Illinois Defense Relocation Corporation. They paid $20,000 for the property. When Powell sold his interest in 1965, he showed a gain of more than $50,000. Powell had received steady annual income of a few thousand dollars a year during that time, as well as income from a hunt club on the same property managed by Marlin.

Powell had two profitable investments in Vienna. Starting in 1961 he owned a half interest in the Mount Funeral Home that paid him almost $44,000 in the years before he died. As part of the liquidation of Powell's estate, the executor sold the interest to the surviving partner, Thomas Mount, for $9,274, after paying Powell's share of 1970 profits of $4,869. With plenty of cash to invest in the early 1960s, Powell put $25,564 in a Vienna apartment building venture. The annual income payments totaled about $10,000 before his death. That investment was with long-time friend Joe Throgmorton, local druggist. According to friends of Mount and Throgmorton, the investments may have been kindly financial assists from Powell.

Periodically his returns told part of a tale about complicated business dealings while he also served as an elected official. Such was the case with an item on his returns of 1961 and 1962 that simply stated, "Robert Crain, finder's fee." In 1961 the finder's fee amounted to $2,000, and in 1962 the line item showed $7,656. Crain was a partner in the Centralia, Illinois, law firm of Crain and Hall. Correspondence in Powell's files indicates a business relationship between Crain and Powell that began in the early 1960s and continued until at least 1967.

While Powell served as minority leader of the House of Representatives in 1963, he corresponded with Crain and Ray Dickirson, the head of Dickirson-Davis, a firm that rigged and sold trucks throughout the Midwest, about appointments Powell arranged with prospective customers. Powell wrote directly to prospects asking for an appointment with Dickirson, and in other letters Crain asked him to make specific contacts. Powell almost always included a paragraph in his letters similar to this from 1963: "There certainly will be no obligation on the part of your company to purchase anything whatsoever, but I do hope that you will see to it that an appointment is made for Ray Dickirson."[5]

During 1963 the contacts that Powell made for Crain and Dickirson included Commonwealth Edison of Chicago, FS (Farm Service Company), Illinois Power Company, Central Illinois Public Service, Central Motor Freight Association, and J. D. Barter Construction Company of Harrisburg. Powell became close enough to the Dickirson firm to purchase 250 shares of stock at $1 a share early in the 1960s. While Crain later estimated in correspondence that a share had increased in value to $50, the 250 shares were valued at total of $1,200 on Powell's estate tax form.

Another investment related to a public issue appeared on Powell's tax returns about the same time as the Crain and Dickirson involvement in the early 1960s. Powell apparently had become involved in business matters with Trinity Investment Company, which had offices in Salem, Illinois. In October 1961, Powell interceded in behalf of Jack P. Gibbs, president of Trinity, who had been denied a state license to sell stock in Christian Universal Life Insurance Company. The state said Gibbs once sold stock of another insurance firm without legal permission.[6]

Powell took the matter up with the Department of Insurance and sought a ruling by the state attorney general that would allow Gibbs to sell stock before the company's stock offering was approved. The matter made public news accounts in mid-December that claimed Powell had a business relationship with Trinity and was serving as a public relations counsel for the firm. Angrily, Powell denied knowing Gibbs or having any advisory role with Trinity. Powell's 1961 tax returns showed income received from Trinity Investment of $1,201, and his 1962 return indicated income of $2,277 from Trinity. The issue becomes a bit more involved on Powell's returns for 1962 through 1964.

Powell had sought relief from the attorney general's office for Gibbs so that stock in Christian Universal Life Insurance Company, a southern Illinois firm, could be sold. News accounts declared Powell had an arrangement with Christian Universal Life that would pay him a commission on all stock sold in Illinois by Trinity Investment. In a statement, Powell acknowledged that he owned stock in Christian Universal Life and that he had been assigned a ten-county area over which he acted as district director. He called reports that he would receive from $1,500 to $15,000 in commissions on the sale of stock "wild guesses": "I expect to receive not more than $1,200 toward my expenses and incidentals as a district board member, which will be paid to me over a period of about two years and which will be my only remuneration and will not cover my actual expenses," Powell said. "I do not and will not receive any commission on sales of stock or any insurance sold throughout the state of Illinois."

The small amounts of income from Trinity Investment could well have been reimbursement for expenses, although counted as income on the returns. Powell's receipts from Christian Universal Life for 1962 through 1964 indicate quite a different story from the one he told newspapers late in 1961. Powell showed income from Christian Universal Life of $6,173 in 1962, $11,891 in 1963, and $1,259 in 1964, for a total from the life insurance company of $19,323, in spite of public denials that he had no commission arrangement with Christian Universal.

Without a doubt, the most troublesome business venture in Powell's life began in September 1959, when he and friend, Clyde Choate, became major stockholders in formation of a company named Statewide Tire Sales. For the next decade, Statewide tried to carve a niche in the tire sales business of the Midwest, ultimately failing as an investment and as a company. Powell and Choate, joined by partner Seymour Emalfarb, each purchased 2,500 shares of stock at $25 a share, for a total of $62,500, to begin the firm.[7] Emalfarb ran the business, but correspondence in Powell's papers reveals the elected official's firm hand and political touch.

In a series of letters dated 1964 between Emalfarb and Powell, the subject was the sale of tickets to a fund-raising dinner for Powell's campaign, featuring former President Harry S. Truman. Powell pushed fifty tickets off on Emalfarb to peddle among customers and friends. Another time Powell asked Emalfarb to sell tickets to help defray costs of a movie produced by a Herrin newspaper publisher and Southern Illinois University that promoted Powell and his interest in education. Also in 1964, while Powell campaigned for secretary of state, he wrote Emalfarb on legislative stationery: "I received a letter from Gene Simonds that 10 each 1000 x 20 Single Ply, Road Treat Michelin Tires and Tubes be shipped to attention of Mr. George Johnson. I note where he asks that you give the discount to the Paul Powell Campaign Fund. As soon as these tires are delivered and you receive your checks for both Simonds and J. D. Barter I trust that you will forward your check to me for the discount on both orders."[8]

Before the company ran into trouble later in the 1960s, Powell received an annual salary from Statewide for three consecutive years, although there is little evidence the firm made much money. Powell received $4,000 in 1962, $5,600 in 1963, and $7,325 in 1964. He also charged off various travel and business-related expenses. During that time, Powell served as chairman of the board of directors, and Choate served as associate chairman. Powell stepped down as an officer late in 1964 after winning the race for secretary of state. During the campaign, he promised to resign because of the potential conflict. While he gave up the position, correspondence indicates he maintained an interest in the firm, and his income tax returns reflected involvement as late as 1968.

By the time of Powell's last salary payment in 1964, the firm had hit hard times, and the final years leading up to dissolution in 1968 were filled with litigation and other legal troubles. The first portion of a letter to Albert M. Zlotnick dated May 14, 1968, on Statewide stationery and signed by Franklin H. Weber, reveals some of the tension:

I have enclosed particulars on the tire companies as we discussed over the telephone on Friday, May 10, 1968. The principals, both high ranking state officials, are most anxious that I dispose of the assets of the companies since the
operation has been closed down. The delay in offering assets for sale was due
to the fact that creditors had to be satisfied. The big problem was an exhaus-
tive search to determine both assets and liabilities. The business was operated
by a family group that ran the business for personal gain and I suspect more
material left through the back door than through the front door. . . . My
friends, the principals involved, dropped a lot of money into this venture.
They do have excellent connections in this field and would gladly help any
future operator.[9]

Powell's 1968 federal tax return showed a $40,069 loss for Statewide Tire Sales
for "overdraft, notes, interest." That combined with the original investment
indicated Powell had invested more than $100,000 in the company and had
taken out about $17,000 in the ten-year period. Emalfarb fell upon hard
times after dissolution of Statewide. He was convicted in U.S. District Court
on December 23, 1971, of interstate extortion for accepting money to keep
state policemen from ticketing trucks belonging to an Indiana firm.[10] Powell was not involved in the activities for which Emalfarb was prosecuted, nor
were any specific state policemen implicated.

While most of Powell's income from miscellaneous sources must be
termed modest, there is no doubting the largest source of his wealth over the
years. From all horse racing sources—dividends, interest, rent, breeding
horses, capital gains from stock sales—Powell accumulated a small fortune
in the twenty years from 1950 to 1969. The total amount of gross income,
before taxes, amounted to $862,000—more than the amount of cash found
in his hotel room in 1970.

Racetrack operations, in particular four of them, provided him with huge
sums of money, considering the times. While an annual income of $60,000
today might be considered middle class, in Powell's time that was a handsome amount and put a person in the upper income percentiles. Powell's
gross annual income exceeded $60,000 starting in 1961, with the bulk of that
from racetrack sources. From the tax return figures and their relationship to
the passage of legislation in which he had a strong hand, the conclusion can
be drawn that Powell was not only the father of harness racing but also the
beneficiary.

But he alone did not reap profits. Many legislative friends earned substantial dividends from Chicago Downs stock purchased at the same time as
Powell. In the case of Egyptian Downs, the beneficiaries included most of his

racetrack friends and associates from southern Illinois; and the same was true of the dividends and interest paid on Cahokia Downs operations. Powell simply had more stock than his fellow investors.

When Powell helped drive through the harness racing pari-mutuel racing bill in 1949, then subsequently became the largest stockholder of Chicago Downs, he assured himself of wealth beyond anything he had imagined as a struggling cafe owner or young legislator from Vienna. The investment opportunity at Chicago Downs, created by the legislation and the offering of stock at $.10 a share, paid dividends and other sources of income amounting to at least $625,320 over a twenty-year period. Powell did not live a fancy lifestyle; consequently, he reinvested much of the income in other income producing stock and savings institutions.

Here is an accounting of Powell's income from the Chicago Downs connection as shown on tax returns:

- The stock Powell held paid at least $465,000 in dividends from 1950 to 1969. The lowest annual dividend was $11,550, and the highest in any year was $55,300. Although not included in this computation, Powell's estate received a payment of $63,200 for his dividend in 1970.
- He received $92,200 in "finder's fees" from Sam Wiedrick, beginning in 1956 and concluding in 1966. The annual amounts of fee splitting by Wiedrick for his friend and associate Powell varied from $4,200 to $10,000. The money was paid to Wiedrick for consulting by Chicago Downs.
- From 1967 to 1969, Powell received $20,000 a year in consulting fees directly from Chicago Downs.
- Over the years, Powell sold small amounts of Chicago Downs stock for gains, and he showed a salary of $4,200 from the track in 1953, without an explanation for services rendered.

The next largest amount of track income came from his stock in Egyptian Trotting, which began as a venture at the Cahokia Downs track in East St. Louis, then switched to Chicago area tracks. The association paid no dividends until it moved away from East St. Louis. The first dividend amounted to $1,350 in 1963. In a very few years, it became the second most productive dividend total next to Chicago Downs.

As with Chicago Downs, the income opportunity from Egyptian Trotting was not limited to stock dividends or interest on loans. Starting in the year of the first dividend payment, 1963, Powell went on the payroll of Egyptian Trotting with a $3,000 annual payment for public relations work. There is no indication of services rendered for the payment, nor was the work in behalf of Egyptian known publicly at the time. Powell watched carefully over the interest of racetracks as long as he served in state government, and he received additional pay for those efforts.

Powell could thank his associations with Chicago interests—including the owners of Sportsman's Park and Wiedrick—for his investment opportunity in Fox Valley Trotting Club, Inc. Powell appeared, from the tax returns, to be just an investor in stock of the harness racing company and not a holder of debentures or the recipient of consulting arrangements. From the first dividend paid in 1960 to his death, Powell received $66,667.

In terms of income produced for all the effort and political schmoozing, the biggest disappointment for Powell had to be his holdings in Cahokia Downs racetrack. Presumably this was the experience of most of those who started the enterprise in 1953 with high hopes of a major payoff from thoroughbred and harness racing operations. Instead, the various forms of income from Cahokia Downs paid to Powell from 1954 to 1969 amounted to only a little more than $42,000. Most of that—$23,222—came from the Cahokia Downs Land Trust, which essentially amounted to rent paid by the track operations organization. Powell received $14,224 in interest payments on debentures he held. There were only five of those fifteen years in which Cahokia Downs, Inc., paid dividends, and they amounted to just $5,300.

During the twenty years in which Powell established his reputation as racing's biggest booster and supporter, he held stock in other lesser racetrack operations that paid little in dividends. Nevertheless, the tax return information on this income does give a picture of the breadth of his interests. Without question, he benefited from stock purchases at low initial prices. Although Powell's returns did not show any dividend income from Suburban Downs—one of the state's first pari-mutuel racetracks in the Chicago area—he bought stock in 1956 and sold it in 1961 for a gain of $16,883, on an original investment of just $2,000. The returns do not indicate how many shares he purchased in 1956.

One of the most curious transactions on his returns occurred in 1963, when Powell bought stock in the Washington Park Trotting Association, started in the early 1960s by Marje Lindheimer Everett. Four years after he purchased the stock for $7,000, Powell sold it for $42,000, with a taxable gain of $35,000. The timing of this transaction overlays the period in which Everett was engaged in a stock deal with then Gov. Otto Kerner that eventually led to his conviction on federal charges.

Evidence is lacking that Powell had a deal similar to Kerner's. In fact, Kerner's stock ownership was in Chicago Thoroughbred Enterprises, a holding company for all of Everett's racetrack operations at Washington Park and Arlington Park. The Kerner stock deal involved stock options, which were exercised in 1966 for a gain of $150,000. Powell's purchase occurred after Powell ended two consecutive terms in the legislature as Speaker. He was secretary of state when he sold the stock. Everett's harness racing venture succeeded wildly, and those who held stock did very well. Contacted twenty-five years after the conviction of Kerner, federal co-prosecutor Samuel Skinner said there never was a serious investigation of Powell's dealings with Everett because he had died before the probe gained momentum.[11]

Powell's returns indicate occasional forays into the breeding of horses. Most of them failed to earn profits but resulted in a tax write-off. One that never appeared to work was Powell's ownership of a horse named Sylvester. The total tax liability from 1950 to 1969 amounted to a loss of $5,720.

The investment of cash in the stock of small southern Illinois banks and cash held by various savings institutions paid a steady income to Powell, especially after the flow of cash began from racetracks. The growth in earnings from the bank investments occurred mostly in the mid to late 1960s, when Powell's cash flow increased substantially. In 1961, when his annual income took a jump over levels during the 1950s, Powell received $1,130 in dividends from stock in banks in Paducah, Kentucky, Marion, Vienna, and Cobden. His cash holdings were in two savings and loans and an account at City National Bank. By 1964, he appeared to have about the same level of stock investments in small banks, but his interest income reflected a major increase in cash investments. He earned more than $4,600 in interest.

The picture changed dramatically by 1969, reflecting not just increased cash holdings in banks but stock investments as well. He counted dividends from bank stock of $4,035. The list had grown from 1961 to include banks in Harrisburg and Carbondale. The cash holdings produced $12,700 in interest from most of the same banks. At the going rate of 5 percent annual interest, that would represent income on more than $250,000 in cash.

By the end of his life, Powell's twenty-year involvement with racetracks had turned him into a virtual moneymaking machine, not just with dividends and interest from track investments but also with annual payments for consulting work performed while he served as an elected state official. On the other hand, his tax returns reveal nothing to explain the accumulation of $800,000 in cash found in his hotel closet.

9

Hide and Seek: The Story of $800,000

P AUL POWELL'S DETERIORATING HEALTH TOOK HIM BACK TO ROCH-
ester, Minnesota, and the Mayo Clinic in October 1970, for diagnosis
and treatment. He had been there in September, and the return visit so concerned his friends that they urged him to check into the hospital rather than
be treated as an outpatient.

Typically, Powell resisted, and his friends knew he would only be angered
and more resistant if they persisted. Nevertheless, Powell was sick. He had
become increasingly aware of his vulnerability, beginning in 1963, when he
suffered a heart attack. He may have had a premonition about this trip to the
Mayo Clinic because he took a copy of his will along.[1]

With this heightened sense of mortality, Powell frequently reminded Mrs.
Margaret Hensey, his secretary and traveling companion, of things to be
done "if something should happen to me." This was more than just a cau-
tionary comment to the person he held dear. He was the only person who
had a full understanding of his complex personal and business interests.
Also, only Powell understood what the public reaction would be when everyone discovered all that he had done or was doing.

One of Powell's requests to Hensey was that items be removed from his
personal locked file cabinet in the secretary of state's office and be turned
over to John S. Rendleman, executor of Powell's estate and longtime personal
attorney. Hensey had heard Powell discuss the subject just a few days before
the trip. Little by little Powell was making arrangements for what appeared
to be closing in on him.

On Thursday, October 8, 1970, Powell and Hensey flew to Rochester on
a commercial flight via Minneapolis and checked into the Kahler Hotel. Only
a few of Powell's close associates knew he was out of state and seeing doctors. Lucille Koval, a former personal secretary and close friend, said she
talked to Powell the day he left for Rochester: "He told me he wasn't feeling
well and was out of breath. . . . I asked him if he needed any company. He
gave me an abrupt no, and it was then I knew Mrs. Hensey was with him."[2]

The trip to Rochester and subsequent events from Thursday through Saturday are largely a mystery today, mainly because Hensey was the only other

person with Powell. She never publicly told her version of the story. In January 1971, long after events in Rochester, she testified under oath and answered questions about Powell's death. A transcript of her remarks is part of Powell's papers now at the Illinois State Historical Library.

Therefore, the only known account of what happened in the hotel suite on October 8 and 9 and until the evening of October 10 is what Hensey told interrogators from the Sangamon County state's attorney's office in January. Events in Rochester, as contained in Hensey's account—true or false—were only the first in an incredible sequence of events over a period of almost three months.[3]

Powell arrived with a suitcase of personal belongings, a tote bag, and a separate suitcase containing applications for license tags. Hensey and Powell worked on these requests Thursday night and Friday, according to her account. Powell personally handled all requests to the secretary of state's office for low and special license numbers, including the highly cherished first 15,000. Powell took this business seriously because it was one of the ways he could dispense special favors to friends, campaign contributors, associates, and cronies. He wrote instructions on the requests and handed them to Hensey for processing. Apparently he took those applications along to have work to do while waiting for treatment and tests at the Mayo Clinic.

Powell carried a large amount of cash with him and, after arrival, put most of that and some other personal belongings in the hotel safe. Hensey said: "After we came down from dinner on Thursday night, he said he was going to put the money in there [the safe] that he didn't want to have it on his person while he was going through the clinic, and then he asked the clerk if I could sign for it also, that if I needed it I could get it, and she said yes." Hensey estimated the roll of bills might have been worth $3,000–$4,000, although a later accounting fixed the total at $6,600. It was not unusual for Powell to carry large amounts of cash on trips. When Powell went to dinner with a guest or bought an item personally, he paid cash, if he paid. Powell was a notorious moocher.

Their Kahler suite was roomy, consisting of a large living room connected to separate bedrooms and baths. There were three telephones in the suite, one in Hensey's bedroom, one in Powell's bedroom, and one in the living room. All had separate numbers. About 10 P.M. on Friday, October 9, Powell and Hensey said good night and went to their bedrooms, she testified. It was the last time she saw him alive. Hensey remained awake until about 1:30 A.M. and then turned out the light.[4]

About 10 o'clock Saturday morning, the telephone in the living room rang three times. "Mr. Powell didn't answer, so I went out and answered the phone." She saw Powell sitting in a chair against a wall. The caller was Nicholas Ciaccio, assistant to Powell, who was in Springfield and apparently had called to check up on the boss. He asked about the secretary, and that is when Hensey looked more closely at Powell. "Oh, my God, Nick, I don't know. Wait a minute," she remembers saying. She left the phone and went to Powell. He was cold. She shook him and saliva came out of his mouth. After trying to get a pulse without success, she returned to the telephone: "My God, Nick, I think he's dead."[5]

Hensey told Ciaccio she needed to get a doctor and that she would call him back. "I got on the telephone and got the [hotel] operator and told her I needed a doctor right away, and she tried to locate Mr. Powell's doctor over at the Mayo Clinic, but he wasn't in, and this was Saturday." An assistant manager at the hotel came to the room and started trying to get a doctor to come to the hotel. Ultimately a doctor came and declared Powell dead.

Hensey returned to the phone and called Ciaccio, telling him, "Yes, I know the secretary is dead." She told Ciaccio about Powell's request to empty the file cabinet in his office and give the contents to Rendleman. "Would you do it?" she asked Ciaccio.[6] She was the only person other than Powell who had the combination to the three-drawer file cabinet in the office, and she gave that to Ciaccio. He said, "Do you want me to come up?" and Hensey said yes.

Ciaccio needed a key to gain entry to Powell's office, but the closest one was in the custody of Marilyn Towle, a secretary in Powell's office who was about two hundred miles from Springfield, in Eldorado, northeast of Harrisburg. Ciaccio said he would charter a plane. "I'll get Miss Towle and I'll get her keys. We'll be up in the afternoon," Hensey quoted him as saying.[7]

The three-drawer file cabinet in Powell's office, which Hensey directed Ciaccio to clean out, became an object of intense interest during inquiries after his death and during testimony given by Hensey. Clearly there were sensitive documents in the file cabinet, but there is no evidence that cash was among them. However, these are presumptions because neither Ciaccio nor Hensey made a precise inventory, and no individuals ever were held responsible.

To this day, we have to take on faith that whatever was removed by Ciaccio ultimately was turned over to Rendleman and became part of the estate. All Ciaccio ever said was that he and Towle took two suitcases full of ledgers, a checkbook, and sealed envelopes from the locked cabinet.[8]

Actually, there were two other safes in the secretary of state's office, Hensey said, but they contained official office information and nothing of a personal nature. They never were the object of Powell's request to Hensey. Under questioning, investigators learned that the locked file cabinet contained mostly personal items in red envelopes that tied and around which Hensey had placed rubber bands. She said the cabinet contained securities for his holdings in banks and racetracks, time deposit certificates, and campaign documents and records including receipts, canceled checks, and invoices. Ciaccio told investigators later that the items included a gray ledger, a brown ledger-type book, and fifteen brown envelopes, which most likely were the "red envelopes."

While there was no loose cash in the file, she said, Powell apparently had placed a manila envelope with *M-A-R-G-E* written in the upper right-hand corner in one of the drawers. This contained $55,000 in $100 bills. Hensey recalled after Powell returned from the September Mayo Clinic trip that he was depressed and told her he had put an envelope in his personal file cabinet that "would take care of me until the will was settled."[9] She did not discover the money until the return to Springfield. Although Hensey's claim to this money ultimately was upheld, there were numerous attempts to deny her the funds or otherwise diminish the value to her.

Ciaccio's versions of what happened Saturday afternoon, evening and, early Sunday morning must be weighed carefully. In all, Ciaccio gave at least three different accounts of events. The first occurred in the days immediately after Powell's death. A second variation was given in an interview with a *St. Louis Post-Dispatch* reporter on January 7, 1971, and finally Ciaccio gave a third explanation to Illinois attorney general's investigators on January 8.

Even taking Ciaccio's last account as the real story is risky, because there is little corroborating evidence from other sources. In the days immediately after Powell's death, Ciaccio said that his wife, Towle, and he were in Rochester when Powell died and that they chartered a plane to return to Springfield. He failed to mention a charter plane trip to Rochester, a call from Hensey, or the entering of Powell's office and taking items from the locked file cabinet.[10]

In the second version, which was told to a reporter for the *St. Louis Post-Dispatch* on January 7, Ciaccio said he received the news from Hensey, chartered a plane, and traveled with his wife and Towle to Rochester, then returned to Springfield in the wee hours of Sunday. Amazingly, Ciaccio still did not have the story straight—at least not the story told by Hensey. Ciaccio's second version was that the group returned to Springfield and then removed contents from the file cabinet. He said that between 12:30 and 1 A.M. on Sunday, he, his wife, and three Powell aides went to Powell's Springfield office to remove documents they did not believe should be made public. "To my knowledge there was no cash in the file," he said in response to questions.

Ciaccio's third version—the one that agreed the most with Hensey's—was given to attorney general's investigators in a seventy-five-page statement a day after his conversation with the reporter. The contents of this statement became the basis for a complaint filed by Atty. Gen. William J. Scott against Ciaccio, Hensey, Ciaccio's wife, Powell's driver Emil Saccaro, and Towle to obtain documents that had been taken from the locked file cabinet.

Later confronted by the differing versions, Ciaccio admitted that he lied to keep Powell's memory and Hensey's reputation clean. "What I did for him when he died was the last thing in the world I could have done," Ciaccio said. "I created an impression that I was in Minnesota at the time of the death with my wife, Marilyn Towle and Marge Hensey out of a sense of human charity for a public official," he told a press conference. "I didn't think it would be good reading for eleven million Illinoisans that he was up there with his personal secretary."[11]

Be that as it may, Ciaccio added immeasurably to the confusion for weeks after the death and gave rise to speculation about a conspiracy to conceal documents or remove cash from the file cabinet. Because Ciaccio never implicated anyone else in his lie, the presumption is that he concocted the story on his own. Certainly he took all the blame for the erroneous tale. At no time during the account given by Hensey to state's attorney's investigators did she refer to Ciaccio's initial story, nor did she mention conversation among the principals of October 10 about what story to tell. The net effect of Ciaccio's string of tales is to raise doubt about all of them and shatter his credibility.

After talking to Hensey on the telephone Saturday, Ciaccio said in his January 8 statement that he went about the business of chartering a plane. Nothing was available to charter in Springfield, but he found one plane in St. Louis. The plane picked up Towle in Harrisburg and flew back to Springfield, where Ciaccio and she entered Powell's office, cleaned out the three-drawer file cabinet, and put all those items into two suitcases.

He described the cabinet as "a three-drawer file safe with combination. I think it's really more fireproof, but in any event the contents for the most part consisted of large brown manila envelopes. These were rather bulky and they were all sealed . . . . My recollection was there may have been 15."[12] Ciaccio said he also called Joe Belair, public information person for the secretary of state. "I asked him if he would be available through the day, but I told him I would call him back. I had something to discuss with him, but I didn't say what."

In the version that conformed with Hensey's account, Ciaccio said he, his wife Jean, and Towle were aboard the charter plane when it left for Rochester. The flight from Springfield to Rochester, which began about 3 P.M., took two and a half hours. The group, with the contents from the three-drawer file, arrived at the hotel about 6 P.M..

Ciaccio said he took Towle to Rochester because of her long association with Powell and Hensey: "She had worked for Mr. Powell for about 11 years. She had been closely associated with him . . . for many years past, Miss Towle, Mrs. Hensey, the secretary myself and my wife had attended annually secretary of state's conventions together and I wanted to create the impression that we were all there together rather than have a story which would indicate that he and Mrs. Hensey were up there alone together."[13] According to Hensey, she had not done much while waiting for the Ciaccios and Towle. She described her condition as "dazed."

Ciaccio knew exactly where to go at the hotel. The suite where Powell died was the same suite Ciaccio and Powell had shared three weeks earlier when Powell went for tests. Upon reaching the hotel, Ciaccio placed calls for Gov. Richard B. Ogilvie, he said.[14] Finding the governor was complicated by the weekend timing and by having to conduct the search from out of state. But reaching the governor for an emergency is not extraordinarily difficult any time of day or week, it seems in retrospect. Ciaccio said he tried to call the governor's personal secretary, Judy Allen, without success. He also tried to reach Marion Oglesby, the governor's political aide.

Although Ciaccio said he made an effort to reach Ogilvie Saturday evening, few with an interest in the matter would forget that he had waited more than eight hours after learning of Powell's death to try. The delay underscored the importance that Ciaccio and Hensey placed on getting the items from Powell's file cabinet to Rochester before any officials knew of the death. The delays in notifying officials of the death on October 10 always rankled Ogilvie.

Curious about the documents taken from the file cabinet, Ciaccio reported Hensey as asking if he brought them along. "I said yes, they were in suitcases and were locked up in the plane. I told her that I'd gotten the material and that it was on the plane." The exact location of the suitcases in Rochester never has been resolved between Ciaccio's version and Hensey's. She said the suitcases were brought to the hotel.

Gathered at the hotel, they talked about funeral arrangements and related matters. A funeral director in Rochester was contacted and began working on plans with a funeral director in Vienna for return of the body to Illinois on Sunday. Hensey called Powell's personal physician and told him of Powell's death. Ciaccio arranged for a public information officer in the secretary of state's office to meet them upon the return to Springfield so that a press release could be written and sent.

After several hours together in Rochester, they decided to return to Springfield. Hensey said she signed for the hotel bill, and they took Powell's suitcases and personal belongings, hired a cab, and left for the airport.[15] When asked by interrogators, Hensey could not recall looking at the items Ciaccio brought from Powell's office.

From the outset of official inquiry into Powell's affairs, suspicions existed about the location of the suitcases during the trip to Rochester and back to Springfield and during the time when the suitcases were later at Hensey's home. During Hensey's January testimony, interrogators probed the whereabouts of the suitcases and when they were in or out of her sight or control. According to the principals, the suitcases left Springfield in the hands of Ciaccio on Saturday, were taken off the plane to the hotel in Rochester, then were taken back to the plane three or four hours later.

Back in Springfield, the four took the suitcases to Powell's office and later to the apartment at the St. Nicholas Hotel. Finally, the suitcases were taken from the hotel to Hensey's home. No wonder that the state's attorney asked if Hensey had opened the suitcases, taken inventory, discussed the contents with the others, or carried the suitcases herself.

The interrogators asked about the location of the suitcases when she first saw Ciaccio and others who arrived on the plane. Hensey was vague about the suitcases and could not recall having opened them or checked the contents while they were in Rochester. She could not remember the precise location of the suitcases on the plane and who may have put them on the plane or taken them off. At one point an interrogator asked where the suitcases were placed after they were taken off the airplane in Springfield. Hensey said, "Well, they were placed in the trunk of Nick's car and there could have been some in the back seat because I really don't remember the ride from the airport down to the capitol building." She added that at no time did she handle the suitcases. Hensey said she did not open the suitcases or look at the contents of the safe until the suitcases were taken to her home on Sunday.

Nobody talked on the plane ride to Springfield. They were exhausted and in shock. It was twelve hours after Hensey had found Powell dead, and very few people knew yet what had happened in Rochester.

According to their statements, the quartet—Ciaccio and his wife, Towle, and Hensey—arrived back in Springfield shortly after midnight. They drove to the capitol building, entered on the north side, and walked to Powell's office without registering or being stopped by a guard. Undoubtedly preferring to keep talk to a minimum, they hurried toward Powell's office, down the darkened and deserted hallways of the historic capitol, past the murals and formal portraits of state leaders, the silence broken only by an eerie click, click, click of their shoes and maybe a softly spoken word.

They said no one was at the office when they arrived. After a telephone call by Hensey, they were joined at the office by Emil Saccaro, who had worked for Powell as chauffeur since 1986. When he arrived, Saccaro remembered, Hensey was clearly in charge of operations.[16] According to accounts, Ciaccio placed calls to reach the governor, and he also called for a public information officer in Powell's office to join them and prepare a press release. It never was clear how long the five were in the offices alone.

Here is how Hensey remembers those events in testimony: "Well, Nick went into his office and he placed a call, again trying to get the governor, and he may have called Mr. [Joe] Belair [public information officer] and told him to meet him at such and such a time, because Mr. Belair did get down there and they were going to write up a press release, regardless of whether they could get the governor or not. . . . Belair and Nick were going to get together on it. . . . I don't know if he [Ciaccio] got ahold of Mrs. Kolom [Ogilvie's aide at the mansion] or just who it was, but someone at the mansion, and they said . . . well, that they knew where the governor was and they would have him call back. Then the governor called back."[17]

Hensey said she went to her office and made calls, too, and one of the first, after 1 A.M., was to locate Rendleman. Hensey called his Edwardsville home, and one of his children answered the telephone, then woke the grandmother. She told Hensey that Rendleman and his wife were vacationing in New Orleans, but the grandmother did not know where. She expected Rendleman to call about 9 A.M. Sunday, and she promised Hensey she would give him the message. In her January testimony, Hensey was asked why she had not tried to reach Rendleman earlier. "I guess it just didn't dawn on me," she answered.[18]

Others Hensey said she called in the wee hours of Sunday included Wanda Saccaro, the driver's wife, and Bob Walsh, a Powell friend from Mt. Vernon. She also called "Billy Johnston," a longtime horse racing friend of Powell. "He is connected with Sportsman's Park [in Chicago] and I told Billy because I felt sure the secretary would want him to know and not read it in the paper or hear about it over the radio, and I asked Billy if he would be one of the pallbearers."

This was William H. Johnston Jr., operator of Sportsman's Park and Florida dog tracks. After making calls, Hensey, Towle, and Ciaccio spent time working on a pallbearer list, having apparently discussed it in Rochester.

Hensey also removed a brown envelope containing personal papers of Powell's from her desk drawer and put it with items that later were taken to her home.

Traffic at Powell's office increased substantially as Sunday wore on. Larry Richardson, a top aide in Powell's office, Tom Owens, in charge of government buildings for Powell, and Circuit Judge William H. Chamberlain all came to the office. Then workmen arrived to pack Powell's personal items in the office. Hensey remembered: "They started packing up his mementos like . . . all kinds of them sitting around which were personal, and plaques, and started taking pictures off the walls."

Hensey separated these mementos from two boxes of Powell's income tax forms and papers. She asked Saccaro to deliver the tax materials to her home. Hensey asked Saccaro to take the boxes because she did not trust them in the hands of someone she did not know. Saccaro said he took two of Owens's employees with him, in Owens's car, to deliver boxes containing tax ledgers and personal records to the house. They returned to the capital.[19]

As investigators eventually asked questions later about activities in Powell's office that night, the appearance of Judge Chamberlain came under special scrutiny. Judge Chamberlain did not tell his version of the night in Powell's office until it became public in statements given by Powell's aides in January 1971. At that time he hastened to justify his appearance as advisory to the group of aides, although those present that night said he took an active role in cleaning out Powell's desk. After receiving a telephone call from Hensey about midnight, the judge said he arrived at the offices about 1:10 A.M.: "Mrs. Hensey was opening and closing drawers and cabinets and Ciaccio was on the telephone. Together, they placed a number of large manila envelopes in several big cardboard boxes."[20]

Chamberlain said he stayed about forty minutes, while Ciaccio and Hensey searched through desks and filing cabinets. "I heard Mrs. Hensey tell Ciaccio there was a large amount of money belonging to Powell in Powell's hotel suite in the St. Nicholas Hotel," Chamberlain said. He saw the three-drawer filing cabinet, but he did not remember seeing it open.[21] Saccaro said he saw Chamberlain helping clear out Powell's desk. Chamberlain said, "Mrs. Hensey and Ciaccio asked me a number of questions on what should be done and what is usually done before the appointment of a secretary of state. . . . It wasn't legal advice that I gave them. I gave them some suggestions and told them what the laws were."

Ciaccio asked Chamberlain to call the governor's mansion and pass on word of Powell's death. "After a series of calls I got through to Margaret

Kolom, the mansion secretary, whom I met when Kerner was governor. I passed the word on and I understand Fred Bird, the governor's press secretary, called back about 3 A.M." Ciaccio's version had him making the contact with Bird.

The remaining boxes filled in the dark of early Sunday morning apparently were stored in the capitol basement, then sometime after the middle of October were taken to Hensey's home. She believes there may have been as many as twenty that later were placed in the basement storage area of her condominium. She said boxes with campaign information were taken upstairs to her residence, and she looked through those. When asked if she had destroyed any of Powell's files, Hensey said, yes, that after conferring with Rendleman, she got rid of telegrams, memorial cards, perpetual blessings cards, and thank you letters.

Hensey, Ciaccio, Saccaro, and Towle (Mrs. Ciaccio became ill and went home) stayed at Powell's office until nearly 5 A.M. All others had left, and after turning off the lights, the four went to cars driven by Saccaro and Ciaccio. The time element has always remained vague, in spite of agreement in their accounts. The next destination, directed by Hensey, was the St. Nicholas Hotel and the suite Powell had rented for years.[22] Again, Hensey relied on what Powell apparently told her to do, should something happen to him. In this case, Powell said there were two metal containers and two briefcases in the apartment closet that she was to retrieve and deliver to Rendleman.

Because Hensey had a key to the apartment, they did not stop at the hotel desk but went directly to the elevator and took it to the fifth floor. She told investigators that Powell and she were the only people who had keys to the outer door. Ciaccio, Saccaro, Towle—who was going to stay the night at Hensey's duplex—and Hensey entered Powell's apartment. Hensey located his key to the closet door in the bedroom, and while the others remained in the outer apartment room, she opened the closet door. The movements of the group in the apartment and the report by Hensey about what she saw and took from the closet had serious implications for future investigators. As far as is known, they were the only people in the apartment before John Rendleman opened the closet on Tuesday afternoon.

This is how Hensey described to the grand jury her actions upon entering the apartment: "I went into the bedroom and then I went through his [Powell's] key case and found the key to the closet. I opened the closet, there were two briefcases, he had told me that there were some briefcases, he didn't tell me what was in them. . . . I think he might have said 'I've got a little money,' I don't really remember. I took the briefcases and I got a metal box, and then I called Mr. Saccaro because I felt another metal box, and he had some whiskey, cases of whiskey, stored and I asked Mr. Saccaro if he would move the whiskey. I said 'I think there is a box there' and he came in and he felt, and he got the box out and he put the whiskey back."

She recalled that the closet was about the normal size for a hotel room. There were three or four cases of whiskey there, some items of clothing on hangers, and the objects that Powell had said would be there: two metal boxes, two briefcases, and a tote bag. The metal boxes were about the size of an average safe deposit box. She looked to see what else might be in the closet. She got a chair and stood on it to see if there were any items on the shelf, and there were none. State's attorney investigators asked if she saw any cardboard boxes the size of the metal boxes in the closet. "No, sir, I never even really looked."

She said there were some things on the closet floor, but she didn't pay much attention. "I just took what he had told me to take." Before leaving the apartment, she took a small television that she said Powell had told her she could have. All this activity was accomplished quickly. "I don't think we were there over fifteen minutes."

Saccaro's version agreed on most points with Hensey's: "She went into the bedroom and summoned me minutes later. She told me to remove two strongboxes hidden behind a pile of liquor cases in the small closet. Then she took the strongboxes and I left the bedroom. I did not see what she did with the strongboxes, but I did carry suitcases out of that room that were big enough to hold them." Ciaccio said they had taken a suitcase to the hotel room. Saccaro disagreed: "We just carried things out. Three of us stood around doing little else while Mrs. Hensey packed in the bedroom." He never saw strongboxes open and did not see any money after giving the strongboxes to Hensey.

They left in two cars—Hensey could not remember in which they put the items from Powell's closet—and went to Hensey's home. When they unloaded the cars, the items left in her living room included the two suitcases Ciaccio had filled with items from the locked file cabinet; the suitcases taken from the Rochester hotel room; the two boxes Saccaro had delivered with tax forms; and the metal boxes, briefcases, and tote bag from the closet. She recalled there wasn't much room left in her living room when all the items were placed there. Saccaro reported that Ciaccio, Towle, and he left Hensey's immediately, and he got home about 7 A.M.: "I took my orders from them. It was my job. They were my bosses and I didn't question it."[23]

In about twenty hours, these friends, associates, confidantes, and companions of Paul Powell had seen their lives flash before them. They had lost their boss, protector, and dear friend, one of the most influential people in the state of Illinois. They faced probable unemployment because a replacement would be appointed by a Republican governor. They were left to explain the actions of a man whom they loved but about whom they had less than full information.

Rather than thinking for themselves, they characterized their moves for those hours as having been almost entirely influenced by the words of a dead man. He had told them to take items from the file cabinet and make sure certain items were taken from the closet at his hotel apartment. All those things they had gathered in his name were to be delivered to Rendleman. If we believe what they said, the four did not know what was in the containers, and they did not make inventories.

Rendleman and his wife were in New Orleans on a brief vacation and were staying at the Royal Orleans Hotel. They actually had started toward New Orleans several days before from St. Louis, on a barge excursion down the Mississippi River with another couple, Mel and Zella Lockard of Mattoon.[24] Zella and Rendleman were cousins. After a few days on the barge, the Rendlemans left the Lockards and the barge at Memphis and flew on to New Orleans, where they intended to meet again and fly back to Illinois. Lockard, then president of the First National Bank of Mattoon and a longtime friend and associate of Powell, heard about the death several days later in a telephone conversation with Rendleman. Lockard's bank eventually was named to administer trusts set up by Powell's will.

About 9:30 Sunday morning, Rendleman took a telephone call from his secretary at Southern Illinois University in Edwardsville. She had been called by the mother of Mrs. Rendleman, who was staying at the family home with the Rendleman children. After that telephone call, Rendleman called Hensey in Springfield and learned firsthand of Powell's death. Before the day was over, the two talked several times, mostly about funeral arrangements and pallbearers, according to their testimony.

During one of the Sunday conversations with Hensey, Rendleman said he asked if she had been to the hotel and had retrieved items from the closet. "She said yes, so I seemed quite relieved and proceeded very leisurely back to Illinois," Rendleman recalled.[25] Some years earlier, Rendleman remembered, Powell and he were sitting in the St. Nicholas Hotel apartment having a drink before attending an office Christmas party hosted by Powell. "He told me as we started out to go to the party that I was executor of his will and that if anything should ever happen to him that he kept a little cash in the closet for emergencies."

He made only one other telephone call on Sunday regarding Powell's death. That was to his father, Ford Rendleman, seeking legal advice about his responsibilities as executor. That night the Rendlemans had dinner in New Orleans with friends from New Orleans, and during the evening, they discussed the turn of events. On Monday the Rendlemans, still not in contact with many people about Powell's death, left New Orleans and flew back to Edwardsville.

After sleeping for just an hour Sunday morning, Hensey said she took a telephone call from Rendleman and told him about Powell's death in Rochester. When Rendleman asked her to go to the hotel room and look for money, she said, "John, I've already been over there." They also talked about funeral services, and he accepted her invitation to serve as a pallbearer at the Tuesday service. Hensey said she spent the rest of Sunday greeting friends and callers at her home and meeting with the funeral director from Vienna, who had flown to Springfield to take the body to Vienna.

Details about what Hensey and Rendleman did on Monday are sketchy, other than general information about Rendleman's return trip and that Hensey, resting at her home from the ordeal of Saturday and Sunday, took telephone calls and talked to well-wishers. Acting on Rendleman's request, she made arrangements for movers to meet him at the St. Nicholas Hotel apartment on Tuesday.

To interrogators, she steadfastly denied looking through the boxes, files, and suitcases that filled her living room. If she thought there was money in them, she never indicated any curiosity or that she even peaked to see what they contained. This behavior seemed almost abnormal to those who questioned her or speculated about what happened in her home.

Adding to the confusion over whether she looked through the boxes was her testimony later about finding the envelope—containing $55,000—that Powell had marked with the letters M-A-R-G-E. This is how she explained to investigators finding the money on Monday night: "I got a box, I believe was on Monday night, and I had some of these file boxes, several of them at home, and I got one and emptied the contents into them. I didn't look through them to see what they were, because I figured they were . . . I did take this one brown envelope that Mr. Powell had, that had the $55,000 in it." She put the envelope in a desk drawer and later put it in a bank safe deposit box.[26]

First news accounts of Powell's death were broadcast on Sunday, and initial newspaper accounts appeared on Monday. From the first, there were suspicions about the accuracy of information and speculation about the action of Powell's associates. Ted McCoy was working on the air at a Springfield radio station when a one-paragraph statement came over the Associated Press wire announcing Powell's death. Within an hour after reading the bulletin on the air, McCoy remembers taking a telephone call. A caller in a gruff voice asked two questions: "Is it true Paul Powell has died"? and "Have they found the money yet?"[27]

Newspapers carried the traditional obituary information and recounted highlights of Powell's career. Governor Ogilvie and Lt. Gov. Paul Simon issued statements that skirted controversy and political history. "His death marks the passing of an era," Ogilvie said. "The state has lost a loyal servant whose outstanding record of service will be very difficult to equal." Simon, who clashed repeatedly with Powell during legislative battles, said, "Paul Powell, for nearly four decades, was in the forefront of nearly every battle that has brought help to the helpless and given hope to our young and old." It was time to speak well of the dead.

Other articles appearing on Monday questioned events of Saturday and Sunday and reported rumors of files being taken from the secretary of state's office. The *St. Louis Post-Dispatch* noted that after receiving anonymous reports of files being taken away, Illinois Bureau of Investigation agents monitored Powell's offices. The same account referred to events in Rochester on Saturday and quoted Ciaccio in his first version. He said the delay in reporting Powell's death occurred because of the inability to inform Governor Ogilvie. The news article identified Ciaccio as "one of four persons who discovered the secretary's body."

Picking up on the inference that Ogilvie was not reachable until early Sunday morning, an aide to the governor demurred, saying the governor was easily within reach of the aide to Powell. Ogilvie's schedule revealed that he was in Chicago that day. During the afternoon, he attended a football game at Northwestern University. From there he went to a political rally at a downtown Chicago hotel and then retired around midnight in a suite at the Bismarck Hotel. The first call from Ciaccio was recorded by the governor's aide at 7:30 P.M. Saturday, but the caller did not say Powell had died. "All he said was that he had an important announcement to make and needed to get in touch with the governor," the aide said.

On Tuesday, dozens of elected and appointed state and local officials throughout Illinois began three days of mourning the death of Paul Powell. There were memorial services Tuesday in Springfield, a day for moving the body to Vienna, and final services and burial on Thursday. On Monday and until services Tuesday at the state capitol, Powell's body lay in state while thousands of citizens filed past. Ciaccio had suggested the public visitation to Ogilvie, who approved.

Powell's friends, associates, and political enemies paid their respects and went on praising his record of public service. Mayor Richard J. Daley of Chicago called Powell "a leader of men. He loved politics and was proud to be called a politician." Speaker after speaker referred to his touch with the common man, his loyalty to southern Illinois, and his word of honor. Ogilvie said: "No handshake was necessary; only his plain statement of his intentions. And he could always be counted on—always—to honor the commitment he made."[28]

Paul Simon, then lieutenant governor, tells of a conversation with Mayor Daley at the services in Vienna two days later, which puts a different cast on the mayor's attitude about Powell: "There I am talking to Daley next to the open casket. Daley said, 'You know I believe if you're honest, then the people below you are going to be honest.' He said Powell took money and everybody took money. I thought Powell would rise up at that moment."

Rendleman left Edwardsville on Tuesday morning and drove to Springfield in his father's car. There he met with a number of Powell aides and associates, and he saw Marge Hensey for the first time since Powell's death. After the services, they talked briefly. They agreed to meet and dismantle the Powell hotel apartment later that day, and she gave him keys to the apartment.[29] Rendleman learned later that the hotel had changed the locks. Hensey also gave Rendleman a wad of bills—later said to total $6,600—that she had carried with her since leaving the hotel in Rochester. Rendleman soon would see much more of Powell's cash.

After the services, Hensey completed duties at the capitol and went to the St. Nicholas Hotel, where she ate lunch in the dining room. Meanwhile, according to his testimony, Rendleman had arrived about 12:30 P.M. and had been let into the apartment by an assistant hotel manager. Afterward, Rendleman repeatedly told investigators he was alone in the apartment about fifteen minutes before an inspector for the secretary of state's office arrived. In that time, Rendleman said he found the suite in a mess, and he started to straighten it up. A final inventory of the suite and storage area turned up 49 cases of whiskey, 14 transistor radios, 154 shirts, and two cases of canned corn.

Rendleman recalled: "Mr. Powell was kind of a pack-rat; he had *Reader's Digest*s from ten years back, the sofa was full of shirts—there were things all over the apartment and I tried to figure out what best to save and what we could dispose of. Eventually I went to the closet."[30] Shortly after arrival of the inspector, movers arrived and began packing Powell's belongings for shipment to Vienna.

Hensey went to the apartment after eating, arriving about the time that Rendleman started looking in the closet. He apparently was in the apartment about an hour before opening the closet door. There he found cases of whiskey, and clothes. For state investigators, Rendleman later explained his actions this way: "When the first [whiskey] case was removed, I saw the shoe box, and I thought that strange because I'd seen good shoes kept in the bedroom which we had packed. I opened the shoe box and I saw it stacked with money and became frightened. . . . As I recall I got a shirt box and put the shoe box in the shirt box, and the shirt box on the bed, and then became doubly concerned that there might be even additional ones, which there were."[31]

Hensey remembered when she first learned of the cash: "Well, we talked just general conversation because there were movers in and out, I mean, nothing of a personal nature was discovered until he said—he called me into the bedroom, and he said, 'My God, look what I found.' And he opened a shoe box and I was just amazed and I believe he had found another container or so, a metal box."[32] It was similar to the metal boxes she had taken from the closet Sunday morning. In fact, little of the money was actually in shoe boxes, contrary to common belief. Rendleman found the cash stuffed in strong boxes, a leather briefcase, and loose envelopes.

Rendleman, in testimony to Internal Revenue Service agents and investigators for the Illinois Bureau of Investigations, said he was staggered by the discovery—he thought Hensey had removed anything which contained money—and immediately he began to pile the items on Powell's bed and conceal them from view by others in the suite. "I began to take it out of the closet and put it on the bed with some other things, then I began to gather some other personal effects of his so that just boxes sitting there wouldn't look unusual." He told the movers he would take care of those items personally.

Hensey was just as shocked, she remembered. Rendleman had found containers in a closet she thought had been cleaned out on Sunday morning: "I presumed they [the containers] would have been on the floor, maybe behind something that wasn't moved out, because I did look on the shelf and there was nothing on the shelf." While Rendleman's and Hensey's accounts compare well, there is no explanation for how the money got to the hotel suite, or when. The presumption from their testimony is that Powell must have placed the money there for others to find. Longtime friends and associates of Powell found that unlikely. Once again, there is nothing on the record to counter the stories by Hensey and Rendleman, and they offered no response to speculation.

After collecting their wits, Rendleman and Hensey began an afternoon-long process of dodging movers and well-wishers who came to the suite, consolidating the money in shirt boxes and putting them in his father's car, which was parked on the street. Rendleman called it playing "hide and seek." Asked by investigators how many trips he made, Rendleman said: "I frankly went into a state of shock. . . . I can't tell you the sequence of events. It seemed to me my duty then was to try and get this money and get it into a safe place."[33]

By about 7 o'clock, the movers had finished their work, and Hensey and Rendleman had taken all the money to the car. They locked up the suite and prepared to take the car to her duplex and put together all the items she had taken from the closet with those they found Tuesday afternoon. A heavy rainstorm had hit the Springfield area, Rendleman remembered for investigators, adding an element of gloom.

When the two walked to the street just north of the hotel, they discovered the car—a white Cadillac—was gone. Rendleman had parked it in a zone where no parking was permitted from 4 to 6 P.M. Police had towed the car away with all the money in the trunk. Rendleman very nearly panicked, but he recovered quickly and realized the police had towed the illegally parked car. Hensey called a taxi to go home, and after Rendleman called the police station, he took a cab there. The complications had only begun. "I identified the car, and of course I had some concern about that since it was my father's car and I did not have the registration with me." But he identified the car and gave the license number and they released the car to him. He paid a $15 towing charge.[34]

Rendleman remembered taking the cab to a remote unlighted part of Springfield where the car was parked. Nervous beyond belief, Rendleman told the taxi driver to wait while he found the car and got in, without checking to see if the money was still in the trunk. He drove to Hensey's house, arriving about 8 P.M. When asked later why they agreed to take the newly found cash to Hensey's house, Rendleman said the intent was to put it with the containers Hensey had removed on Sunday. Also, the secretary of state's office had stationed a guard at her house since Sunday, and Rendleman believed that provided security. He was not asked by investigators if he thought of taking the money straight to a banker or to some official for counting.

Here is what Rendleman and Hensey faced after what must have been some of the most incredible eight hours of their lives—for Hensey, even eclipsing the twenty-four hours after Powell was discovered dead. According to their testimony, they had discovered an unbelievable amount of cash in the hotel apartment, had lost it, found it again, and now they wanted to count it.

Hensey had returned to her home first, and already it was full of friends giving comfort and reminiscing about Powell. When Rendleman arrived at Hensey's duplex, he found people visiting and a security agent from the secretary of state's office in the house. Rendleman opened the trunk of the car and began taking the containers of money into the kitchen, where he put them on the kitchen table. Hensey joined him, and they locked the door to the kitchen and began to count the money, just a few feet from friends of Powell. As incredible as it seems, there is no indication that anyone, including the security guard, had an inkling of what was occurring in the kitchen.

There were two hurdles to clear before the two could accomplish their counting task. First was the sheer volume of money and the time that would be required to count it, without people discovering them. Second, the only way to the bathroom was through the kitchen. Rendleman explained to investigators how the rooms were organized: "The kitchen is off the dining room. The real point is to get to the bathroom from the living room, you have to go through the kitchen. So when anyone had to use the bathroom, then we had to bundle this stuff all up again and put it away so that it couldn't be seen."[35]

Hensey described under oath what she remembered happened in the kitchen: "Well, I got the containers I had obtained from the hotel, and brought them out and Mr. Rendleman got the keys and started going through them to find the ones that opened the containers. He was going to count the money and then he decided it was going to be too much of a job and he said he was going to get ahold of somebody at the bank."[36] She remembered there were four containers and two briefcases. They had commingled the money she had brought to her home on Sunday and the money Rendleman brought from the hotel. There was never any way to determine how much was found on Saturday and Sunday and how much was found on Tuesday.

The account of Rendleman's activity at Hensey's home and afterward comes from testimony on two formal occasions, during which his stories were virtually the same. Shortly after arriving at Hensey's, Rendleman called the home of A. D. VanMeter, president of Illinois National Bank in Springfield and a friend. VanMeter's wife told Rendleman her husband was at a Cub Scout meeting and would not return until about 9:30 P.M.

Adding to the pressure at the Hensey duplex was the knowledge that she planned to drive to Vienna that night for services on Thursday. She expected Saccaro and his wife and Marilyn Towle to pick her up at the home soon for the drive to Vienna. "We could be here all night" counting the money, Rendleman said. At that point, he put the money back in the containers and closed them. They had not spent much time counting the money.

Rendleman tried to reach VanMeter again, and he still had not returned. "I'm coming right out on a matter of some importance," he said he told Mrs. VanMeter. He took the containers back to his car and drove to VanMeter's house. The banker had arrived, and Rendleman took one container into the home and showed him the money. "Look, look at all this," Rendleman said. They agreed the money had to be put in a safe place. VanMeter called a bank employee and asked him to meet them at the bank. Then he drove his own car and Rendleman drove his father's to the bank, arriving about 10 P.M. They put the money in a vault and left, after agreeing to meet the next morning at the bank to count the money.[37]

Rendleman drove to the St. Nicholas Hotel, where he went to the fifth floor apartment of Powell and entered. He stayed the night.

Many weeks after these events, political critics accused Rendleman of rushing to put the money in the bank instead of waiting and recording serial numbers. After consulting with VanMeter and with attorney and friend Robert Oxtoby, they all agreed that the prudent step was to get the money in a safe place. "This was a matter of mutual discussion, that as long as we kept that money intact and as long as it wasn't accounted for, there would always be the question as to how much there really was, and the best thing to do was to take it and deposit it," Rendleman said. He never explained why that thought had not guided his actions before Tuesday night.

On Wednesday morning, Rendleman met at the bank with VanMeter and Oxtoby, the bank controller, and three tellers, selected by VanMeter, to count the money. An account for "John Rendleman, Trustee"—he was not yet appointed executor—was opened at the bank. Oxtoby, who participated in the counting, had been an assistant U.S. attorney and was familiar with federal inquiries. He knew the IRS would want all evidence possible of the money. "I told the people who were counting the money to save the straps around the bills, to save everything that there was." Oxtoby told those at the bank to preserve all evidence, including suitcases and the shoe box.

Before the counting was concluded, Rendleman left for the drive to Vienna, where he planned to attend the wake that night and services on

Thursday, at which he was a pallbearer. He arrived in Vienna about 3 P.M. and filed the will in Johnson County Circuit Court; after two hours there, he called VanMeter for an accounting. The cash amounted to $654,844, of which $567,900 was in $100 bills.[38]

That did not surprise Saccaro, who said, "$100 bills ran in the Powell family." Apparently Daisy Powell often stayed in Powell's Chicago apartment, and every time he visited, he would give her shopping money. But Daisy rarely went shopping. "She never needed for anything," Saccaro said. After her death in 1967, Powell went through her closets in the Chicago apartment. Saccaro stated, "I think she had 38 $100 bills pinned inside of her sweaters."[39]

Unofficially, Rendleman had been executor of the Powell estate since Powell's death in Rochester, and every action he took was done as an officer of the court, although he had not officially been appointed. Nonetheless, every step had to be viewed later as an act of authority and responsibility. He discussed the role of executor with his father, Ford, on Sunday, and on Wednesday morning before the counting of money began, he talked with VanMeter and Oxtoby. They agreed that in order to avoid potential liabilities and tax claims, Rendleman should take precautions to preserve the assets of the estate.[40]

Although Powell's hotel apartment had been searched thoroughly, he also maintained an apartment in Chicago and a home in Vienna. Having found $654,844 at one location, Rendleman said in testimony that he feared there might be substantial cash at the others. If the hotel find were made public, Rendleman thought there was a chance other locations would be ransacked. He mentioned this often as justification for waiting to announce the cash horde. Rendleman said that he and his advisers concluded that no public disclosure would be made until he had searched the other premises.

His advisers also pointed out to Rendleman that he was not officially appointed as executor. He said later: "My obligation was to make a thorough, honest accounting and inventory of the Powell estate. It would have weakened my ability to meet that obligation if I had publicized the fact of the $800,000 prematurely in order to avoid subsequent criticism."

Thus Rendleman, an attorney having consulted other attorneys, decided on a legal strategy, without serious concern for public reaction or the counsel of top elected officials in Illinois. Curiously, this was the action of an experienced political operative who had worked in the public arena for nearly two decades. Because of this decision, Rendleman learned the hard way that secrecy, even in the name of prudence, is a liability in the court of public opinion.

Rendleman wrote a first will for Powell in 1960, just before the Democratic National Convention in Los Angeles—at which John F. Kennedy was nominated for president. Powell feared for his life on a plane trip to California, although he said his wife Daisy was more fearful, and he wanted a will drawn. Rendleman complied—and revised the will frequently over the years. Rendleman told investigators: "I made that will, and Mr. Powell began to treat his will as a kind of biography. He'd change it every little bit. He'd get mad at somebody and take them out, or he'd get happy with somebody and put them in, and get happier with somebody and up their amount, writing and rewriting wills all the time."[41] When Daisy died in 1967, Rendleman handled legal affairs for her estate, which turned out to be a prelude to an estate decision by Powell. In 1969 Rendleman wrote the final will for Powell and was told that he had been named executor.

Rendleman's reaction to being chosen was prescient. He objected to the selection and screwed up his courage to confront Powell. He told his friend, "I am chancellor of the university now, I have moved away from the area and maybe you'd rather have someone down there [southern Illinois]." Powell said he trusted Rendleman and thought it would be nice to have a chancellor as an executor, and besides, Powell inferred, he had done Rendleman favors for which he should be remembered.[42] "When Mrs. Hensey called me and told me he had died, she indicated that he had the will with him and that I was the executor."

While cast in the primary role in the post-death drama, Rendleman claimed to have been something less than a close associate of Powell through the years. Associates of the two and those familiar with public affairs activities in behalf of Southern Illinois University over the years disclaimed Rendleman's version. Nonetheless, Rendleman insisted that he was a distant admirer who only occasionally had contact with Powell.

As Rendleman told in testimony, the two families were acquainted first through Powell and Ford Rendleman, the father, who were Democratic politicians in adjoining southern Illinois counties. They were not close, the son said. John Rendleman and Powell became better acquainted beginning in 1951, when Rendleman joined SIU as assistant professor of government and acting legal counsel after graduation from the University of Illinois College of Law. In that position, Rendleman began to do the legislative work for the university under President Delyte Morris.[43]

Mel Lockard, who served on the SIU Board of Trustees during Powell's years in the legislature, praised Rendleman's service to the university: "He was one of the smartest boys we ever had in the organization. . . . He was a good lawyer and a good lobbyist."

Rendleman liked Powell, especially his homespun humor and folksiness. The relationship prospered when they worked together on legislation: "I would draft legislation for him or give him advice as a young lawyer. You know about young lawyers; they are the smartest lawyers in the world, and I talked to him in that way." After he became Powell's estate lawyer, they saw each other socially but not frequently, according to Rendleman. After Powell's death, Rendleman said: "I've been to one football game with him. I've been to a dinner a couple of times. I've been to his Christmas party. We were friends, but we were not bosom buddies."[44] Those who watched the two at work suggested a much closer personal friendship.

Whether the course he had already set ever caused him second or third thoughts is not known. Rendleman conducted his duties as executor as he saw them, and eventually, when he had to put his reputation and career on the line, he did it. By the time of Powell's funeral service and burial in Vienna, Rendleman had decided not to make the discovery of cash public for some length of time. This act alone tied him ever closer to the four associates of Powell who staggered through the hours after Powell's death.

Whatever the four had done or not done, Rendleman's actions, his story, and his conduct put him in the same category with them. The suspicions and whispers that have persisted down through the decades blackened them all. Something tied them together—maybe nothing more than extreme loyalty to Paul Powell.

During the next days after the funeral in Vienna, Rendleman tended to a mixture of executor duties and responsibilities as chancellor of SIU at Edwardsville. In Vienna he sorted assets of Powell. He deposited $6,100 of Powell's money in a trust account for immediate expenses of the estate. He started an inventory of the assets. On October 26, Rendleman met with John A. Stelle, son of the former governor and Powell associate, about racetrack holdings.[45]

After the funeral and before public disclosure of the cash discovery, Rendleman said he and Hensey spoke occasionally on the telephone but saw each other just a few times. Those conversations were related to additional money found by Hensey and turned over to Rendleman for deposit. While this appears there was some distance between the two, that apparently was only on the surface. Rendleman acknowledged subsequently that he felt a responsibility for her well-being, based on her closeness to Powell.

In testimony to the IRS, Rendleman explained his watchfulness this way: "Mr. Powell had told me during his lifetime, and this had been two years ago, that Marge Hensey had been very good to him and that if anything should ever happen to him, treat her like she's my wife. He made it clear to me that she had been an important person in the last years of his life." When queried about why he called her with regularity, Rendleman told investigators he tried to console her.

Curiously, though, Hensey kept her own counsel on some matters. One was knowledge of the $55,000 Powell had put in an envelope for her. At the time of the funeral, Hensey had put the money in a bank safe deposit box and had not mentioned it to the executor. He learned of the money in newspaper accounts in January. "Mr. Powell had told me that on occasions he gave Mrs. Hensey money and Mrs. Hensey indicated, at one point when I was consoling her, that she was out of work and that she did have money that Paul had given her, but there was no discussion, specific amounts or anything of that nature," Rendleman said.

If Rendleman thought there might be other cash in Powell's apartment in Chicago or his home in Vienna, that was not so. One report about the Chicago apartment said that all they found were two cases of canned cream-style corn, minus four cans. Powell friend Lockard wrote, "We never knew whether Paul ate the corn cold or had it heated or ate it out of the can or what the hell happened, but he had two cases minus four cans." Subsequent amounts of money did surface, causing Rendleman no end of distress.

The first occasion was a few days after the funeral, when Hensey started going through the boxes that contained Powell's personal items and papers. She found a cardboard box similar to those in which they had found the money in Powell's apartment, and it contained more cash. She called Rendleman, who exclaimed, "My God, I'll come right up and deposit it." On October 27 he went to Hensey's home again and retrieved the box, which they agreed must have been overlooked in their haste the night of October 13. A deposit made in the First National Bank of Springfield that day was for $90,050, of which $69,000 was in $100 bills.[46] A day later he added another attorney to the estate team, East St. Louis lawyer and friend Joseph Lowery.

Rendleman's routine at Edwardsville was shattered again within a few days, when Hensey called on November 9 to report finding additional money. This time she had discovered money among items taken from Powell's office file cabinet that had been among the boxes stored at Hensey's home.[47] Rattled at another discovery, Rendleman told Hensey to look through Powell's items and make sure this was the last.

He drove to her house in Springfield on November 10 and was presented with two accordion-type folders. One was marked "Five Years of Progress," and the other was unmarked. They determined the "Five Years" file contained contributions to a political fund-raiser held by Powell. The other file was assumed to be miscellaneous cash. Rendleman went through the now familiar procedure of depositing the money in VanMeter's bank, with Oxtoby as witness. The deposit for "Five Years" was $6,919, and the unmarked cash deposit was $48,924, of which $31,000 was in $100 bills.[48] The total amount of unidentified cash attributed to Powell now totaled $800,419.

No further cash was found that could be said was from the hotel closet or the locked file cabinet in Powell's office—or was discovered in the first days after his death. As time passed, Rendleman must have relaxed in the knowledge that he had exhausted all sources of additional cash. As it turned out, he was wrong.

Sometime after the second telephone call from Hensey about newly found money, Rendleman testified he received a telephone call from Mrs. Winifred Morris at University City, Missouri, a niece of Daisy Powell and an heir to Powell's estate. Rendleman said Mrs. Morris told him of one more location where he should look for money: Powell's home in Vienna. Rendleman already had searched the house three times looking for any sign of loose cash, without success. But Mrs. Morris insisted that Daisy had told her that she kept money in a closet between the two bedrooms. He told her he had been through the closet at least twice without finding anything.

Rendleman and his attorney, Lowery, were in Vienna on Saturday, January 16, shortly after talking to Mrs. Morris. Rendleman went back to the closet. He removed all the quilts, all the bedding, and everything else in the closet, but then he saw what looked like a board. He explained, "When I got everything out I could remove the board and I saw some additional quilts covering a lockbox." He found the combination to the lock and opened it. "I found myself in the very unusual position of not wanting to find any more money—I just didn't want to find any more money, but there was $3,000 in it."

The bills were in small denominations, and some of the cash was in an envelope marked "Easter, 1955."[49] More careful than before, Rendleman and Lowery recorded the serial numbers and took the bills in the lockbox to the Drovers State Bank in Vienna. That was the last time Rendleman found cash that Powell had stashed.

According to Rendleman's accounting of time spent on the estate, he worked almost every day during November and December on duties as executor. The estate value grew relentlessly, as he discovered Powell's holdings in bank accounts, bank stocks, and racetrack stocks. The unraveling of Powell's affairs, including determining what stock he had listed in the names of others, took time. After he had become Powell's lawyer in the early 1960s, Rendleman remembered telling Powell and Daisy that they should make a list of their assets and put it in a safe deposit box. They made up the lists, and he remembered that the estate amount at that time was about $575,000. Even with that information and knowledge of some of Powell's financial affairs, Rendleman testified that he was surprised by the size of the estate.

On December 2, Oxtoby, working as attorney for the estate, filed a preliminary tax notice with the IRS. After conferring with Rendleman, Oxtoby determined the value, including the $800,000 in cash, at $2,100,000.[50] Oxtoby wrote on the bottom of the report to the IRS: "These are preliminary figures, no appraisal of certificates has been made." The estimate turned out to be far short of the final inventory.

Although more and more people became aware of large amounts of cash being found and the increasing size of the estate, Rendleman kept quiet when it came to the press. He also was careful with whom he talked among public officials. There were only two highly placed elected state officials who knew of the cash discovery. On November 7, Oxtoby and Illinois Atty. Gen. William J. Scott attended the Regional Conference of United States Attorneys in Springfield. Oxtoby met with Scott and VanMeter at the Illinois National Bank, where Oxtoby told Scott of the Powell money.[51]

Before the November 3 elections in 1970, Rendleman and Lt. Gov. Paul Simon talked, according to Simon. Rendleman asked if Simon remembered a conversation the two of them had previously in Rendleman's apartment in Carbondale. Rendleman said that Simon had called Powell a crook, and Rendleman vehemently denied the accusation, Simon remembered.

Rendleman then said, according to Simon, he was calling to say Simon had been right about Powell. The executor then told Simon of finding the cash at the St. Nicholas Hotel. Simon said later: "John said there was a strong feeling that Powell had stashed more cash other places, and he wanted to know if I could suggest some spots to look. The only thing I replied was that I thought he should go through Powell's house in Vienna. John also said that day that he was going to inform Scott, but also asked him not to say anything about it."[52]

Rendleman later said only three people outside the inner circle knew of Powell's cash, and one was Scott. He identified the third as Clyde Choate, longtime southern Illinois politician and Powell associate.

As December wore on, there was less justification for Rendleman to keep the Powell cash secret, and official agencies such as the IRS were showing increased interest in the estate. Rendleman decided to put his full version of the story in print by confiding in a journalist he knew and trusted, rather than call a press conference. He never fully explained why he gave the story to one newspaper first, but control of information must have been one reason.

John C. Gardner was editor and publisher of the *Southern Illinoisan* in Carbondale, home of the main campus of Southern Illinois University. Gardner, a respected journalist and businessman, maintained a visible image in the community and among newspaper people across the state. The *Southern Illinoisan*, a daily newspaper, was owned by Lindsay-Schaub newspapers, with headquarters in Decatur. The chain also owned papers in Decatur, Edwardsville, Champaign-Urbana, and East St. Louis. Rendleman knew that all those papers would pick up the story from the *Southern Illinoisan*, and he would have his story told across the state.

Although Gardner and Rendleman were acquainted, the relationship was not extraordinary. Gardner was a newspaperman, and Rendleman was a highly placed official of the university. "We knew each other through business, but also he had included me on a dinner list or two at his home and had stopped by my home from time to time to discuss university or community matters," Gardner recalled.[53]

If Rendleman trusted Gardner, the publisher respected Rendleman. "He was a skilled politician, sometimes mentioned as a potential governor, and obviously was close to Powell. . . . He was, in my mind, never regarded as shady, but was regarded as clever," Gardner said. "I always considered Rendleman honest."

On Saturday, December 26, Gardner and his wife Ann entertained a number of friends and acquaintances at a holiday open house. Rendleman and his wife were invited, and they came. At one point during the evening, Rendleman asked Gardner to step into the kitchen with him. There, while guests wandered about, Rendleman said he had come to Gardner with his story because he knew and trusted him to handle it completely and fairly, Gardner said later. Gardner did not want to take notes in front of guests, so he listened intently as Rendleman spoke.

"He pledged me to silence until he had a chance to make another search of Powell property in Vienna, expressing concern that the townfolk would tear the place apart if they thought there was more stashed away there," Gardner stated.[54] Gardner's wife, seeing the two men whispering in the kitchen, reminded Gardner he was not a very good host, "before I explained to her what was going on."

Rendleman said he would let Gardner know when the story could be published. Gardner did speak to Rendleman at least once more by telephone to clarify a few points. Gardner recalled: "He answered all my questions. It was my choice to tell the story as it was written, not having taken sufficient notes there in the kitchen to use many, if any direct quotes." Gardner asked Rendleman in the kitchen if he gave any thought just to pocketing the $800,000 once he could find no records to trace its source. "He smiled and said the thought had crossed his mind, but, still smiling, said he just knew that if he did, someone somewhere would turn up a notebook describing each dollar, its source and its purpose."[55]

Meanwhile, Gardner waited, fearing that the story might break elsewhere before Rendleman gave him approval. On Tuesday, December 29, Rendleman called to say he had made the visit to Vienna and had not found any more money. They spoke for two hours, and Rendleman gave more details of the story. Gardner could publish the account. The *Southern Illinoisan* was an afternoon newspaper, and the articles by Gardner appeared Wednesday afternoon.[56] Gardner had the exclusive story of his career. Rendleman had his story out in his words, eighty-one days after the death of Paul Powell.

As to why Rendleman chose Gardner, the editor wrote: "He told me he came to me because he felt he knew me and that I would handle the story both completely and fairly. He wanted to get it all out at one time in one place. He expressed concern over bits and pieces leaking out, increasing the chance of error. And he felt that getting it all out at one time in one publication would assure at least that the initial story would be complete, something that a news conference would not guarantee, and it would have more credibility than a statement he might draft."[57]

Over the years Gardner has contemplated Rendleman's story. "I never reached any conclusion about Rendleman having any more involvement in the episode than he shared with me. I am sure Rendleman had his theories, as many did, about the source of the money. But he never shared those theories with me. . . . If he was aware of Powell's activities beyond what he told, I know not."[58]

The account as related by the editor was the same story that Rendleman told thereafter until his death from cancer in 1976, whether in sworn testimony, press conferences, or interviews. The details varied little, and Rendleman refused to make excuses for waiting nearly three months to tell the story.

The *Southern Illinoisan*'s articles started a firestorm of reaction accompanied by speculation and gossip across the state, along with the predictable political sniping. The day after publication, Rendleman spent six hours answering telephone calls about the estate; on December 31 he spent four hours talking to news reporters and appearing on television. The beat continued after New Years. On January 5 he appeared before TV cameras for three hours.

Among those wounded by the revelation was Republican Governor Ogilvie. On one hand, Ogilvie remained irked that nearly thirteen hours had passed before he was informed of Powell's death. At the time Ogilvie complained that aides to Powell had not made a timely effort to inform him. As much as that lack of protocol and courtesy bothered Ogilvie, the personal slight regarding the cash discovery was more than he could contain.

The governor learned of the Powell money virtually along with the rest of the world, after publication in the *Southern Illinoisan*. Fred Bird, press secretary to the governor, explained the notification: "We did not learn of the $800,000 find until the news story broke December 30 in the Lindsay-Schaub newspapers. I was called by Richard Icen, a Lindsay-Schaub reporter, and told about the story about twenty minutes before it hit the press. I immediately notified the governor. The next day the governor arrived at his office in Springfield to find a note from Rendleman saying Rendleman was sorry he hadn't notified the governor of the discovery sooner."[59]

Public disclosure of the $800,000 discovery and Rendleman's explanation of his actions since October 11 stunned Illinois citizens and the press. It unleashed reactions and confusion that lasted for most of the month of January and in some quarters well beyond. Hardly a day passed without a rumor of more Powell money being uncovered.

Ogilvie reacted quickly. On January 4, steaming from the presumed insult by Rendleman, Ogilvie and Attorney General Scott held a joint press conference at which they carelessly threw about rumors and gossip and left the impression that Rendleman may have committed the crime of the century. Notable among the misinformation spread by Scott was his report that an additional $700,000 in securities, certificates of deposit, and cash had been found. If he wanted headlines, he got them.

Within hours after, contacted by the media, Rendleman set the record straight: "This latest $700,000 was part of the overall nearly $2 million estate that I reported originally. I knew about it and can't understand why it should be brought up as a new find. I'm not sure the $700,000 is correct—it may be more or less. This is in time certificates and some in cash." Rendleman began commenting publicly on a trend of criticism aimed at him by top state officials: "I don't know what I have done to warrant this criticism. I was appointed to serve the assets of Mr. Powell's estate, and that's what I am doing. I have an obligation to a man deceased, and I am fulfilling that obligation."[60] Rendleman noted that he had not been contacted by Scott before the press conference.

Scott, a highly partisan politician with a reputation as a publicity seeker and political opportunist, predictably called for a state investigation of the whole issue. Ogilvie, aiding and abetting, granted use of the Illinois Bureau of Investigation. The investigative work out of the attorney general's office was assigned to Waldo Ackerman, a Springfield lawyer named recently as a deputy attorney general. Ackerman was a prosecutor in the trial and conviction of former state auditor Orville E. Hodge for the theft of state funds.

At the same time, the first political criticism of Rendleman came from a state legislator. Rep. Gale Williams, a Republican from Murphysboro, garnered statewide headlines by calling for Rendleman to step down as chancellor of SIU at Edwardsville and appealing to a handful of state and federal agencies to investigate. Williams accused Rendleman of poor judgment in keeping his discovery of the money secret so long. Williams's statement prompted two SIU trustees to respond with support of Rendleman. Lindell Sturgis, chairman, said the board had no intention of asking Rendleman to resign.

The state investigation moved rapidly. On January 8, Ackerman interviewed Ciaccio at length in what became the unraveling of his lies about events surrounding Powell's death. In a seventy-five-page document, Ciaccio put his own spin on the events of nearly three months. The IRS let little time pass before going after tax records. The agency subpoenaed documents from Hensey and Rendleman. On January 15, the IRS took twenty-five boxes of documents from Hensey's duplex, and on January 19 Rendleman accommodated agents by turning over tax information that had been removed from Powell's file cabinet after his death.

Ogilvie let Scott take the offensive in the first days of the month, but on January 8 he unleashed his full fury in a statement criticizing Rendleman for his lack of candor and performance of duty:

I do not think that John S. Rendleman has demonstrated in this matter either the candor or the spirit of public service which we have a right to expect in our public officials. Rendleman is not only a public official but also one whose conduct should inspire the respect and confidence of young people under his jurisdiction. Waiting as long as he did to make a public disclosure of the astonishing discovery he made of Powell's huge cash accumulation contributes nothing of value to the position of chancellor of a major university. . . . It is not whether Rendleman is open to charges of wrong-doing. It is rather whether his actions inspire confidence in him as a public official. In my view, his actions have in fact caused a degree of public cynicism and distrust we can ill afford now or ever.[61]

Ogilvie's criticism became part of a growing effort to force Rendleman to step down as chancellor of SIU at Edwardsville, suggesting that he could not continue as leader of the school and be executor of the estate.

Rushing to Rendleman's defense were a number of editorial pages throughout the state. The *St. Louis Post-Dispatch* led the way with a slap at the governor for being "out of order" in criticizing Rendleman: "Perhaps Mr. Rendleman would agree in retrospect that he should have disclosed the existence of the money much sooner, but he was under no obligation to do so. As executor, his obligation was to locate the assets of the estate, act to preserve them and compile an inventory of them, all of which he did. . . . If there has been a loss of public confidence, it has taken place at the level of state government, not where Mr. Ogilvie claims. After all it was not Mr. Rendleman but Mr. Powell—30 years a member of the House and six years secretary of state with 4,000 patronage employees—who accumulated the enormous sum of money.[62]

By early January two trends had developed. First, the central players in the drama were being extremely careful about what they said publicly. Rendleman responded to criticism and offered some minor clarifications to his newspaper account. Hensey refused to comment publicly or privately. Towle had sent a written statement to state investigators. That left Ciaccio and Saccaro to attract the media. Rendleman could not let that go far. He had to defend his actions to the SIU trustees and make further public statements to head off the assault by Scott and Ogilvie. He could not depend on Ciaccio or Saccaro, and he knew Hensey would hide out as long as possible.

Second, investigations proliferated. The IRS had started; the attorney general and IBI reacted quickly; the FBI had taken up the hunt. Before the month ended, a federal grand jury started in Chicago, and a state grand jury began early in February. Quickly it became apparent that they all were scrambling for the same documents and the scant public statements. They all had one outcome in common: Nothing resulted from the probes.

Rendleman, infuriated by the attack on his character and performance, answered charges with a counterattack on his critics. He took his case directly public. On January 9, one day after Ogilvie's chastisement, Rendleman began a public relations onslaught. He read a statement at a press conference, then answered questions about his role as executor. He was accompanied by his attorneys. They included Oxtoby and Lowery. Newspapers published his statement in full, and a transcript of the press conference appeared quickly.

At the press conference, Rendleman gave the explanation he would repeat frequently: "I have attempted to act honorably at every step in this matter. I have done as I was advised by competent people."[63] Rendleman refused to step down either as chancellor or executor. He expressed puzzlement over being in the eye of the storm: "I cannot understand why public criticism of the cash hoard is being directed not at Mr. Powell but at the executor of his estate, a man who had nothing whatsoever to do with the money or with Mr. Powell's political activities. . . . Criticism of this kind resembles the reaction of the kings who used to chop off the heads of messengers if they brought bad news to the court."

He addressed the source of Powell's money with this statement: "I have no idea where the cash came from, how it was accumulated, or what purpose Mr. Powell had in mind." He added, "I really don't want to speculate about something—about a man who is dead and can't explain. I don't want to speculate about where it could have come from."

At one point in the press conference, the subject turned to Ogilvie's criticism. Rendleman said that since the money disclosure he had offered "to go over everything I knew about the matter." Oxtoby told reporters he and Van-Meter had met with Scott and Ogilvie since the disclosure: "I went over to see the Governor and the Attorney General, and of course what we are discussing here and the $800,000 at the St. Nicholas was common knowledge and he just wanted to know the facts from Mr. VanMeter and myself as to what we knew." Oxtoby said the governor did not mention that Scott had known about the money since November.

Rendleman expressed surprise at the attack by Ogilvie. He said there had been no quarrels in the past over administration of the university. "I think the Chief Executive of the state has the obligation to comment upon any matter of state government," Rendleman said. "I obviously am a public official and if he feels that I had acted improperly, he, of course, has his right to that opinion. I don't think that any one of the four of us [those at the press conference] think that I had acted improperly."

Rendleman captured headlines and temporarily disarmed the critics. Ogilvie kept up a barrage, but he toned down the rhetoric. A day after the SIU appearance, Ogilvie said, "I think people are pretty damn mad about the Powell matter." Mad, maybe, and surrounded by mysteries that defied explanation.

Less than a week after the press conference on January 15, Rendleman continued his public explanations to a meeting of the SIU Board of Trustees in Edwardsville. Before the board, a large assemblage of reporters, and members of the university administration, he made a statement that repeated much of what he had said at the press conference. At the outset, Rendleman explained that he had a close personal association with some members of the board. The meeting minutes read: "Chancellor Rendleman commented that he thought it should be noted that he did have certain personal and business relations with individual Board members. Trustee [Dr. Martin V.] Brown and Chancellor Rendleman and two others own a farm near Carbondale, and Chancellor Rendleman serves on the Board of Directors of both the First Granite City National Bank of which Mr. [Harold R.] Fischer is Chairman and the First National Bank of Cobden of which Mr. [Melvin] Lockard is Chairman."[64] He failed to mention that Lockard's wife was a cousin of Rendleman. Others on the SIU board were William W. Allen, Ivan A. Elliott Jr., F. Guy Hitt, and Lindell W. Sturgis, chair.

Toward the end of his statement, Rendleman said: "I want to affirm to you my honest conviction that I have handled all matters connected with Mr. Powell's estate with firmness, prudence and dispatch. In following the orderly course prescribed by law, I have called on the advice and counsel of distinguished and competent people." At the conclusion of Rendleman's statement, Elliott called for an expression of the board's confidence in Rendleman, and the vote of trustees was unanimous.

Unknown to the public or media, Rendleman and Hensey testified under oath and gave the most thorough accounts of their actions up to then, or later. These accounts were not made public until after the estate was settled. Rendleman testified twice, the first time on January 6 to officers of the IBI. His second testimony occurred on January 18 before officials of the IRS. Basic facts did not vary.

The IRS went after more information regarding Powell's income, documents that could trace his financial activity, and whether money was concealed or raked off. In terms of depth questioning and length of interview, the IRS probe was more extensive. Hensey steadfastly refused to provide documents beyond the IRS demand. On January 25 she underwent hours of interrogation by officials of the Sangamon County state's attorney's office.

In these lengthy sessions, where Hensey and Rendleman were under oath, interrogators probed the witnesses about the sources of Powell's cash and events of the first hours after his death. Not surprisingly, the two offered little on the record to explain the cash or the actions. But, for the record, Rendleman did speculate further than Hensey.

The Sangamon County state's attorney questioners thought that Hensey's access to Powell, knowledge of the secretary of state's office operations, and awareness of the boss's political activity should give her some insight. Her curt answer to almost every question about the source of cash was "I haven't the slightest idea where it came from." They wanted to know about the mail she opened at Powell's office and whether it ever contained cash. No, she said, not the mail she opened. She did say that much of Powell's personal mail went to the St. Nicholas Hotel. They asked about his associations with people who might have paid him money for favors, but she expressed no knowledge of them or their business with Powell.

Under questioning by the IBI, Rendleman could not offer any specific thoughts about how Powell accumulated the cash. He thought the cash came as a complete surprise to Hensey because Powell was so secretive about his personal affairs. "I think he was so closed mouthed about it that it just wasn't known," Rendleman said. Did Powell give any hints about his wealth? "He'd say things like, if they think they're going to send me back to Vienna hungry, they've waited too long."

On how Powell accumulated the money, Rendleman followed the same line of comment that he used in public. He told IBI interrogators: "I would hate to speculate about the source of the money with as little knowledge as I have. I would observe that it's an extremely large amount of money in cash for a person to have."

Wasn't that much cash hard to accumulate for someone who never earned more than $30,000 a year in public salary? Rendleman responded: "Well, his annual salary really has no bearing on it. He had many business ventures. He was going to pay $100,000 in income tax this year, so his salary was a very small portion of his income." Then he gave just a hint that he knew something: "I have some private feelings about the matter, but I wouldn't want to express them about a man who is not here to defend himself. As Mike Howlett [then state auditor] said, if Paul was here he'd explain where that money came from and 90 percent of the people would believe him."[65]

The questions got around to the behavior of Hensey and her friends before Powell's death was known publicly. Why did these people enter Powell's office? Were they looking for cash? Rendleman replied: "No, I think that no matter what the figure's going to be, somebody's always going to say, well, some was skimmed off the top or something was done, but now, damn it, you don't deal with a group of people and come out with $800,000. He just couldn't have accumulated much more than that. If you know the people that were around him, they were scared to death of him. Not fearful from a physical standpoint, but if he'd say jump, they'd say how high, and my guess is that they weren't quite sure that he wasn't going to walk out of that casket sometime . . . . They might take a dime, but I just don't believe that they did."[66]

Rendleman offered one further comment on the action of the others: "I think it is unfortunate, and this is a personal opinion, that they went in there and took those things out of that office because now this casts a shadow over them, and I think if they had known there was all this money they wouldn't have done it because I think they were thinking they were doing the man a favor."

Events of January 1971 proved inconclusive on virtually every other front. There was no way the citizens of Illinois could place confidence in public authority and elected officials that answers would be found regarding Powell's fortune. They surely were ambivalent about Powell, who had not been convicted of any crime but had been painted almost daily as having taken advantage of his position to increase his wealth. John Rendleman, not known statewide before Powell's death, was a sympathetic character and survived mostly because no one seemed strong enough to remove him from responsibilities as chancellor or executor. The investigations staggered forward.

10

Handouts from a Lifelong Democrat

IN PAUL POWELL'S WILL AND TESTAMENT, THE FIRST ARTICLE DIRECTED "that a proper marker be placed at my grave. I further direct that on that marker appear an appropriate replica of the State Seal together with the statement, 'Here Lies a Lifelong Democrat.'"[1] That epitaph has received special attention for decades, but if Powell were around to comment today, he might want it known what else is on the gravestone.

The portion that was not stipulated in his will adds texture to the remembrance of a colorful politician, who had his own views of posterity. "A Great American," it says. And further, "Never known to refuse a generous donation to any worthwhile organization, handicapped person, underprivileged child." Also, it commemorates his six years as mayor of Vienna and six years on the Vienna school board.[2] Indeed, he wanted to be remembered as a faithful party member. But others who put the words on stone could not let it go with just a party loyalty oath.

Just as there often was an untold story behind Powell's words and actions, his epitaph is no exception. The idea for the gravestone did not originate with Powell. He, or someone else, found the words *He was a lifelong Democrat* on a gravestone in Saline County, and that provided the inspiration for his variation. Captivated by the discovery, Powell displayed a photograph of the Saline grave site on his wall in the secretary of state's office. He told reporters and visitors that he wanted an inscription about his party loyalty because "if that won't get you to heaven nothing will."[3]

The will and codicil of Powell, which executor Rendleman said had been revised countless times over the years as Powell changed his mind about people and organizations, did contain a number of original ideas along with surprises, last minute changes, and disappointments. Powell signed the frequently rewritten will in Johnson County on August 11, 1969, and the codicil, containing one major change and several smaller alterations, on September 23, 1969. A little less than nine years later, the final estate documents were filed and accounts were settled.[4]

The will took care of all those who meant anything to Powell. He had no close relatives left—two wives preceded him in death and the marriages were childless. It provided for two dear woman friends, the Democratic party, a few remaining distant relatives, his executor, his doctor, his wife Daisy's relatives, and a number of institutions that he knew would be thankful for the donations. The will provided funds to establish a shrine to Powell at the homesite in Vienna.

There was one notable deletion from the will, brought about in the codicil. In the will of August 1969, Powell had bequeathed $50,000 to the Southern Illinois University Foundation to establish the Powell Memorial Fund. Proceeds were to be used for study of science of politics and government and for the intercollegiate athletic program. The codicil language reversed that decision in no uncertain terms: "It is now my wish that the Article Fifteen covering the bequest be stricken from the will." This reflected Powell's anger and unhappiness with antiwar demonstrations on campus in 1968 and 1969, and constituted a reversal of loyalty and sentiment for an institution that he helped build.[5]

Among the largest individual beneficiaries of the estate were two women whose close personal relationships with Powell were well known. The greatest take of all went to Marge Hensey. She received 15,800 shares of Chicago Downs racetrack stock—which once was held in Daisy Powell's name—valued at $695,200, cash totaling $15,000, Powell's Buick worth $3,000, and the $55,000 Powell left for her in an envelope. The bequests totaled $760,401. Lucille Koval, who preceded Hensey in Powell's affections, received $15,000 in cash and 6,838 shares of Fox Valley Trotting Club valued at $75,970, for a grand total of $90,970. The net numbers for both were less after taxes.

Anticipating that Hensey would receive the shares of Chicago Downs in the final estate settlement, a circuit court judge approved the payment of annual dividends as an advance while the settlement awaited legal action. For Hensey, beginning in 1972 and ending six years later in 1977, this meant total dividend payments of $442,400, for an average of more than $73,000 per year. The largest single-year dividend of $110,600 was paid in 1977. Over the same period, also as an advance against final settlement, Koval received $63,251.50 in dividends from Fox Valley.[6]

The two women shared the affections of Powell over almost a twenty-year period, and they also shared in his estate, although not equally in either case. The more recent woman friend, Hensey, received more, although there is evidence that Powell continued a close relationship with Koval up to his final days. She claimed to have talked with him on the day he left Springfield for Rochester. While Powell was a common interest to them, there was no common ground between the women.

Animosity between the two women was apparent from an interview Koval gave the *Chicago Tribune*'s Michael Sneed in January 1971.[7] She leveled a blast at Hensey that the latter did not return publicly: "Three words could describe this woman—self-centered, greedy and mercenary. She had a terrible influence on him. Powell dreaded getting old and she was a great party girl. She threw herself at him. Many of Powell's friends could not understand why he became so attached to her. He told me at one time that he wanted to get rid of her. She was rough talking and was not an asset in his office. She had a terrible temper and it was not unusual for her to yell and scream at him in public."

Rendleman benefited, too, from the will, with bank stock in University Bank of Carbondale valued at $19,187 and 20 shares of First National Bank of Cobden worth $2,000. The will stipulated the amount was to be included as part of his compensation for serving as executor. He did far better than this as paid executor, receiving more than $200,000 for his services.[8]

Those who played such a major role in the hours after Powell's death received minor amounts. Towle, Saccaro, and Ciaccio each got $2,000. Powell's longtime physician, Dr. Harry Grant, received $7,500. Only one Powell relative received anything from the will. Lillie Panghorn, a cousin from Marion, Illinois, received 3,000 shares of stock in the Bank of Egypt at Marion, valued at $105,000. Two relatives of Daisy received funds. Anna Roddy of Carmi got $20,000 and Winifred Morris of St. Louis got $50,000 and Powell's personal clothing and jewelry.

Assuming no challenges, the will is the last word of the decedent, and often as not some words are meant to perpetuate the dead person's memory. Whether the bequests are justified, proper, or logical is beside the point. Thus, beneficiaries of Powell's mysteriously earned dollars went to organizations that would keep the benefactor's name alive. He set aside $105,000 in trust for scholarships to the Amvets of Illinois, Veterans of Foreign Wars of Illinois, the American Legion (Boys State and Girls State), Fraternal Order of Eagles, Loyal Order of Moose, and the Illinois Drum and Bugle Corporation Association. All were scholarships in Powell's name. He gave to the Shriners Crippled Children's Hospital of St. Louis ($10,000), the Christian Church of Vienna ($25,000), the First Methodist Church of Vienna ($5,000), the Masons ($10,000), and the Vienna Cemetery Association ($10,000 for blacktopping the road).

Powell perpetuated his memory in a trust established at the Bank of Mattoon to hold the Powell family home in Vienna, plus all furnishings and political mementos, for use as a museum for the citizens of Illinois. He set aside $15,000 in perpetual trust for payment of care to the Cairo Cemetery Association for the Butler (Daisy's family name) cemetery lot in Villa Ridge, Illinois, and for the placement of flowers on the Butler cemetery lot, for Easter, Mother's Day, Memorial Day, and Christmas. He provided $10,000 to pay for poinsettias to be given to all shut-ins in Johnson County at Christmas, specifying that flowers must be purchased from the Bellamy Floral Shop in Vienna. He apparently had a political difference of opinion with another florist in town.

Finally, to cement the memory of his deeds as a Democrat for at least a short time, he gave $200 to each of the Democratic Central Committees in the 102 counties of Illinois and $10,000 each to the Democratic State Central Committee of Illinois and the Cook County Democratic Committee of Chicago.

Bequests to all beneficiaries totaled $1,330,000, a little more than a third of the total value of the estate at Powell's death.

Those were Powell's expressed wishes, although he could not guarantee their payment. His beneficiaries could do no more than watch as the money battle played out among the titans for almost eight years before final settlement. Until the end, there was a possibility that not enough money would remain to pay the heirs. The principal contenders for the fortune were the Internal Revenue Service, the state of Illinois, and administrators of the estate.

In the race of government agencies to be first in line for a major portion of Powell's estate, the Internal Revenue Service was swiftest. The state of Illinois, the other entity in pursuit of Powell's riches, never caught up but also may have had a weaker claim. The IRS proved ably that the holder of the documents gets to the tape first.

An early contact with the IRS by agents for the estate occurred on December 2, when Robert Oxtoby, one of Rendleman's attorneys, filed a State Tax Preliminary Notice. The document set forth the name of the deceased, the executor, attorneys, and a preliminary estimate of the estate. Although the $800,000 had not been made public, the estimate included the amount. Oxtoby, telling at a 1971 press conference how he filled out the first estimate, said:

> I put residence and lots, Vienna, Illinois, amount—unknown. I don't know what the value of the house is in Vienna. Stocks and bonds, I put down $600,000. That just seemed like a ballpark guess as to the stocks and bonds that we knew of. And then, as to mortgages, notes and cash, I have down $1.5

million. . . . I ran a tape on the certificates of deposit because those are cash. That came out to about $700,000. . . . So, I totaled the figures of $2.1 million and then I wrote at the bottom "these are preliminary figures, no appraisal of certificates has been had."[9]

That got the attention of the IRS. However, as later was shown in the shocking news of December 30 and progressive estimates of the estate, Oxtoby's numbers truly were guesses. While Rendleman had found most of the documents by early December, some of the racetrack stock certificates proved hard to locate. Powell had registered most of his racetrack stock in the names of friends, and it took time to get accurate estimates of the stock value.

IRS eyes lighted up fast when it became apparent that Powell had not paid taxes on all his income in recent years, meaning the $800,000. While the Illinois attorney general had known of the Powell cash as early as the first week of November, there is little evidence the state prepared a case against the estate or had mobilized to seek its portion of the estate. As soon as the public disclosure occurred, Scott called for investigations, but the IRS already had a head start on the state.

Hensey complied to an IRS demand for papers, and on January 15 IRS agents carried away twenty-five boxes of documents from her Springfield duplex. On January 19, Rendleman met with agents in East St. Louis and turned over all the documents he had collected.[10] By that date, the IRS had the bulk of evidence it needed to make a case against the estate. Meanwhile, the state found itself without documents to study, let alone make a case.

Jay G. Philpott, Springfield district director for the IRS, said: "This is not a joint investigation and our policy is such that we can't permit anyone else to see these records while we have them. The state people also will not be present at interviews we may conduct in connection with the records." Proof of his statement came on January 18 when Rendleman testified before IRS agents, without the state being present. The best Philpott did was offer documents later.

While Rendleman and his attorneys struggled to get their arms around the rapidly growing estate value, they were faced increasingly with legal tactics of the IRS and the state to pick the bones clean. The distracting episodes, complicated by other suits against the estate and claims of fraud, took a toll in time. In work on large estates, time is money, and as administrative costs mounted to cope with delays, observers wondered if there would be sufficient resources to pay heirs.

Throughout 1971, the IRS laid out its case in legal documents and press releases. In court filings, the IRS accused Powell of fraud in settlement of Daisy Powell's estate in 1968.[11] The IRS contended that Daisy, "in contemplation of death," transferred her property to Powell on April 26, 1965. As a result, she and her husband should have been listed as joint tenants and the property was not deductible from her estate.

The IRS said, "It is determined that all or part of the tax required to be shown on the estate tax return is due to fraud." Daisy's estate tax return listed a gross estate of only $41,202.54, when it should have been $1,707,840.49, according to the IRS, which argued Powell's estate owed $370,568 in taxes and penalties. Estate attorneys answered the IRS by saying the agency had overestimated the gross estate, including some of the stock at the time of Daisy's death. They also said the tax commissioner erred in citing fraud. Rendleman was Powell's attorney for Daisy's estate.

The IRS bill amounted to $3,500,000 and, if allowed, would have wiped out most of the estate. In addition to the back taxes for Daisy's estate, the IRS wanted $705,884 in estate taxes and back taxes and penalties of $1,103,790 from the Powell estate. Also, the IRS claimed $1,058,056 for taxes in 1971, 1972, and 1973. In a report filed with the Circuit Court in Vienna in February 1973, Rendleman valued the estate at $3,300,000.

The persistent state kept up pressure to capture a huge piece of the estate. Nearly three years after the state's suit to obtain tax documents from Hensey and others was filed, a circuit court judge in Johnson County approved an agreement between Scott and Rendleman that would pay the state $1,600,000—maybe.[12] The understanding identified $100,000 to be paid into the state's general revenue fund as punitive damages for misappropriation of funds, such as the pocketing of proceeds from capitol vending machines under Powell's control.

The remaining $1,500,000 was depleted by payment of federal and state inheritance taxes before anything could be set aside for a state trust for grants to the Illinois State Historical Library, the Illinois State Museum, and various bequests to organizations such as the Powell family home in Vienna. Agreement or not, the state would get what was left over after federal taxes and administrative costs. The claims of heirs to Powell's estate awaited a final accounting, too. They could not be paid until all other claims were settled.

The idea of a state trust apparently came from Atty. Robert Oxtoby, on the theory that a large portion of the estate would come to the state of Illinois and proceeds should go to the places that Powell liked. No specific recipients were included in the will, so there was a bit of guesswork in determining which might benefit from the funds. After discussion, the attorney general's office agreed to consider funds for the Illinois State Historical Library, the state museum, and the executive mansion, those being favorites of Powell. Daniel Walker, governor at the time, refused the offer, saying he did not want any part of the Powell estate for the mansion. The museum and library both accepted.[13]

At that time, Robert Howard, former Springfield correspondent for the *Chicago Tribune*, was chairman of the State Museum Society. He joined Milt Thompson, director of the museum, and Bill Alderfer, the state historian, on a trip to Vienna to testify in circuit court on the Oxtoby idea. The trip did not accomplish anything. "It turned out it was a wasted trip because when the lawyers got through with the case there wasn't that much money anyway. By the time the Internal Revenue Service got its hands on it and the lawyers took care of the rest there was none at all for these causes," Howard said.[14] A few thousand of the dollars received by the state were set aside in trust for the museum and library, but the proceeds fell short of the expectations of Oxtoby and Howard.

From the beginning, the state struggled over its case for jurisdiction and in the end had only the state inheritance tax law on which to stand. No criminal jurisdiction existed, and the state's investigation had a narrow focus. William Nettles, assistant attorney general and chief investigator for Attorney General Scott, recalls the first serious department discussion about jurisdiction: "When Scott found out about the discovery of the money he called a 2 A.M. meeting at the Bismarck Hotel in Chicago. I went with Wally Ackerman [another assistant attorney general in Springfield] and there were maybe 18 to 20 people there. The first subject was our jurisdiction."[15] Nettles suggested the inheritance tax angle, and that prevailed as the state's reason for entering the case.

Nettles said Governor Ogilvie joined in the investigation by committing as many as twenty-five agents of the Illinois Bureau of Investigation. In spite of the action, Nettles said no one came forward with evidence of wrongdoing by Powell during his tenure as secretary of state. "I always thought he was an honest guy and didn't steal from the state," Nettles said.

On the other hand, Nettles believes Powell did receive kickbacks from Chicago trucking firms.[16] Nettles, who investigated dozens of rumors, said Powell got kickback money from trucking firms whom he allowed to register in Indiana instead of Chicago, thus saving the trucking company money. Licenses cost much less in Indiana. Nettles says some of the savings went back to Powell for his willingness to look the other way.

The first grand jury that looked into the Powell matter ended its inquiry in the same manner as later investigations. The *Springfield State Journal* headline on May 29, 1971, told the story: "No Indictments Returned in Powell Case." The Sangamon County grand jury concluded its session by saying there was not sufficient evidence to indict anyone. The grand jury started its work on January 13 and spent most of its thirty-four meeting times on Powell issues. The state's attorney promised a deeper look by a new grand jury.

The IRS claim dangled in court until October 1975, when all parties reached an out-of-court settlement. The federal government received $1,500,000, or a little less than half what the IRS wanted. On the claim against Daisy's estate, the IRS got $121,379. On back taxes and penalties against Powell's estate, the IRS received $974,959 instead of $1,103,790. Instead of giving the IRS $1,058,056 for estate taxes after Powell's death, the agreement provided $434,809 net to the government. As part of the settlement, the court approved release of the $55,000 to Marge Hensey.[17]

While the contest raged in court for the leftovers, Rendleman and his attorneys had determined the estate's value at the moment of Powell's death. This would not change, even if court battles continued. Delay did have a positive impact on the total estate by increasing the total value, however, and at the conclusion this factor weighed heavily in the payoff for heirs. In an amended inheritance tax return filed June 3, 1976, more than five and a half years after Powell's death, details of the value were spelled out. In 1970 dollars, at a time when a salary of $50,000 a year was a princely sum, Powell had accumulated an estate of $3,292,959.[18]

Among the astonishing details was that Powell held stock in seven horse racing organizations, both harness and thoroughbred, worth more than $910,000, or 27 percent of the total assets. They were Chicago Downs (15,800 shares worth $695,200); Fox Valley Trotting (6,838 shares worth $75,970); Egyptian Trotting (6,750 shares worth $27,000); Chicago Harness Racing (7,500 shares worth $46,350); Maywood Park Trotting (354 shares worth $5,664); and Mississippi Valley Trotting (750 shares worth $750). Powell's remaining racetrack holdings were in Cahokia Downs, the racetrack across the Mississippi River from St. Louis. He owned 5,365 shares of Cahokia Downs stock valued at $7,376. But Powell's certificates of ownership in the Cahokia Land Trust totaled $52,500.

While the $800,419 in loose cash discovered in the seventy-two hours after Powell's death received enormous attention, and still does, total cash in various forms exceeded the "shoe box" tonnage. In checking accounts spread mostly throughout the southern half of Illinois, Powell had stashed $176,221.

He had interest-bearing certificates of deposit in the same banks totaling $392,055, bringing this cash to $568,276. The list of banks in which Powell placed funds reveals how he spread the amounts around so that no single bank had enough to raise eyebrows.

The banks and amounts listed in the tax return were Illinois National Bank of Springfield, $50,000; City National Bank of Metropolis, $40,000; Drovers State Bank of Vienna, $141,371; First State Bank of Springfield, $44,881; The Bank of Harrisburg, $176,378; First State Bank of Vienna, $23,795; Peoples National Bank of Springfield, $10,000; Bank of Egypt, Marion, $20,000; Bank of Paducah, $9,111; and First National Bank of Chicago, $5,646.

Powell's dedication to the banks of southern Illinois extended to a sizable investment in stock of banks in which he also had savings or checking accounts. The shares were valued at $183,887. Stock holdings and values were Bank of Egypt, Marion, 3,000 shares valued at $105,000; First State Bank of Springfield, 100, $3,000; Bank of Harrisburg, 198, $24,750; City National Bank of Metropolis, 25, $5,000; Paducah Bank, 118, $20,650; Peoples National Bank of Springfield, 180, $6,300; First National Bank of Cobden, 20, $2,000; and University Bank of Carbondale, 125, $17,187.

Separate accounts marked as campaign contributions disclosed the success of Powell fund-raising capabilities but raised other questions. These separate accounts totaled $538,573. Of that amount, the "Five Years of Progress" fund amounted to $186,282; there was $75,000 in "dinner committee" accounts; and campaign fund cash totaled $277,573. The half million in campaign funds existed less than two years after Powell's 1968 statewide campaign, testimony to his perseverance in attracting contributions well in advance of a reelection campaign. Nevertheless, the total reflected only what Powell declared as campaign funds. Campaign accounting was so slipshod in those times that there is no way of knowing what percentage of total contributions this represented.

Powell tapped all sources for campaign funds, often well in advance of an election. With more than 2,700 employees on the secretary of state's payroll, he had a built-in revenue stream. About two years after his election in 1964, he scheduled something called a "garden party," for employees at the state fairgrounds. They were treated to entertainment and food and Powell, all for a contribution.

All those earning up to $300 a month were asked to purchase one $20 ticket. Those earning $301 to $500 were asked to buy three tickets at $20 each. And so until up to those who drew more than $1,000 a month and had to buy ten tickets for a $200 total. Thomas J. Owens, chairman of the party, said employees were sponsoring the party to help "Powell defray the tremendous financial burdens, other than political, imposed upon persons holding public office." The party was expected to gross $150,000.[19]

Marge Hensey gave a glimpse of how Powell and she handled campaign funds from 1964 to his death, during which he was secretary of state. She had no involvement with his campaign funds before 1964. In January testimony, Hensey explained that her responsibility was limited to depositing money in three campaign accounts, reconciling the funds, and writing thank-you notes.[20] She did not solicit funds or plan or carry out fund-raising events. At her hearing, she was asked, "So what you are telling me is that it was your responsibility to look at these checking accounts and to reconcile the campaign fund, but any other operation they had for collecting money, you don't know anything about?" She answered, "No, sir."

This is how Hensey described the procedure for handling funds from campaign dinners: "Well, sir, when they had a dinner, somebody else would handle that, and then after all expenses and that they would deposit it in some bank, I don't know which bank, because I never wrote any of those checks of that. What money was left over they would deplete the account, they would give me a check on it made out to the Paul Powell Campaign Fund, which would be deposited in the fund." When Powell wanted to put funds in a certificate of deposit or a bank account, he instructed Hensey to make the transaction.

The three campaign checkbooks she kept were for the Capital Bank, the First State Bank, and the First National Bank of Chicago. Powell gave her deposits to make in cash and checks. She said that these were the only campaign records she knew of and that she was the only person to keep records for Powell. Only Powell and she could write checks on the accounts. She did not indicate that anyone had records except perhaps people who put on a dinner or cocktail party for Powell.

"Was there any kind of a file or book or compilation kept of people who made contributions to Mr. Powell's campaigns?" She answered, "No, sir." The only record, she said, was for thank-you letters she sent. "As a general rule was there a letter sent out to everybody that made a contribution to Mr. Powell?" They tried to, she said, "but we didn't keep them all, because, as I said, space just—we just didn't have the space." Some copies of letters were kept, some were thrown away. She acknowledged that the files she threw away after Powell's death contained many thank-you letters.

Finally, the stage was set for settlement of the estate. By 1978, interest payments during the long delay had pushed the estate's value to $4,700,000 and had allowed claims to be adjusted and administrative costs to be paid so that enough remained to pay the heirs in full.[21] The judge stated that had the estate not grown, the payoff to heirs might have been as low as 21.5 percent of the original amounts. The ranks of principals were depleted, too. Executor Rendleman died in 1976 of cancer, and his father Ford died in 1977. Although the division of the estate for tax purposes was accomplished in 1976, it still took two more years to complete the settlement and pay expenses.

As previously determined by the court, the federal government received $1,529,000 in taxes, representing less than half the amount sought by the IRS but still supporting the government's contention that Powell had a large accumulation of wealth on which he paid no taxes before his death.

Attorney fees, aside from the fees paid Rendleman for being executor, amounted to $305,000. The largest amount paid to any individual attorney or law firm went to Rendleman's father. Before his death, he had collected $125,000. Other lawyers and firms included Joseph R. Lowery and his firm, Pope and Driemeyer of East St. Louis. Springfield attorney Robert Oxtoby and the Chicago law firm of Jenner and Block also received payments.

Rendleman, who surely must have felt that his fees for duties as executor were far too little for the burdens he carried, received $140,000 before his death on March 4, 1976. The final settlement provided an additional $67,000 for his estate. After the revelation of Powell's $800,000 in cash and the incredible story Rendleman told, and subsequent political criticism, the cry quickly became a whimper. By all accounts, Rendleman carried out his prescribed duties as executor without serious issues or questions. Whether he was adequately compensated for the stress and strain as well as the administrative responsibilities, it is easily argued that there was not enough money in the whole estate to ease his pain.

Only the state of Illinois had to wonder about fairness. Throughout the years, the state contended that Powell literally had stolen from the citizens of Illinois. In William J. Scott's initial suit, the state argued that Powell gained his wealth through misappropriation of funds, such as payments for vending and concessionaire privileges under his control at the capitol, and influence payments from special interests. In reaction to the case built by the state, the settlement called for a $100,000 payment to the state's general revenue fund as damages for contracts awarded by Powell without competitive bidding.

The estate also paid $222,000 in inheritance taxes, and that left about $480,000 for a state trust fund. Although Scott estimated in 1973 that the state would receive $1,600,000, the total was about half that much. After deducting expenses for investigators, lawyers, and miscellaneous staff, the state may have done well to break even.

The trust fund had to set aside about $200,000 to maintain Powell's home in Vienna as a state museum, and the scholarships and contributions to charities took another $155,000. This left the state with a little more than $100,000 for a trust fund to benefit state historical and museum societies. Circuit Judge Robert Porter from Vienna, who issued the final settlement and declared the legal fees not excessive, expressed displeasure with the provision that required Powell's home to be established as a museum: "That money could have educated two or three doctors. But Powell loved his home."[22]

11

Powell's Secret

IT IS POSSIBLE THAT ANYONE WHO KNOWS THE NAME PAUL POWELL HAS a theory about the origin of money found in his hotel closet. They may also have a conspiracy theory about those close to Powell and their actions in the hours after his death. Or they may have reached a conclusion about the sources of his wealth. The lingering mysteries about Powell and his money encourage guesses and beg for explanations.

In the days immediately after disclosure of the $800,000 in cash, nearly everyone in Illinois had an answer to each question, and many of them were expressed through news accounts. As time passed and the story faded from the headlines, the guessing lessened and eventually stopped. But on the anniversaries, when the media go back to the files to find a new angle for public consumption, the old theories resurface and the speculation is revived.

Remarkably, almost thirty years after Powell's death, there is widespread awareness of the man and, more so, the $800,000. The mystery surrounding the money and its origin remains one of the great riddles of Illinois history. There are some answers to the lingering questions, and more is known now about Powell and his money than in the months immediately after his death. Still, after settlement of the estate eight years later, there was little interest in pursuing answers to the questions.

There is uncertainty in the quest for answers now. In the absence of believable information, or fresh revelations, the tendency is to rely too heavily on what we know, rather than consider and pursue what we don't know. This gap grows as the years separate us from Powell's death. These facts remain, however:

• We do not know the specific origin of the $800,000.
• We do not know what happened for sure in the hours after his death or even up to the moment of public disclosure.

The specific sources of Powell's cash are unknown. Investigators for the Illinois attorney general's office, the state's attorney of Sangamon County, and the Internal Revenue Service spent years and large sums of money trying to identify the sources, mostly without success. They hoped the probes would uncover criminal acts by Powell or his subordinates that would account for the money. They went through his papers, his tax returns, the endless expense receipts, and bank accounts. They quizzed those close to him and those not so close. In the end, the investigators had their suspicions, but they did not have enough evidence to indict anyone close to Powell or account for significant parts of the $800,000.

The original claims of federal and state tax authorities were reduced because they could not substantiate them. They did little more than add to the suspicions already existing about Powell and his business dealings. What we know from the unearthing of petty graft and occasional payoffs to Powell is that by themselves they are unlikely to have amounted to $800,000 or more.

Within the cautions mentioned earlier, we can, however, speculate with a measure of confidence about the likely sources of cash that made up some of the total. Powell clearly had access to huge amounts of cash during his two campaigns for secretary of state and his campaigns for the legislature. With virtually no required accounting of campaign income or expenses, Powell could do what he wanted with the money. He put some in bank accounts clearly marked as campaign contributions, and the purpose could have been to keep the Internal Revenue Service off balance. Those probably represent legitimate contributions and proceeds from fund-raising events and contributions from the Democratic party. But we know from those around him that he received unsolicited cash with frequency throughout his career. He contributed some of that money to the campaigns of friends and associates, and several people have testified that they either received such contributions or knew when he made them.

Just as there are uncounted stories about Powell and his politics, there are almost as many about Powell and his money. Longtime Central Illinois legislator Martin B. Lohmann, who served in the House and Senate during Powell's time, remembers being called to Powell's office once to discuss legislation: "He called me in one time and says, 'Let me show you something, but they won't believe it.' He showed me—that fellow had about $450,000."[1] Asked what it was used for, Lohmann said: "Paying it off to the different candidates. . . . That's what that money was for." Asked where Powell got it, Lohmann added: "From different fellows. A shakedown, of course; naturally, big donors, looking for big jobs."

What does a statement like that tell us? The significance of Lohmann's comment is not his guess about the origin of the money but that he saw a huge sum of cash on hand in Powell's office. At a minimum, we need evidence that Powell kept large sums of cash in his office, in part for use in political campaigns. And he probably did receive large sums from those seeking favors. He was willing to accept money for his influence, and we know there were those willing to pay. We should believe that he was capable of amassing extremely large sums.

Evidence abounds of Powell's inclination to talk about big sums of money to friends and even acquaintances. Mel Lockard, banker, friend, and SIU booster, writes in his autobiography about Powell's preparation for the 1964 campaign for secretary of state against Elmer J. Hoffman: "Of course, the Democrats in Chicago were very much in favor of Paul winning, so before he ever started they told him they'd give him three hundred thousand dollars. He told them he didn't want any checks or IOUs, he wanted the currency. He wanted the money. He wanted the cash. And he told me, he said, 'Old Paul is going to have some of this money left over when this race is done, 'cause I'm not going to spend it all.'"[2] Even discounting for his boasting, Powell undoubtedly kept a tidy sum from the campaign. And there were two secretary of state campaigns.

William J. Nettles, who investigated Powell's affairs for the state attorney general's office, believed the state did all it could in the investigations because it lacked criminal case jurisdiction: "We did as much as we could do under the circumstances, when he's dead and we don't believe others were involved." After more than two decades had passed, Nettles pronounced this judgment on Powell and his money: "I always thought he was an honest guy, who didn't steal from the state of Illinois. He just took kickbacks. I think that's where all of that money came from."[3]

As to other sources, we know from Powell's income tax returns and the large amounts of dividends and interest he received from racetrack stock holdings, particularly in the last six or eight years of his life, that he had huge amounts of cash on hand. But this presumably was legitimate money, reported to the IRS. He watched how other more careless officials, such as Orville Hodge, fell prey to the IRS, and he covered his tax tracks. Powell did not have any aversions to using banks, or savings and loans, or investing in stocks and bonds.

Those who knew Powell and those who knew of his inclinations have never been able to accept that he put $800,000 in a suite closet at the St. Nicholas Hotel. The consensus, again without any real proof, is that the money was moved to the hotel and had not been there any length of time when discovered by John S. Rendleman. They argue there is no logic to having the money at the hotel, where presumably it could be found by someone cleaning the suite or there on routine inspections. The preponderance of this opinion is best summed up by Shelby Vasconcelles, who spent a lifetime working in the capital pressroom in Springfield, where he watched Powell in action for many years:

> Well, I'd bet my life that Paul Powell never put a nickel in a shoe box, let alone eight hundred thousand dollars. He might have put it in a safe somewhere, but he wouldn't put it in shoe boxes; not in a hotel room. Knowing that the maid and everything comes to clean up your hotel; why that just don't make sense. If I live to be a hundred years old, I'd never believe it. . . . It made good writing, good copy. It sounded good. . . . Somebody had to put that money in the shoe box, but it wasn't Paul Powell. . . . What he couldn't carry in his pocket he'd put in a safe, that's where he'd put it. I'd say that the money rightfully belonged in the safe in the secretary of state's office.[4]

Yes, but the closet where the money apparently was found by Hensey and Rendleman could be locked (Hensey had a key) and could have been put off limits to cleaning people, visitors, and other casual acquaintances.

The theory most often repeated by those familiar with Powell, or familiar with the secretary of state's office and his attitudes toward money, is that Powell might have had a few dollars at the hotel, but the bulk of his cash was in the locked file cabinet in his office when he died. If that is accurate, the money had to get from the locked file cabinet to the hotel in order to be discovered by Rendleman and Hensey. That account immediately implicates the handful of people who had access to the safe, the money, and the hotel room in the hours and days immediately after Powell's death.

From conversations, public statements, private and off-the-record communications, and oral histories, a story emerges. There is no proof that it happened this way, and those who could have addressed the details refused to comment when asked.

Nevertheless, by taking the events as they were explained publicly by several of the principals and adding a different story of the movement of the money, this theory is possible: Ciaccio and Towle went to Powell's office the afternoon after his death and opened the locked file cabinet that contained $800,000, or maybe more, and some documents. They removed the contents and put them into suitcases that were taken on the airplane to Rochester, Minnesota. Those two, Hensey, and Ciaccio's wife returned to Springfield later that night with the money in the suitcases and put it in Ciaccio's car, which they had left at the airport. They went to Powell's office at the capitol and proceeded to make sure there were no other critical documents or money. They conferred with Judge William Chamberlain and asked him about the procedures for transition to a new secretary of state, principally to give themselves cover of his legitimacy. After everyone had left except the principals, they took two cars to the St. Nicholas Hotel. They did not find any money there, because there was no money at the hotel. The money remained in Ciaccio's car. On Tuesday, Rendleman was told of the scheme and maybe a plan to divide the money, but he refused to go along. That day the money was transferred from Ciaccio's car to Rendleman's father's car. The money never was taken to or from the hotel room.

The implications of this scenario are considerable, especially for the relatives and friends of the people involved. For instance, those who knew Rendleman well and trusted him absolutely refuse to believe that he was involved in anything other than the story he told. But the actions, vague statements under oath, and incomplete explanations of those involved make such a story plausible.

In the final analysis, Thomas A. McGloon of Chicago, who served in the Illinois senate for twelve years until 1970, did as good a job as anyone of summarizing the speculation, theories, and possibilities of Paul Powell's cash: "I think that the secret of Powell's money will remain a mystery for the rest of time."[5]

Notes
Select Bibliography
Index

Notes

1. A Son of Southern Illinois

1. Much of the early history of southern Illinois and the people of the region is based on works by historians with Illinois interests and roots: Ray Allen Billington, *Westward Expansion: A History of the American Frontier* (New York: Macmillan, 1949); John W. Allen, *Legends and Lore of Southern Illinois* (Carbondale: Southern Illinois University Press, 1963); Robert P. Howard, *Illinois: A History of the Prairie State* (Grand Rapids: Eerdmans, 1972); Paul M. Angle, *Bloody Williamson* (New York: Knopf, 1969); John H. Keiser, *Building for the Centuries: Illinois 1865 to 1898* (Urbana: University of Illinois Press, 1977); and Allan Nevins, "The Frontier in Illinois History," *Journal of the Illinois State Historical Society*, 13.1, (Spring 1950): 28–45.

2. Billington, *Westward Expansion*, 293.

3. Keiser, *Building for the Centuries*, 10.

4. Edgar G. Crane, ed., *Illinois: Political Processes and Governmental Performance* (Dubuque: Kendall/Hunt, 1980), 156; and Billington, *Westward Expansion*, 294, 296.

5. Billington, *Westward Expansion*, 293.

6. Angle, *Bloody Williamson*, 72–88.

7. Howard, *Illinois*, 163. He cites supporting works by Paul M. Angle, and Katherine and Will Griffith, *Spotlight on Egypt* (Carbondale, 1946).

8. Allen, *Legends and Lore of Southern Illinois*, 48.

9. George Washington Smith, *A History of Southern Illinois: A Narrative Account of Its Historical Progress, Its People and Its Principal Interests*, vol. 1 (Chicago: Lewis, 1912), 492.

10. Mel Lockard, *. . . and even the stump is gone* (Tucson: Pepper), 1.

11. Gary Harker, personal interview with author, Vienna, Illinois, 21 Feb. 1998. Harker has conducted extensive oral histories about Vienna and Johnson County, Illinois.

12. The early history of Vienna and Johnson County is chronicled in detail in *Johnson County, Illinois, History and Families* (Paducah: Turner, 1990); and Smith, *A History of Southern Illinois*.

13. James Pickett Jones, *Black Jack: John A. Logan and Southern Illinois in the Civil War Era* (Reprint, Carbondale: Southern Illinois University Press, 1967); U. S. Grant, *Personal Memoirs*, vol. 2 (New York: Charles Webster, 1886), 245, 246; and Smith, *A History of Southern Illinois*, 494.

14. Information on the early history of the Thomas Powell family is scant. Anecdotal information is available from Paul Powell comments. Background on Thomas B. Powell is from Mrs. P. T. Chapman, *A History of Johnson County Illinois* (Herrin: Press of the Herrin News, 1925); from the souvenir edition of the *Vienna Democrat*, 18 Mar. 1898; and from Thomas B. Powell's certificate of death, 28 May 1924.

15. Smith, *A History of Southern Illinois*, 495; Chapman, *A History of Johnson County Illinois*, 421; and John Clayton, *The Illinois Fact Book and Historical Almanac 1673–1968* (Carbondale: Southern Illinois University Press, 1970), 111.

16. Chapman, *A History of Johnson County Illinois*, 421.

17. Harker, in personal interview with author, cited an oral history tape made by Herbert Hook with Levi Locke of Vienna. In Chapman, *A History of Johnson County Illinois*, there is no mention of the specifics of the accident. Royce Hundley, in personal interview with author, Vienna, Illinois, 21 Feb. 1998, recalled the accident occurred as Hartwell tried to cross a fence.

18. Thomas B. Powell, Last Will and Testament, Johnson County Circuit Court, Thomas B. Powell, filed 29 July 1924.

19. "Johnson County Honors Speaker Paul Powell," *Vienna Times* 24 Mar. 1961: 1; James Walker, personal interview with author, Vienna, Illinois, 21 Feb. 1998 (from tape recording of Powell's dinner speech on March 24, 1961).

20. Hundley, interview with author; Walker, interview with author.

21. Walker, interview with author (from tape recording of Powell's dinner speech on March 24, 1961).

22. Hundley, interview with author; and Delbert and Edith Brown, interview with author, 21 Feb. 1998.

23. Michael Sneed, "Inside the Shoe Box Scandal," *Chicago Magazine* Oct. 1978: 247; and Hundley, interview with author.

24. Jerry W. Venters, "Vienna Won't Forget Powell," *St. Louis Post-Dispatch* 7 Jan. 1971: 3A.

25. Powell's cafe papers, Personal File, 1910–1967 (hereinafter PP Personal File); Paul Powell and Estate Papers, 1910–1976, Illinois State Historical Library (hereinafter PP Papers).

26. William Griffin, "A final round of applause for Powell," *Chicago Tribune* 16 July 1978: sec. 1, p. 5.

27. Hundley, interview with author.

28. Sneed, "Inside the Shoe Box Scandal."

29. Walker, interview with author (from tape recording of Powell's dinner speech on March 24, 1961).

30. Daisy Butler's certificate of birth, Villa Ridge, Illinois, filed 11 Aug. 1897, PP Papers, PP Personal File; "Services Set Saturday for Mrs. Powell," *Chicago Tribune* 27 Apr. 1967, PP Papers.

31. Sneed, "Inside the Shoe Box Scandal."

32. Dr. Thomas J. Coogan, letter to Paul Powell, 6 May 1967, PP Papers.

33. Hundley, interview with author.

34. Daisy Powell, letter to Paul Powell, 16 Oct. 1962, PP Papers.

35. Daisy Powell, letter to Paul Powell, 25 Mar. 1963, PP Papers.

36. Daisy Powell, letter to Paul Powell, n.d., PP Papers.

37. Daisy Powell, letter to Paul Powell, 15 Nov. 1960, PP Papers.

38. Paul Powell, letter to Daisy Powell, 6 Mar. 1963, PP Papers.

39. Paul Powell, letter to Daisy Powell, n.d., "Sunday afternoon," PP Papers.

40. "Huge Throng Fills Vienna High School Gym for Powell Services," *Harrisburg (Ill.) Daily Register* 1 May 1967, PP Papers.

41. "Vienna Won't Forget Powell," *St. Louis Post-Dispatch* 7 Jan. 1971.

42. "A Final Round of Applause for Powell," *Chicago Tribune* 16 July 1978. A similar version was told by Paul O'Neal, *Chicago Magazine* Oct. 1978.

43. Lockard, . . . *and even the stump is gone*, 274.

44. Information in the following paragraphs of text came from Walker, interview (and tour of Vienna) with author (from tape recording of Powell's dinner speech on March 25, 1961.) Walker played a tape recording of a dinner honoring Powell, took the author to the cemetery where Powell is buried, and told of his experiences with Powell.

45. Walker, interview with author.

46. Walker, interview with author.

2. A Full Life of Politics

1. Conditions in southern Illinois during the 1920s and 1930s were described for the author by longtime residents and in memoirs, including Lockard's . . . *and even the stump is gone.*

2. Clyde Lee, *Memoir* (Springfield: Sangamon State University, 1982–1983), 103.

3. Samuel K. Gove and James D. Nowlan, *Illinois Politics and Government: The*

Expanding Metropolitan Frontier (Lincoln: University of Nebraska Press, 1996), 79–81.

4. Robert W. Sink, "Where Did Powell Get the Money," Lindsay-Schaub newspapers, 10 Jan. 1971.

5. Paul Powell, federal individual income tax return, 1945, PP Papers.

6. Anthony Scariano, *Memoir* (Springfield: Sangamon State University, 1988), 121.

7. Gove and Nowlan, *Illinois Politics and Government*, 80.

8. Clayton, *Illinois Fact Book*, 194.

9. Information about cumulative voting in the Illinois Constitution of 1870 is from Clayton, *Illinois Fact Book*, 191; Howard, *Illinois*, 335; Paul M. Green, "History of Political Parties in Illinois," in Crane, *Illinois*, 170–71; and Richard H. Icen, "Paul Powell story: Cumulative voting kept him going," *Metro-East Journal* 26 Jan. 1971: 3.

10. Illinois Legislative Council, "Legislative Membership," memo to Paul Powell, 10 Mar. 1954, PP Papers.

11. Clayton, *Illinois Fact Book*, 194.

12. Paul Powell Biography, Secretary of State's Office, 1965.

13. Thorough accounts of the Henry Horner administration can be found in Thomas B. Littlewood, *Horner of Illinois* (Evanston: Northwestern University Press, 1969); Robert P. Howard, *Mostly Good and Competent Men: Illinois Governors 1818 to 1988* (Springfield: Illinois Issues, Sangamon State University, Illinois State Historical Society), 253–60; and Roger Biles, *Big City Boss in Depression and War: Mayor Edward J. Kelly of Chicago* (DeKalb: Northern Illinois University Press, 1984).

14. The enmity felt for Stelle in Democratic party circles is described by John Bartlow Martin, Adlai E. Stevenson's biographer, in *Adlai Stevenson of Illinois* (New York: Doubleday, 1976). On page 363, Martin wrote, "Stelle was considered a spoilsman and a party wrecker."

15. Howard, *Mostly Good and Competent Men*, 261–66.

16. "John Stelle Dies; Illinois Ex-Governor," *St. Louis Post-Dispatch* 6 July 1962: 3.

17. Howard, *Mostly Good and Competent Men*, 262; Clayton, *Illinois Fact Book*, 143.

18. Biles, *Big City Boss in Depression and War*, 53.

19. Littlewood, *Horner of Illinois*, 117.

20. "Funeral Monday at McLeansboro for Illinois Ex-Gov. John Stelle," *St. Louis Post-Dispatch* 7 July 1962: C4.

21. Howard, *Mostly Good and Competent Men*, 263.

22. Littlewood, *Horner of Illinois*, 244.

23. Robert E. Hartley, *Big Jim Thompson of Illinois* (Chicago: Rand McNally, 1979), 59–60.

24. Littlewood, *Horner of Illinois*, 244.

25. Howard, *Mostly Good and Competent Men*, 264.

26. Egyptian Trotting Association stockholder and debenture ownership list, 1 Jan. 1962, PP Papers.

27. "Stelle Left $1.5 Million," *East St. Louis Journal* 5 July 1962: 3.

28. Howard, *Mostly Good and Competent Men*, 271; Robert J. Casey and W. A. S. Douglas, *The Midwesterner: The Story of Dwight H. Green* (Chicago: Wilcox & Follett, 1948).

29. Martin, *Adlai Stevenson in Illinois*, 433.

30. Martin, *Adlai Stevenson in Illinois*, 362.

31. Robert P. Howard, *Memoir* (Springfield: Sangamon State University, 1982), 184, 185.

32. Martin, *Adlai Stevenson in Illinois*, 467.

33. William "Smokey" Downey, *Memoir* (Sangamon State University, 1982), 51.

34. Lee, *Memoir*, 161.

35. Scariano, *Memoir*, 119.

36. David Kenney, *A Political Passage: The Career of Stratton of Illinois* (Carbondale: Southern Illinois University Press, 1990), 166.

37. Marion R. Lynes, "Powell Calls Gov. Stratton Tough to Beat," *St. Louis Globe-Democrat* 22 Nov. 1959.

38. Kenney, *A Political Passage*, 202.

39. Martin, *Adlai Stevenson in Illinois*, 392, a quotation from Rep. Abner Mikva.

40. Hartley, *Big Jim Thompson of Illinois*, 51–53.

41. Howard, *Mostly Good and Competent Men*, 304.

42. Robert D. Reid, "Powell's philosophy: Making money hadn't been 'declared a crime'," *Metro-East Journal* 30 Dec. 1970: 3.

43. Lockard, *. . . and even the stump is gone*, 265.

44. Abner Mikva, telephone interview with author, 27 Dec. 1997.

45. Sneed, "Inside the Shoe Box Scandal."

46. Reid, "Powell's philosophy."

47. W. J. Murphy, letter to Paul Powell, 28 July 1969, PP Papers.

48. Paul Powell, letter to Murphy, 11 Aug. 1969, PP Papers.

49. "Legislator's Wife Owns Track Stock," *Chicago Daily News* 21 Aug. 1951: 5.

50. Howard, *Memoir*, 84.

51. Abner Mikva, telephone interview with author, 27 Dec. 1997; and Abner Mikva, letter to author, 18 Dec. 1997.

52. Comments in the next several paragraphs are from Anthony Scariano, *Memoir*.

53. Martin, *Adlai Stevenson in Illinois*, 362.

54. Martin, *Adlai Stevenson in Illinois*, 362.

55. "Speaker Powell's Typical Day Starts with Talks Night Before," *St. Louis Post-Dispatch* 7 June 1961: 5A.

56. Maurice Scott, *Memoir* (Springfield: Sangamon State University, 1984), 64.

57. Jean H. Baker, *The Stevensons: A Biography of an American Family* (New York: Norton, 1996), 320.

58. "Paul Powell, American," *St. Louis Post-Dispatch* 24 Jan. 1971: 2D.

59. Reid, "Powell's philosophy."

60. Howard, *Memoir*, 164.

61. Reid, "Powell's philosophy."

62. Shelby Vasconcelles, *Memoir* (Springfield: Sangamon State University, 1979), 84.

63. Thomas B. Littlewood, "Impact of the Media: Analyst or Interest Group?" in Crane, *Illinois*, 204.

64. Scariano, *Memoir*, 123–24.

65. "The Danger in Paul Powell," *St. Louis Post-Dispatch* 11 Dec. 1949.

66. "Payoff at a Race Track," *St. Louis Post-Dispatch* 24 Aug. 1951.

67. "Gifts for Favors," *Chicago Daily News* 24 Aug. 1951: 12.

68. "Is Happiness Paul Powell?" *Chicago Daily News* (reprinted in the *St. Louis Post-Dispatch* 14 Apr. 1966).

69. Sneed, "Inside the Shoe Box Scandal."

70. Howard, *Memoir*, 185.

71. Reid, "Powell's philosophy."

3. The Pinnacle: Mr. Speaker

1. The discussion of Illinois political history and background about state government covered in the early part of this chapter is aided by three articles in Crane, *Illinois*: Samuel K. Gove, "The Illinois General Assembly"; Alan D. Monroe, "Elections: Political Culture, Public Opinion, Sectionalism and Voting"; and Paul M. Green, "History of Political Parties in Illinois." Also helpful are Clayton, *Illinois Fact Book*, 190–94; Donald E. Tingley, *The Structuring of a State: The His-*

tory of Illinois 1899–1928 (Urbana: University of Illinois Press, 1980), 183, 190, 348–49, 359; and Howard, *Illinois*, 459–83.

2. Martin, *Adlai Stevenson in Illinois*, 362.

3. "The Danger in Paul Powell," *St. Louis Post-Dispatch* 11 Dec. 1948.

4. "Paul Powell Denies Wishing Dire Fate upon Republicans," *St. Louis Post-Dispatch* 30 Dec. 1948.

5. George Tagge, "Powell Assured of Election as House Speaker," *Chicago Tribune* 4 Jan. 1949: 1.

6. Charles Wheeler, "Assembly Meets Amid Flowers," *Chicago Daily New* 5 Jan. 1949: 32.

7. Charles Wheeler, "Legislature Gets 1st Workout Jan. 25," *Chicago Daily News* 7 Jan. 1949: 3.

8. George Thiem, "Powell Speaks Up for Legislature," *Chicago Daily News* 31 May 1949: 9.

9. Martin, *Adlai Stevenson in Illinois*, 394.

10. Adlai E. Stevenson, speech before American Bar Association, 19 Sept. 1950, Princeton University, Adlai E. Stevenson Papers.

11. Martin, *Adlai Stevenson in Illinois*, 395.

12. Martin, *Adlai Stevenson in Illinois*, 397; Kenney, *A Political Passage*, 117. Howard, *Mostly Good and Competent Men*, 278.

13. Martin, *Adlai Stevenson in Illinois*, 509–10.

14. Betty Mitchell, *Delyte Morris of SIU* (Carbondale: Southern Illinois University Press, 1988), 9.

15. Clayton, *Illinois Fact Book*, 141.

16. Excellent explanations of the history of reapportionment of the legislature can be found in Howard, *Illinois*, 554–56; Gove, "The Illinois General Assembly," 95–97; Kenney, *A Political Passage*, 116; and Clayton, *Illinois Fact Book*, 192.

17. Kenney, *A Political Passage*, 117.

18. Kenney, *A Political Passage*, 131.

19. The following text paragraphs on Richard J. Daley are aided by Roger Biles, *Richard J. Daley: Politics, Race, and the Governing of Chicago* (Dekalb: Northern Illinois University Press, 1995), 26–30; references in Len O'Connor, *Clout: Mayor Daley and His City* (New York: Avon, 1975) and Clayton, *Illinois Fact Book*; and research by the author for two previous Illinois political books.

20. Martin, *Adlai Stevenson in Illinois*, 359.

21. Abner Mikva, oral history, in Milton Rakove, *We Don't Want Nobody Nobody Sent: An Oral History of the Daley Years* (Bloomington: Indiana University Press, 1979), 318–30.

22. Alan Dixon, telephone interview with author, 14 Apr. 1998; and Paul Simon, interview with author, 20 Feb. 1998. A number of members of the legislature during the 1950s, including Simon and Dixon, commented to the author about the relationship of Powell and Richard J. Daley in the early years of Daley's reign.

23. Kenney, *A Political Passage*, 166.

24. Mikva, telephone interview with author.

25. "Downstate Still Here, Rep. Powell Says," *St. Louis Globe-Democrat* 9 Jan. 1959: 8.

26. George Tagge, "Powell Seen as Speaker in Legislature," *Chicago Tribune* 7 Jan. 1959: 1.

27. Accounts of the House floor voting for Speaker are contained in articles by George Tagge of the *Chicago Tribune*, Robert Howard of the *Tribune*, Marion Lynes of the *St. Louis Globe-Democrat*, and dispatches from the Associated Press.

28. Marion Lynes, "Powell Wins New Victory in House," *St. Louis Globe-Democrat* 13 Jan. 1959: 1.

29. Mikva, telephone interview with author.

30. Thomas B. Littlewood, "Sales Tax Voted," *Chicago Sun-Times* 27 June 1959: 1, PP Papers.

31. Robert Howard, "House Passes 1/2 Cent Boost in Sales Tax," *Chicago Tribune* 26 June 1959: 1, PP Papers.

32. George Thiem, "Sales Tax Hike Votes, But Date Is in Doubt," *Chicago Daily News* 27 June 1959: 1, PP Papers.

33. Scariano, *Memoir*, 119.

34. Except as noted, accounts of the controversial election of Powell as Speaker are by Robert Howard of the *Chicago Tribune*, Marion Lynes of the *St. Louis Globe-Democrat*, O. T. Banton of Lindsay-Schaub newspapers, and dispatches of he Associated Press and United Press International. Although events were confusing at times, reporters at the scene agreed on the sequence and details.

35. Mikva, telephone interview with author.

36. Scariano, *Memoir*, 117.

37. Mikva, telephone interview with author.

38. Scariano, *Memoir*, 118.

39. "Powell Rejects GOP Action Against Four," *St. Louis Globe-Democrat* 19 Jan. 1961.

40. "Mayor Daley Boosts Powell as Dirksen Foe," *St. Louis Globe-Democrat* 10 May 1961.

41. Edward L. Schapsmeier and Frederick F. Schapsmeier, *Dirksen of Illinois: Senatorial Statesman* (Urbana: University of Illinois Press, 1985), 127–49.

42. James Deakin, "Powell Says He May Run for Senate in 1962," *St. Louis Post-Dispatch* 2 Aug. 1961.

43. Schapsmeier, *Dirksen of Illinois*, 141–44.

4. Secretary of Trouble

1. Dixon, telephone interview with author.

2. Robert E. Hartley, *Charles H. Percy: A Political Perspective* (Chicago: Rand McNally, 1975), 69–77.

3. "Secretary of State," *Metro-East Journal* 25 Oct. 1964.

4. Clayton, *Illinois Fact Book*, 15.

5. "Powell Defends Strength," *Metro-East Journal* 17 Jan. 1964.

6. "Secretary of State," *Metro-East Journal.*

7. State Board of Elections, Springfield, Illinois, official vote count for November 3, 1964.

8. "Why Was Paul Powell Paid $8,000," *Chicago Daily News* 15 June 1965: 1.

9. "Deals with Wiedrick Fully Legal—Powell," *Chicago Daily News* 23 June 1965: 1.

10. "Wiedrick Payments to Powell: $70,000," *Chicago Daily News* 22 June 1965: 1.

11. "Paul Powell: a Talent for Big, Big Spending," *Chicago Daily News* 18 June 1965: 1.

12. "Secret Tapes Bare Story of Payoffs in Legislature," *Chicago's American* 23 June 1965: 1.

13. "Powell Hits Stories, Denies Bill 'Favors,'" *Chicago's American* 23 June 1965: 3.

14. "Horse Trading Put Powell on Top," *Chicago's American* 24 June 1965: 3.

15. "Is Reform losing Steam?" *Chicago's American* 28 June 1965: 8; "House Pushes Bribe Probe of Members of Legislature," *Chicago Daily News* 25 June 1965: 1.

16. "Charlie Smith's Salary Bigger Than His Boss," *Chicago Daily News* 12 Oct. 1966.

17. "Porcaro Quits As Powell Aide," *Illinois State Register* 7 Mar. 1966.

18. "Porcaro Gets 1 to 5 Years," *Chicago Tribune* 8 Sept. 1966.

19. "Inside Story of Bribes and Mob's Influence," *Chicago Tribune* 2 Oct. 1966: 1.

20. "Juries Quiz Powell, Porky," *Chicago Daily News* 11 Oct. 1966: 1.

21. "Link Powell's Top Aide and VIP Auto Plates Obtained for Giancana," *Chicago Sun-Times* 8 Sept. 1967.

22. "Giancana-Linked License Form Found, Turned Over to FBI," *Illinois State Journal* 12 Sept. 1967: 3.

23. "Powell: Missing Plate File Found," *Springfield State Register* 11 Sept. 1967.

24. "Powell Has Eye on Re-Election," *Springfield State Register* 10 May 1967: 6.

25. Simon, interview with author.

26. "On This One, We Pass," *Chicago Daily News* 30 Oct. 1968: 8.

27. State Board of Elections, Springfield, Illinois, official vote count for November 5, 1968, 26.

5. A Helping Hand for SIU

1. Dr. Leo Brown, telephone interview with author, 7 Feb. 1998, and in Carbondale, Illinois, 22 Feb. 1998; and David Kenney, *In It, to Win It: A Personal Memoir* (Carbondale: Sunny Slope Press, 1998). Prof. Kenney, long associated with SIU, provides in his memoir a sample of life as a student and faculty member in the years of growth at the teachers college (in book 2, chapter 6, "Becoming Normal").

2. Lockard, . . . *and even the stump is gone,* 19–49.

3. Paul Powell, "State Rep. Paul Powell Reports on Record in Legislature," *Southern Illinoisan* 27 Oct. 1958.

4. Howard, *Illinois,* 339–41.

5. Leo Brown, interview with author; and Betty Mitchell, *Delyte Morris of SIU,* xiv.

6. Leo Brown, interview with author.

7. Leo Brown, interview with author.

8. Mitchell, *Delyte Morris of SIU,* 3.

9. David Rendleman, interview with author, Carbondale, Illinois, 21 Feb. 1998.

10. O. T. Banton, "Separate Board May Help Answer School 'Politics,'" *Southern Illinoisan* 29 Dec. 1948.

11. "Crisenberry Will Introduce Bill," *Southern Illinoisan* 3 Jan. 1949; and "Senate Passes S.I.U. Board Bill After Lively Discussion," *Southern Illinoisan* 24 May 1949.

12. "Crisenberry Thinks 2-Year Trial Plan Best for S.I.U.," *Southern Illinoisan* 15 June 1949; and "Governor Signs S.I.U. Bills; Board Unnamed," *Southern Illinoisan* 6 July 1949.

13. Mitchell, *Delyte Morris of SIU,* 9.

14. Powell's membership on the Legislative Budget Commission and that of Sen. Everett Peters and their work in behalf of the University of Illinois and Southern Illinois University are mentioned frequently in books, oral histories, articles about Powell, and his papers at the Illinois State Historical Library. A most recent account is in Taylor Pensoneau, *Governor Richard Ogilvie: In the Interest of the State* (Carbondale: Southern Illinois University Press, 1997), 179–80.

15. William L. Grindle, *Memoir* (Springfield: Sangamon State University, 1986), 295.

16. Alan Dixon, telephone interview by author.

17. Scariano, *Memoir*, 121.

18. Mitchell, *Delyte Morris of SIU*, 89; and Pete Goldman, "SIU Rounds Out Dazzling Decade of Growth," *St. Louis Globe-Democrat* 8 July 1957: 1.

19. David Kenney, *In It, to Win It*, chapter 6, 129.

20. James Holloway, *Memoir* (Springfield: Sangamon State University, 1981), 153.

21. Leo Brown, interview with author.

22. Rendleman, interview with author.

23. Rendleman, interview with author.

24. Legislative Council, memo to Paul Powell, 10 Sept. 1957, "Legislation Benefiting Southern Illinois," PP Papers.

25. Leo Brown, interview with author.

26. Simon, interview with author.

27. Henry de Fiebre, "Rendleman kept close area ties," *Southern Illinoisan* 4 Mar. 1976: 1.

28. Holloway, *Memoir*, 153.

29. Paul J. Randolph, *Memoir* (Springfield: Sangamon State University, 1986), 61–62.

30. Grindle, *Memoir*, 293.

31. Leo Brown, interview with author.

32. Grindle, *Memoir*, 153.

33. "Senate Education Committee Vetoes SIU Plea for Agriculture, Engineering," *Southern Illinoisan* 28 May 1953: 1.

34. Pete Goldman, "Legislature Puts Brakes on College Boom; University of Illinois Pressure Blamed," *St. Louis Globe-Democrat* 7 July 1957: 1; and O. T. Banton, "SIU Engineering School Bill Meets Roadblock," *Southern Illinoisan* 2 May 1957: 1.

35. "How Big Can SIU Get?" *St. Louis Globe-Democrat* 7 July 1957: 1.

36. Grindle, *Memoir*, 121.

37. Mitchell, *Delyte Morris of SIU*, 96.

38. John Page Wham and Delyte Morris, letter to Paul Powell, 24 July 1957, PP Papers.

39. "Edwardsville Campus Building Plans Outlined," *Southern Illinoisan* 13 Aug. 1961.

40. Paul Powell, codicil to Last Will and Testament, 11 Aug. 1969, PP Papers: "Whereas, in the Article Fifteenth, I gave and bequeathed the sum of $50,000 to the Southern Illinois University Foundation, a not-for-profit corporation of the State of Illinois, or to its successor, or to the Board of Trustees of Southern Illinois University should the Foundation be disbanded or dissolved or in any way be unable to accept the bequest, it is now my wish that the Article Fifteenth be stricken from my last will and testament and be rendered null and void in its entirety as it might operate in the disposition of my personal estate."

6. Off to the Races

1. Clayton's *Illinois Fact Book* contains a well-researched section on horse racing that includes historical information. The early part of this chapter features excerpts from the section (445–46, 460). Other historical data about horse racing was provided by the Illinois Racing Board, in a letter to the author, 27 June 1997.

2. Gerald F. Fitzgerald, letter to author, 27 Apr. 1998.

3. John W. Fribley, *Memoir* (Springfield: Sangamon State University, 1981), 120.

4. Charles W. Clabaugh, *Memoir* (Springfield: Sangamon State University, 1982), 105.

5. Paul Powell, testimony at hearing of Illinois Harness Racing Commission, Springfield, Illinois, 29 Jan. 1952, PP Papers.

6. Illinois Association of Agricultural Fairs, adoption of resolution, Springfield, Illinois, 9 Sept. 1951, PP Papers.

7. Clayton, *The Illinois Fact Book*, 449–51.

8. Information about the six special funds and dollar amounts for 1962 and 1963 is from Clayton, *The Illinois Fact Book*, 449; and from a series of articles written by William F. Mooney and Walter Pincus, *Chicago Daily News* 21 Mar. 1962 through 27 Mar. 1962.

9. Clabaugh, *Memoir*.

10. Elbert S. Smith, *Memoir* (Springfield: Sangamon State University, 1982), 213.

11. *Illinois Standardbred and Sulky News* Nov. 1981: 28, PP Papers.

12. News articles about Irwin S. (Big Sam) Wiedrick and Paul Powell appeared

in many Illinois newspapers from 1949 to 1969. Aside from articles by Chicago newspapers, one other newspaper in the state that reported with authority about Wiedrick's business affairs was the *East St. Louis Journal* and its investigative reporter Charles O. Stewart.

13. Information about Wiedrick's troubles in New York is from accounts of January 1927 in the *Rochester Democrat and Chronicle*, provided from archives of the Rochester Public Library. Also helpful was Charles O. Stewart, "Ex-convict Was Original Cahokia Downs Promoter," *East St. Louis Journal* 24 July 1963, and "This Is Sam Wiedrick," *Metro-East Journal* 23 June 1965.

14. Stewart, *East St. Louis Journal* 24 July 1963.

15. "Track Stock Paid 1650% in 2 Yrs.; Owners Listed," *Chicago Daily News* 22 Aug. 1951: 1.

16. Paul and Daisy Powell, federal joint income tax returns, 1952–1955, PP Papers.

17. "Track Boss Faces Quiz on Ricca Loan," *Chicago Daily News* 7 Oct. 1950: 7.

18. Carl H. Preihs, letter to Paul Powell, 21 Feb. 1953, PP Papers. The partnership list changed over time. According to Hugo Bennett, letter to Paul Powell, 18 Mar. 1957, PP Papers, the partnership included Dee Stover, Mt. Vernon, a horse trainer.

19. Information about Wiedrick and Cahokia Downs and business relationships with Chicago harness tracks is from Stewart, *East St. Louis Journal* 24 July 1963.

20. Fitzgerald, letter to author.

21. Illinois Association of Agricultural Fairs, 9 Sept. 1951, 1, PP Papers.

22. Illinois Association of County Fairs, minutes of meeting, Springfield, Illinois, 6 Mar. 1949, PP Papers.

23. Illinois Association of Agricultural Fairs, 19 Sept. 1951, 2, PP Papers.

24. Irwin S. Wiedrick, testimony at hearing of Illinois Harness Racing Commission, Springfield, Illinois, 29 Jan. 1952, PP Papers.

25. James S. Kearns, letter to Paul Powell, 13 Apr. 1949, PP Papers.

26. House Bill 1044, 66th Illinois General Assembly, 1949, Illinois State Archives.

27. Clyde Lee, *Memoir* (Springfield: Sangamon State University, 1988), 138.

28. Powell, Public Statement, 29 Jan. 1952, PP Papers.

29. Lee, *Memoir*, 325.

30. Lee, *Memoir*, 350.

31. Clayton, *The Illinois Fact Book*, 297–304.

32. "Officials Own Fourth of Stock in Racing Group," *St. Louis Post-Dispatch* 23 Aug. 1951: 8.

33. Fribley, *Memoir*, 195.

34. Fribley, *Memoir*, 121.

35. Fribley, testimony at hearing of Illinois Harness Racing Commission, 29 Jan. 1952, PP Papers.

36. Adlai E. Stevenson, Illinois State Budget Report, 1949, PP Papers.

37. "8 Legislators on Payroll of Quickie-Law Race Track at Chicago," *St. Louis Post-Dispatch* 22 Aug. 1951; Illinois House and Senate committee roll call votes; final votes of House and Senate, Illinois State Archives; and Illinois Association of Agricultural Fairs, statement, 9 Sept. 1951, 3, PP Papers.

38. Smith, *Memoir*, 134.

39. Downey, *Memoir*, 51.

40. "State's Attorney to Investigate Deals in Stock of Chicago Track," *St. Louis Post-Dispatch* 24 Aug. 1951: 1; "Track Stock Paid 1650% in 2 Yrs.; Owners Listed," *Chicago Daily News*.

41. "Officials Own Fourth of Stock in Racing Group," *St. Louis Post-Dispatch*.

42. "Complete Roster of Stockholders," *Chicago Daily News* 22 Aug. 1951: 1.

43. Fribley, *Memoir*, 121.

44. Randolph, *Memoir*, 116.

45. Paul Powell, "Rep. Paul Powell Explains Illinois Harness Racing Bill," *McLeansboro Times-Leader* 21 Feb. 1952, PP Papers.

46. Powell, testimony at hearing of Illinois Harness Racing Commission, 29 Jan. 1952, PP Papers.

47. "Illinois Legislators, Wives Tell How They Got Race Track Stock," *St. Louis Post-Dispatch* 23 Aug. 1951: 8.

48. Lee, *Memoir*, 137.

49. "Illinois Legislators, Wives Tell How They Got Race Track Stock," *St. Louis Post-Dispatch*.

50. "Track Boss Faces Quiz on Ricca Loan," *Chicago Daily News*.

51. Martin, *Adlai Stevenson in Illinois*, 294.

52. "Find State Lawmakers on Race Track Payroll," *Chicago Daily News* 21 Aug. 1951: 1.

53. *Chicago Daily News* reporters covering sessions of the Senate investigating committee on organized crime in 1950–51, headed by Sen. Estes Kefauver, got the first indications of the Chicago Downs financial windfall and the involvement of state legislators. The investigation led to a series of articles in August 1951 that first exposed the Chicago Downs arrangements. Other newspapers in Chicago and St. Louis soon covered the same subjects.

54. Fribley, *Memoir*, 122.

55. "Some Deny, Some Admit Stock Deal," *Chicago Daily News* 22 Aug. 1951: 8.

56. Martin, *Adlai Stevenson in Illinois*, 485.

57. "Gifts for Favors," *Chicago Daily News* 24 Aug. 1951: 12.

58. "Mr. Mulroy's Bad Investment," *St. Louis Post-Dispatch* 31 Aug. 1951.

59. Martin, *Adlai Stevenson of Illinois*, 485.

60. Walter V. Schaefer, *Memoir* (New York: Columbia University, 1972), 9–10.

61. "Legislator's Wife Owns Track Stock," *Chicago Daily News* 21 Aug. 1951: 8.

62. "Order Probes of Track Deal," *Chicago Daily News* 23 Aug. 1951: 6.

63. Downey, *Memoir*, 51.

64. Information about fee-splitting arrangements between Powell and Wiedrick is contained in Chicago news articles that first surfaced in 1965 and again in 1969. Nevertheless, those sources are often incomplete and misleading when compared to Powell's federal income tax returns during the time of the arrangement and an "affidavit" prepared by Powell in 1969. The document, located in the Paul Powell Papers, carries no specific date of issue, notary seal, or indication of being used officially. News articles from 1969 made no reference to any deposition or legal statement by Powell explaining the fee splitting.

65. "Powell Track Fees Tied to Ex-Convict," *Chicago Today* 4 July 1969: 1, PP Papers.

66. "Hard Times Ahead at Maywood Track," *Chicago Daily News* 26 Mar. 1962: 18.

67. Marje Everett's entry into harness racing, her success with the legislature, and her involvement with William Miller and Gov. Otto Kerner are discussed in Hartley, *Big Jim Thompson of Illinois*; Lee, *Memoir*; "Harness Track Boom—The Race for Profits," *Chicago Daily News* 21 Mar. 1962: 1; and articles by Robert W. Sink of Lindsay-Schaub newspapers, during the trial of Otto Kerner in 1973, contained in the papers about James R. Thompson at the Illinois State Historical Library.

68. Powell, letter to William S. Miller, 6 June 1963, PP Papers.

69. Powell, letter to Thomas Bradley, 7 June 1963, PP Papers.

70. Powell, letter to Senator Arthur Bidwell, n.d., PP Papers.

71. Clyde Lee, remarks on House Bill 884, 11 June 1959, 10, PP Papers.

72. William S. Miller, campaign support letter for Paul Powell, 25 Sept. 1964, PP Papers.

7. Cahokia Downs: In Search of a Parlay

1. John Bartlow Martin, *Butcher's Dozen and Other Murders* (New York: Harper, 1950). In chapter 5, "The Shelton Boys," Martin claims the Sheltons netted between $1,500,000 and $2,000,000 on a gross of $7,000,000 annually from various illegal operations in southern Illinois during the 1930s.

2. Criminal activity of the Wortman mob was exposed during hearings of the

Special Committee to Investigate Organized Crime in Interstate Commerce. The committee, referred to as the "Kefauver Committee," met in St. Louis, Missouri, in April 1950 and February 1951. Also, Estes Kefauver, *Crime in America* (New York: Doubleday, 1951). The Capone connection to East St. Louis is reported by Charles O. Stewart, "Tavern and Juke Box Men Asking Vital Question," *East St. Louis Journal* 27 July 1947. A widely cited reference for listing Wortman's activities is Rube Yelvington, "Police Tolerance Seen as Answer; Career Viewed," *East St. Louis Journal* 19 June 1955.

3. The history of racing wire operations in the East St. Louis area is included in an extensive review of the business on a regional and national scale in "Summary of Certain Evidence Now in Committee Records Prior to December 18, 1950," Exhibit 40, Special Committee to Investigate Organized Crime in Interstate Commerce, proceedings, 1950–51, 1386–90.

4. James E. Sprehe, "Origin of Cahokia Empire," *St. Louis Post-Dispatch* 12 Sept. 1971: 3A; and Charles O. Stewart, "Longshots and Sure Shots," *East St. Louis Journal* 14 July 1963: 1.

5. Paul and Daisy Powell, federal joint income tax return, 1954, PP Papers.

6. Charles O. Stewart, "Always in the Winner's Circle," *East St. Louis Journal*, 15 July 1963: 1.

7. Henry W. Kenoe, "Basic Nature of the Land Trust" (Chicago: Illinois Institute for Continuing Legal Education, 1989), 1.5–1.8.

8. Stewart, "Always in the Winner's Circle."

9. Trust Agreement, Cahokia Land Trust, 15 June 1953, PP Papers.

10. George Edward Day, Andrew Ryan, John A. Stelle, Schaefer O'Neil, and Dan McGlynn, letter to owners of Cahokia Voting Trust Certificates, 2 Aug. 1962, East St. Louis, Illinois, PP Papers.

11. Affidavit, 14 July 1966, attesting to purchase of land trust units and common stock shares, PP Papers.

12. "Powell's Cahokia Shares," *St. Louis Post-Dispatch* 14 Jan. 1971: 1.

13. "Shareholder List on Cahokia Trust," *St. Louis Post-Dispatch* 12 Sept. 1971.

14. "Powell Put Turf Stocks in Other Names," *St. Louis Post-Dispatch* 12 Jan. 1971: 1.

15. Powell, letter to George Edward Day, 22 Dec. 1965, PP Papers.

16. "Daughter of Illinois Official Named as Owner of Race Track Stock," *St. Louis Post-Dispatch* 9 Sept. 1971: 5B; and "Stockholders Linked to Bills Aiding Tracks," *Chicago Daily News* 22 Sept. 1971: 1.

17. Clyde Lee, letter to Paul Powell, 29 Oct. 1963, PP Papers.

18. Cahokia Downs, Inc., 1967 annual report, 1, PP Papers.

19. Charles O. Stewart, "Hoodlums Filter into Jobs at Cahokia Race Track," *East St. Louis Journal* 22 July 1962: 3.

20. George Edward Day, letter to Powell, 8 May 1957, PP Papers.

21. Day, letter to Powell, 17 Apr. 1957, PP Papers.

22. Day, letter to Powell.

23. Clyde Choate, letter to Day, 7 Mar. 1961, PP Papers.

24. Powell, letter to Day, 16 Mar. 1961, PP Papers.

25. Day, letter to legislators, 2 Mar. 1961, PP Papers.

26. Powell wrote notes on the bottom of numerous letters that were forwarded to him by Day for comment. There is nothing among Powell's papers to indicate follow-through by Day or Powell, PP Papers.

27. Day, letter to Clyde Lee, 17 Mar. 1961, PP Papers.

28. Powell's insurance activities in 1963 are indicative of his involvement in administrative activities of racetracks in which he had a financial interest. All of these documents are in the PP Papers.

29. "Trot Meet Set Here This Fall," *St. Louis Globe-Democrat* 14 July 1957; and "Cahokia Opens Season Tonight," *St. Louis Globe-Democrat* 14 Oct. 1957.

30. Egyptian Trotting Association, Inc., list of stockholders, 31 Dec. 1963, PP Papers.

31. George W. Howard Jr., letter to Clyde Lee, 16 Oct. 1963, PP Papers.

32. Powell, letter to Lee, 26 July 1963, PP Papers.

33. Lee, letter to Powell, 29 Oct. 1963, PP Papers.

34. Egyptian Trotting Association, Ltd., East St. Louis, Illinois, statement of profit and earned surplus for the period 1 Aug. 1957 to 31 Mar. 1959, PP Papers.

35. Lee, letter to Powell, 21 Dec. 1963, PP Papers.

8. Creating Cash His Way

1. Paul Powell, inheritance tax return (amended), filed 3 June 1976 by Powell's executor, Illinois State Circuit Court, Johnson County, Illinois. The total fair net market value of Powell's property as of October, 10, 1970, was stated as $3,292,959.89. Information regarding his sources of income is from Paul and Daisy Powell, joint federal income tax returns, PP Papers.

2. Powell filed amended returns in 1953, 1955, 1961, and 1962. In 1953 he added $272.25 in the amendment. In 1955 he added $50 in the amendment. In 1961 he decreased his capital gains by $1,750 for a worthless stock and deducted a bad check that had been claimed under farm income. In 1962 Powell paid an additional tax of $242.45, with interest for minor adjustments (PP Papers).

3. Powell's papers contained no reference to work done for Arketex, except receipts for travel expenses submitted to the company from 1954 to 1957 and paid by check. Telephone calls made in February 1998 to members of the Stelle family turned up nothing to explain the payments.

4. Lockard, . . . *and even the stump is gone*, 273.

5. Powell, letter to Sam Barter, 5 Nov. 1963, PP Papers.

6. News coverage of the Trinity business was extensive. Dispatches used for this account are from the Associated Press and the Springfield, Illinois, State Journal, Dec. 1961, PP Papers.

7. Papers of incorporation, Statewide Tire Sales, Inc., 25 Sept. 1959, PP Papers.

8. Powell, letter to Seymour Emalfarb, 8 June 1964, PP Papers.

9. Franklin H. Weber, letter to Albert M. Zlotnick, 14 May 1968, PP Papers.

10. "Powell Ex-Associate Convicted in Extortion," *St. Louis Post-Dispatch* 24 Dec. 1971: 3a.

11. Samuel K. Skinner, letter to the author, 6 Jan. 1998.

9. Hide and Seek: The Story of $800,000

1. John S. Rendleman, testimony to IRS, East St. Louis, Illinois, 18 Jan. 1971, 45, PP Papers.

2. Sneed, "Inside the Shoe Box Scandal."

3. Margaret Hensey, testimony before the Sangamon County Grand Jury, Springfield, Illinois, 25 Jan. 1971, PP Papers. Among the examiners were Sangamon State's Atty. Richard A. Hollis. The account of Powell's death and events immediately thereafter are from Hensey's testimony. The transcript of her testimony is among the Paul Powell Papers.

4. Hensey, testimony before the Sangamon County Grand Jury, 29.

5. Hensey, testimony before the Sangamon County Grand Jury, 26.

6. Hensey, testimony before the Sangamon County Grand Jury, 28.

7. Hensey, testimony before the Sangamon County Grand Jury, 31.

8. "Ciaccio Quiz—New Powell Revelations," *Chicago Sun-Times* 15 Jan. 1971: 1. Newspapers throughout the state on this date reported on a seventy-five-page statement Ciaccio made 8 Jan. to Hollis. Repeated attempts to obtain a copy of the statement from Circuit Court officials were unsuccessful.

9. Hensey, testimony before the Sangamon County Grand Jury, 18, 109.

10. "Powell Aid Admits Phony Office Search," *St. Louis Post-Dispatch* 14 Jan. 1971: 1.

11. "Ciaccio Quiz—New Powell Revelations," *Chicago Sun-Times.*

12. "Ciaccio Quiz—New Powell Revelations," *Chicago Sun-Times.*

13. "Ciaccio Quiz—New Powell Revelations," *Chicago Sun-Times.*

14. Hensey, testimony before the Sangamon County Grand Jury, 43–44, 47.

15. None of the published accounts gave much detail on what Powell's associates did at the hotel Saturday evening before returning to Springfield.

16. "Ex-Chauffeur Tells of Removing Records," *Chicago Tribune* 15 Jan. 1971: 1.

17. Hensey, testimony before the Sangamon County Grand Jury, 54.

18. Hensey, testimony before the Sangamon County Grand Jury, 57.

19. "Ex-Chauffeur Tells of Removing Records," *Chicago Tribune*.

20. "Judge's Story on Powell," *Chicago Tribune* 13 Jan. 1971: 1.

21. "Ex-Chauffeur Tells of Removing Records," *Chicago Tribune*.

22. Accounts of the time spent at Powell's hotel apartment the morning of October 11, 1970, are from Hensey, testimony before the Sangamon County Grand Jury, 91–104; and published accounts of Saccaro and Ciaccio in the *Chicago Tribune* and *Chicago Sun-Times* 15 Jan. 1971.

23. "Ex-Chauffeur Tells of Removing Records," *Chicago Tribune*.

24. Lockard, *. . . and even the stump is gone*, 267–70.

25. Rendleman, testimony to IBI, Springfield, Illinois, 6 Jan. 1971; and testimony to IRS, PP Papers.

26. Hensey, testimony before the Sangamon County Grand Jury, 109. Hensey said that after Powell had visited the Mayo Clinic in September 1970, he put an envelope for her in the locked file cabinet, saying if anything happened to him the money would carry her until the will was settled.

27. Ted McCoy, letter to author, 4 Jan. 1997.

28. "Paul Powell Is Eulogized, Buried at Vienna, Ill.," *St. Louis Globe-Democrat* 16 Oct. 1970: 1.

29. Hensey, testimony before the Sangamon County Grand Jury, 120; and Rendleman, testimony to IRS, 17–18.

30. Gardner, John C. (as told by Rendleman), "Powell's Stash: $800,000 in Cash," *Southern Illinoisan* 30 Dec. 1970: 1.

31. Rendleman, testimony to IBI, 4.

32. Hensey, testimony before the Sangamon County Grand Jury, 130, 139.

33. Rendleman, testimony to IRS, 21–22.

34. Rendleman, testimony to IBI, 7; Rendleman, testimony to IRS, 24; and John C. Gardner, letter to the author, 5 Feb. 1995, 3.

35. Rendleman, testimony to IRS, 25–27.

36. Hensey, testimony before the Sangamon County Grand Jury, 35.

37. Rendleman, testimony to IRS, 27, 29; Rendleman, testimony to IBI, 6, 11–12; and Hensey, Testimony before the Sangamon County Grand Jury, 141–44.

38. Rendleman, testimony to IBI, 7.

39. "Ex-Chauffeur Tells of Removing Records," *Chicago Tribune*.

40. Rendleman, press conference, Edwardsville, Illinois, 9 Jan. 1971, Southern Illinois University at Edwardsville, Lovejoy Library, Archives; and Rendleman, testimony to IBI, 31.

41. Rendleman, testimony to IBI, 40.

42. Rendleman, testimony to IRS, 45.

43. Biographical sketch, John S. Rendleman, president, Southern Illinois University at Edwardsville, University News Services, Jan. 1976.

44. Rendleman, testimony to IBI, 40.

45. Executor's time log, Paul Powell Estate, 3, PP Papers.

46. Hensey, testimony before the Sangamon County Grand Jury, 147–49; Rendleman, testimony to IRS, 49; and Robert Oxtoby, press conference, Edwardsville, Illinois, 9 Jan. 1971, Southern Illinois University at Edwardsville, Lovejoy Library, Archives.

47. Rendleman, testimony to IBI, 31–32, PP Papers.

48. Rendleman, testimony to IRS, 36, PP Papers.

49. Rendleman, testimony to IRS, 8–9, PP Papers.

50. Oxtoby, press conference, 9–10.

51. "Scott told about $800,000," *Metro-East Journal* 13 Jan. 1971: 1; and Rendleman, press conference, 2.

52. Paul Simon, telephone interview with the author, 24 Jan. 1997.

53. Gardner, letter to author, 4. The author and Gardner were colleagues at the time the *Southern Illinoisan*, where Gardner was editor and publisher, told Rendleman's story of the cash find. They discussed the episode at the time and many times after, and in 1995, Gardner wrote a letter with his account and answered questions for the author.

54. Gardner, letter to author, 3.

55. Gardner, letter to author, 4.

56. Gardner, "Powell's Stash: $800,000 in Cash."

57. Gardner, letter to author, 2.

58. Gardner, letter to author, 5.

59. "Scott Told About $800,000," *Metro-East Journal*.

60. "State Reveals Powell Money, Death Probed," *Metro-East Journal* 5 Jan. 1971: 1.

61. Richard B. Ogilvie, statement to press, 8 Jan. 1971, Southern Illinois University at Edwardsville, Lovejoy Library, Archives.

62. "Mr. Ogilvie's Non Sequitur," *St. Louis Post-Dispatch* 11 Jan. 1971.

63. Rendleman, statement to the press and a press conference, 9 Jan. 1971, Southern Illinois University at Edwardsville, Lovejoy Library, Archives.

64. Board of Trustees of Southern Illinois University, proceedings and minutes of the meeting, 15 Jan. 1971, 2–4.

65. Rendleman, testimony to IBI, 48–49.

66. Rendleman, testimony to IBI, 54.

10. Handouts from a Lifelong Democrat

1. Powell, Last Will and Testament, Article I.

2. Author, notes taken at grave site, 21 Feb. 1998.

3. "Why Was Paul Powell Paid $8,000?," *Chicago Daily News* 15 June 1965: 15.

4. "Paul Powell Estate Finally Settled," *Metro-East Journal* 11 July 1978.

5. Leo Brown, interview with author.

6. Paul Powell estate, Order Approving Final Account and Report and Order of Final Distribution, 13 June 1978, Circuit Court of Johnson County.

7. Sneed, "Inside the Shoe Box Scandal."

8. "Taxman, Lawyers Leave Little of Powell Estate," *St. Louis Globe-Democrat* 15 May 1978.

9. Oxtoby, press conference.

10. "Powell Set 1970 Income at $200,000," *St. Louis Post-Dispatch* 19 Jan. 1971: 3A.

11. "Paul Powell Estate Facing Court; IRS Seeks $370,568," *St. Louis Post-Dispatch* 10 Dec. 1974.

12. "Illinois to Get $1.6 Million in Powell Estate Settlement," *St. Louis Globe-Democrat* 18 Aug. 1973.

13. Howard, *Memoir*, 184.

14. Howard, *Memoir*, 184.

15. William J. Nettles, telephone interview with author, 21 Jan. 1998.

16. Nettles, interview with author. Investigations continued for some time after Powell's death in an attempt to determine if Powell received payoffs.

17. Paul Powell, inheritance tax return (amended), filed 3 June 1976 by Powell's executor, Illinois State Circuit Court, Johnson County, Illinois. Information in succeeding paragraphs about values in the estate is from this version of the tax return.

18. Paul Powell, inheritance tax return (amended).

19. "A Green Garden Party," *Chicago Daily News* 13 Oct. 1966: 1.

20. Hensey, testimony before the Sangamon County Grand Jury, 161–74. In her testimony on January 25, 1971, Hensey answered numerous questions about contributions to Powell's campaigns for secretary of state and her roll as clerk and check writer.

21. "Paul Powell's Estate Finally Closed," *St. Louis Globe-Democrat* 11 July 1978.

22. "Paul Powell's Estate Finally Closed," *St. Louis Globe-Democrat*.

11. Powell's Secret

1. Martin B. Lohmann, *Memoir* (Springfield: Sangamon State University, 1980).

2. Lockard, *. . . and even the stump is gone*, 273.

3. Nettles, interview with author.

4. Vasconcelles, *Memoir*.

5. Thomas A. McGloon, *Memoir* (Springfield: Sangamon State University, 1981).

Select Bibliography

Allen, John W. *Legends and Lore of Southern Illinois.* Carbondale: Southern Illinois University Press, 1963.

Angle, Paul M. *Bloody Williamson.* New York: Knopf, 1969.

Armbrister, Trevor. "The Octopus in the State House." *Saturday Evening Post* 12 Feb. 1966.

Baker, Jean H. *The Stevensons: A Biography of an American Family.* New York: Norton, 1996.

Biles, Roger. *Big City Boss: In Depression and War, Mayor Edward J. Kelly of Chicago.* DeKalb: Northern Illinois University Press, 1984.

———. *Richard J. Daley: Politics, Race, and the Governing of Chicago.* DeKalb: Northern Illinois University Press, 1995.

Billington, Ray Allen. *Westward Expansion: A History of the American Frontier.* New York: Macmillan, 1949.

Casey, Robert J., and W. A. S. Douglas. *The Midwesterner: The Story of Dwight H. Green.* Chicago: Wilcox and Follett, 1948.

Chapman, P. T. *A History of Johnson County Illinois.* Herrin: Press of the Herrin News, 1925.

Clabaugh, Charles. *Memoir.* Springfield: Sangamon State University, 1982.

Clayton, John, compiler. *The Illinois Fact Book and Historical Almanac, 1673–1968.* Carbondale: Southern Illinois University Press, 1970.

Crane, Edgar G., ed. *Illinois: Political Processes and Governmental Performance.* Dubuque: Kendall/Hunt, 1980.

Douglas, Paul. *In the Fullness of Time.* New York: Harcourt Brace Jovanovich, 1971.

Downey, William. *Memoir.* Springfield: Sangamon State University, 1982.

Dunne, George W. *Memoir.* Springfield: Sangamon State University, 1988.

Fribley, John W. *Memoir.* Springfield: Sangamon State University, 1981.

Gove, Samuel K. "The Illinois General Assembly." *Illinois: Political Processes and Governmental Performance.* Ed. Edgar G. Crane. Dubuque: Kendall/Hunt, 1980.

Gove, Samuel K., and James D. Nowlan. *Illinois Politics and Government: The Expanding Metropolitan Frontier.* Lincoln: University of Nebraska Press, 1996.

Select Bibliography

Grant, U. S. *Personal Memoirs*. 2 vols. New York: Webster and Company, 1886.

Green, Paul M. "History of Political Parties in Illinois." *Illinois: Political Processes and Governmental Performance*. Ed. Edgar G. Crane. Dubuque: Kendall/Hunt, 1980.

Grindle, William L. *Memoir*. Springfield: Sangamon State University, 1986.

Hartley, Robert E. "The Administration of Governor James R. Thompson." *Illinois: Political Processes and Governmental Performance*. Ed. Edgar G. Crane. Dubuque: Kendall/Hunt, 1980.

———. *Big Jim Thompson of Illinois*. Chicago: Rand McNally, 1979.

———. *Charles H. Percy: A Political Perspective*. Chicago: Rand McNally, 1975.

Hofstadter, Richard. *The American Political Tradition*. Chapter 7, "The Spoilsman: An Age of Cynicism," 164–86. New York: Vintage Books, 1955.

Holloway, James. *Memoir*. Springfield: Sangamon State University, 1982.

Howard, Robert P. *Illinois: A History of the Prairie State*. Grand Rapids: Eerdmans, 1972.

———. *Memoir*. Springfield: Sangamon State University, 1982.

———. *Mostly Good and Competent Men: Illinois Governors 1818 to 1988*. Springfield: Illinois Issues, Sangamon State University, Illinois State Historical Society, 1988.

Jones, James Pickett. *Black Jack: John A. Logan and Southern Illinois in the Civil War Era*. Carbondale: Southern Illinois University Press, 1995, reprint.

———. "John A. Logan, Freshman in Congress, 1859–1861." *Journal of the Illinois State Historical Society* (Spring 1963).

———. *John A. Logan: Stalwart Republican from Illinois*. Jacksonville: Florida State University Press, 1982.

Keiser, John A. *Building for the Centuries: Illinois 1865–1898*. Urbana: University of Illinois Press, 1977.

Kenney, David. *In It, to Win It: A Personal Memoir*. Carbondale: Sunny Slope Press, 1998.

———. *A Political Passage: The Career of Stratton of Illinois*. Carbondale: Southern Illinois University Press, 1990.

Lee, Clyde. *Memoir*. Springfield: Sangamon State University, 1988.

Littlewood, Thomas J. *Horner of Illinois*. Evanston: Northwestern University Press, 1969.

———. "Impact of the Media: Analyst or Interest Group?" *Illinois: Political Processes and Governmental Performance*. Ed. Edgar G. Crane. Dubuque: Kendall/Hunt, 1980.

Lockard, Melvin. *. . . and even the stump is gone*. Tucson: Pepper Publishing, 1995.

Lohmann, Martin B. *Memoir*. Springfield: Sangamon State University, 1980.

Martin, John Bartlow. *Adlai Stevenson of Illinois.* New York: Macmillan, 1976.

————. *Butcher's Dozen and Other Murders.* New York: Harper, 1950.

McGloon, Thomas A. *Memoir.* Springfield: Sangamon State University, 1981.

Mitchell, Betty. *Delyte Morris of SIU.* Carbondale: Southern Illinois University Press, 1988.

Monroe, Alan D. "Elections: Political Culture, Public Opinion, Sectionalism and Voting." In *Illinois: Political Processes and Governmental Performance.* Ed. Edgar G. Crane. Dubuque: Kendall/Hunt, 1980.

Morton, Richard Allen. *Justice and Humanity: Edward F. Dunne, Illinois Progressive.* Carbondale: Southern Illinois University Press, 1997.

Nevins, Allan. "The Frontier in Illinois History." *Journal of the Illinois State Historical Society* 43.1 (Spring 1950): 28–45.

O'Connor, Len. *Clout: Mayor Daley and His City.* New York: Avon, 1975.

Pensoneau, Taylor. *Governor Richard Ogilvie: In the Interest of the State.* Carbondale: Southern Illinois University Press, 1997.

Rakove, Milton L. *We Don't Want Nobody Nobody Sent: An Oral History of the Daley Years.* Bloomington: Indiana University Press, 1979.

Randolph, Paul J. *Memoir.* Springfield: Sangamon State University, 1986.

Redmond, William A. *Memoir.* Springfield: Sangamon State University, 1986.

Scariano, Anthony. *Memoir.* Springfield: Sangamon State University, 1988.

Schaefer, Walter V. *Memoir.* New York: Columbia University, 1972.

Schapsmeier, Edward L. and Frederick F. Schapsmeier. *Dirksen of Illinois: Senatorial Statesman.* Urbana: University of Illinois Press, 1985.

Scott, Maurice. *Memoir.* Springfield: Sangamon State University, 1984.

Simon, Paul, and Alfred Balk. "The Illinois Legislature: A Study in Corruption." *Harper's* Sept. 1964.

Smith, Elbert. *Memoir.* Springfield: Sangamon State University, 1982.

Smith, George Washington. *A History of Southern Illinois: A Narrative Account of Its Historical Progress, Its People and Its Principal Interests,* vol. 1. Chicago: Lewis, 1912.

Tingley, Donald E. *The Structuring of a State: The History of Illinois 1899–1928.* Urbana: University of Illinois Press, 1980.

Vasconcelles, Shelby. *Memoir.* Springfield: Sangamon State University, 1982.

Index

Index

Connors, William "Botchy," 55
constitutional convention (con-con), 48–49, 51
county fairs, 30, 34, 87, 88–89, 91, 96, 98, 100
Cox, Edward, 130
Crain, Robert, 137
Crain and Hall law firm, 137
crime commissions, 68–69, 111
Crisenberry, R. G., 77, 84, 85
CTE. *See* Chicago Thoroughbred Enterprises, Inc.
cumulative voting, 19–21
Cutler, Reed F., 53, 103

Daley, Richard J., 11, 24, 26, 37, 51, 158; as director of revenue, 53–54; minority leaders and, 29–30; SIU and, 84, 85; statewide candidates and, 63, 65
Davis, Corneal, 55
Davis, Hayden, 88
Day, George Edward, 123, 126, 127–28
De La Cour, Joseph, 29–30, 54–56
Democratic State Central Committee, 27
Democrats, 19–21, 23, 43, 55–56
Devine, John P., 44
Dickirson, Ray, 137–38
Dickirson-Davis firm, 137–38
Dillavou, Ora D., 77
Dirksen, Everett, 31, 62–64
District 51, 20–21
Dixon, Alan, xiii, 34, 65, 66, 79, 116
"do-nothing legislature," 48
Downey, J. Harold, 107, 132
Downey, William "Smokey," 102, 110
driver's license controversy, 70–72
Duff, Brian, 72–73
Dunne, Edward F., 43
Du Quoin state fair, 89

Earl W. Jackson Insurance Co., 129–30
"Easter, 1955" envelope, 167
East St. Louis, 118–20, 126–27
East St. Louis Journal, 122, 125
"Egypt," 3–4
Egyptian Trotting Assoc., 26, 30, 113, 114;

Powell's holdings, 130–31, 141–42; stock arrangements, 95, 124–25, 130–33, 136
Eisenhower, Dwight D., 25, 29, 50
Emalfarb, Seymour, 139, 140
Everett, Marjorie Lindheimer, 31–32, 114–15, 142

Fanta, Joseph F., 128
farm land, 136–37
federal income tax returns, 18–19, 134–36, 141
Fields, Al, 132
"Five Years of Progress" folder, 166–67, 186
Fox Valley Trotting Assoc., 111, 142, 179
Freeman, William E., 130
Fribley, John W., 88, 100–101, 103, 104, 107

gambling, 119–20
Gardner, John C., 169–70
Gateway Amendment, 49, 51
Giancana, Momo "Sam," 71–72
Gibbs, Jack P., 138
Gleason, Martin, 66–67
Gove, Sam, 19
governors, 19–22. *See also individual governors*
Green, Dwight, 21–22, 27–28
Grindle, William, 79, 80, 83, 85
Guild, William, 61
Guy A. Wood Agcy., 130

Hambletonian, 87, 99
Hammond, Albert, 116–17
Harness Horse, (magazine), 98
harness racing, 87–90, 101–2. *See also* racetrack business
Harness Racing Commission, 105, 107, 110, 113, 116
Harris, Lloyd "Curly," 58, 103, 105
Harris, Winifred, 167
Hart, Fred J., 128
Hartwell, Vinna, 6, 7
Henry, David, 84, 85
Hensey, Margaret, 10, 180; campaign funds and, 187; Powell's death and, 144–54,

Index

Index

Robert E. Hartley was a journalist and executive for Lindsay-Schaub newspapers in Illinois from 1962 to 1979. After a career as a public relations executive in Seattle, he moved to Westminster, Colorado, where he writes. He is the author of *Charles H. Percy: A Political Perspective* and *Big Jim Thompson of Illinois*, which won the 1980 Illinois Historical Society Award of Merit.